WHY WAS
CHARLES I EXECUTED?

Carnifex Maiestatis Regis Angliæ.

Sir Thomas Fairfax, Lord General of the Army, as Charles I's executioner (1649)
The imputation of Fairfax's personal responsibility for the execution would
have mortified him. Sir Thomas refused to serve on the court appointed to try
the king or, after the execution, to affirm publicly his support for a non-
monarchical regime. But he was commander-in-chief of the army, the major
force in securing the trial and execution of the king.
(*Ashmolean Museum, Oxford*)

Why Was
Charles I Executed?

Clive Holmes

hambledon
continuum

Hambledon Continuum
A Continuum imprint

The Tower Building
11 York Road
London, SE1 7NX
UK

80 Maiden Lane
Suite 704
New York, NY 10038
USA

First Published 2006

ISBN 1 85285 282 8

A description of this book is available from the
British Library and from the Library of Congress.

Typeset by Carnegie Publishing, Lancaster,
and printed in the United Kingdom by Antony Rowe Ltd, Wiltshire.

Contents

Illustrations

Acknowledgements

The research and writing of a historical work – creating a complex narrative or analysing skeins of data – can be a solitary experience. But writing this study has been neither dull nor lonely: it has been a hugely enjoyable co-operative endeavour. This is a book that focuses on *argument*, argument about the key events – the killing of a king; the rejection of a crown – of a turbulent, contentious and fascinating period. My library reading has involved debate, creative and critical, with pastmasters and colleagues in the historical profession, and this process has been reinforced by public discussions at lectures and seminars at Oxford, London and Cambridge. A number of these have been influential – provoking argument as often as commanding assent – in the development of my ideas: here I should mention presentations involving Ann Hughes, Jason Peacey, David Scott, John Adamson, David Cressy, Blair Worden, Sean Kelsey, Ronald Hutton, John Morrill, Quentin Skinner and Mark Kishlansky.

More of the ideas have been tested and refined with a different group of colleagues, in various teaching contexts since my move back to England. Several of my Oxford graduates – Andrew Warmington, Sarah Mortimer, Youngkwon Chung and, particularly, Henrik Langelueddecke – have worked on topics related to this book and have given focus to my ideas. For several years I have taught an undergraduate Special Subject concentrating on the period, giving lectures, and expounding and arguing in seminars and tutorials. Student discussion in the latter, and, more directly, of draft sections of this book, has been a major influence on its development. I dedicate this book to all my Oxford students, but some deserve special mention for their interest and involvement in the project – so particular thanks to Grant Tapsell, George Southcombe, Lara Hays, Emma Furness, Narmi Thiranagama and Jon Fitzgibbons.

Kate Heard of the Print Room at the Ashmolean Museum was exceptionally helpful in finding the prints with which the work is illustrated.

Two people have played central roles in the final production of the work. Martin Sheppard is an exceptional editor, with an ear for language and an eye for the most nuanced formulation of argument: reading recent studies of the period suggests that such skills are regrettably uncommon in modern publishing. Felicity Heal has read, criticised and encouraged – the latter in some bleak moments: a wonderful colleague and more.

Introduction

For most of the twentieth century, the narrative history of the English Civil War and Interregnum was secure in the magisterial volumes of S. R. Gardiner. The main task of historians until a little over thirty years ago was to elucidate the *causes* of the breakdown of royal government and the flux of political experiments which followed it, events which had been so comprehensively described by the Victorian master. The aim was to locate the inception of the crisis and its subsequent development in shifts in the deep structures of English society and political culture in the century following the Reformation.

In 1972 Lawrence Stone produced a book, *The Causes of the English Revolution*. With his argument firmly located in the conceptual schemes of the social sciences, Stone sought to explain the Revolution in terms of a threefold hierarchy of causes. Stone's analysis concentrated on the first two aspects of his aetiological triad, the 'Preconditions' and 'Precipitants' of the Revolution, and concerned the developing fissures and dysfunctions in English social and political structure. The events of the immediate period were examined only as 'Triggers' to the crisis. Stone's analytical scheme had little room or need for a narrative of the short term. It could be treated as a given.

Even as Stone's book appeared, however, many of its assumptions were already being questioned. The challenge had a number of dimensions, some philosophical, some simply material. Certainly the sheer increase in historical knowledge was an important stimulus. Changing patterns of higher education, the growth in the numbers of academic historians, and a professional career path commencing with the doctoral thesis, ensured that new studies of incidents within the narrative provided by Gardiner were undertaken. And the growing availability of archival material, particularly from local collections, ensured that the work could be done in ever greater detail. Philosophically, the challenge was the product of a growing suspicion of the causal skeins enshrined in Stone's book.

Critics, troubled by determinist presumptions in the methodology of the social sciences, increasingly approached issues of causation with a caution remarkable in its chastity. Conrad Russell argued that we need look no further than the battlefield of Newburn to understand the reasons the English lost the Second Bishops' War. Hypotheses about the inadequate provision and funding of the king's army, or about unwilling troops and political disaffection, were otiose and confusing: quite simply the English 'drew up for battle in a position where even the best of armies would have been likely to lose'.[1] But the move away from discussion of causal sequences was not just a matter of epistemological fashion. It was a reaction, if an extreme one, to the *progressive* assumptions on which the history of the seventeenth century had been written, not only from the perspective favoured by Stone but from Gardiner's older political and constitutional focus, upon which the modish social science analyses largely depended. Gardiner's account, it was argued, was polemically charged. It was not an objectively true story, but written in the light of the assumed consequences of the Civil War; consequences which were essentially the central values of the Victorian state – parliamentary government and religious toleration. In reaction to this unstated but powerfully shaping teleology, it was argued that historians must write as though in ignorance of outcomes. And this injunction against hindsight was extended from long-term desiderata – the rule of law or the rise of the middle class – to events far more immediate. Serious charges of 'ahistorical determinism' might be levelled against any account that appeared to assume the inevitability of an outcome.[2] Detailed research, producing a series of microstudies, combined with an antipathy to both hindsight and to long-term causal analysis, typified the work of a group of scholars – the 'revisionists' – who fundamentally deepened and complicated the older account.

Substantively, the revisionists attacked the older certainties about the history of the seventeenth century from three distinct perspectives. First, historians of the localities – a growth industry driven by the archival revolution – denied that people were particularly well informed about, or even interested in, national events. In the provinces parochial issues took precedence, and national policies were evaluated by the county elites only with respect to their local impact. England, for Alan Everitt, the intellectual progenitor of this 'localist' reading of the early modern period, was 'a union of partially independent county-states'.[3] Gardiner had written of the legal and constitutional concerns expressed by 'the nation' in response to Charles I's policies in the 1630s. Localist historians, by contrast, saw only local powerbrokers peeved by the expense and disruption that attended the king's fiscal and administrative experiments.

The second strand of the critique was provided by historians of ideas and political thought. Gardiner had seen the political developments of the early seventeenth century that culminated in the Civil War as fuelled by a fundamental fissure in ideas of constitutional law. For him, and for a distinguished coterie of American historians who developed his arguments, royal absolutism confronted constitutionalism. Revisionists like Glenn Burgess now argued that this was based on a blinkered, a priori misunderstanding. Members of the political elite essentially shared a 'broad consensus and agreement on fundamental issues'.[4] Their views were uniformly paternalist and hierarchical, and based on a common conceptual structure rooted in key theological and legal texts. These views were more generally articulated and internalised throughout society: the commonplaces of the shared contempory understanding justified social subordination, and this was practically manifested in the deference accorded to the elite. Disagreements would occur, but over matters of emphasis not essentials. In this world, the 'opposition' on which older accounts had concentrated was almost a philosophic impossibility.

Yet tensions had obviously disturbed the calm of early Stuart politics. The arguments and breakdowns in, for instance, the parliaments of the 1620s had been at the heart of the older interpretation. How was this record compatible with the general commitment to a hegemonic ideology argued by the revisionists? The answer to this question forms the third strand of the revisionist critique. Tensions might occur intermittently, but the structures of political association were designed to restore the basic consensus. The actors within those structures also subscribed to the consensual ideology. The occasional (and over-emphasised) instances of political conflict were to be understood as the struggles of cliques or factions, centred upon the royal court and seeking to dominate the making of policy and, more particularly, the control of the pork barrel of patronage. The revisionist emphases – localism, ideological consensus, the politics of faction – could, sometimes uneasily, be welded into a unified account. So a detailed narrative of high politics might occasionally turn up moments of intense competition, such as in the challenges to the dominance exercised by the duke of Buckingham in the 1620s. But these instances were to be understood as moments of particularly feverish factional competition. They did not change basic political assumptions. Nor – to add in the localist dimension – did they have much impact upon introverted provincial societies, their political horizons limited by the boundaries of their own communities.

Revisionism, then, changed the landscape of early Stuart studies. How did it affect interpretations of the two central decades of the century? Revisionists tended to assert the continued power of hierarchy, the institutional structure of consensus and the local focus of politics, despite the war. But, as John Morrill has wryly noted, it was easier within their conceptual schema to explain why the Civil War did *not* occur. But it did. Revisionists, disposed to emphasise high politics and to downplay ideological conflict, tended to see the war, and the flux of events that followed it, as almost accidental. After the breakdown, its essential landmarks destroyed or irrelevant, England entered the dominion of Machiavelli's bitch-goddess 'Fortuna': events, even critical events, like the execution of the king, were 'highly adventitious'.[5] As matters of chance and contingency, they were, to that degree, unpredictable. The revisionist reluctance to address issues of causation ensured that it was the interplay of individual character and chance that dominated discussion. In consequence, students and those with an intelligent interest in the period were, and often are, confronted with dense narratives, strong on the denunciation of the lack of archival rigour or the philosophical naivety of the older accounts but weak on anything resembling explanation beyond the contingent.

Historical study moves on. Scholars, some the leading formulators and practitioners of the revisionist approach, some marching under the inelegant banner of 'post-revisionism', have begun to interrogate the period afresh. The power of competing ideas, particularly religious ideas, has been reaffirmed. The dissemination of these ideas to social groups below the level of the elite has been demonstrated, as has their potency in provoking action. The interaction between the agendas of local rulers and the central authorities has been shown. It is clear that competing views of the structure of society, of national identity and political culture, of the role of the church, must be addressed in any account of the developments of the period.

Questions still need to be asked about these processes, but they can be asked – and they can be answered.

1

Why Did Charles I Call
the Long Parliament?

On 2 March 1629, in scenes of unprecedented and chaotic confrontation, the third parliament that Charles I had called since his accession four years before was dissolved. MPs barred the door against Black Rod, held the weeping Speaker in his chair and passed by acclamation three resolutions denouncing as traitors those who proposed or supported innovations in religion, and those who ordered the payment of, and even those who simply paid, taxes that had not been approved in parliament. A week later Charles, to answer, as he asserted, the tissue of rumour and lies propagated by the 'turbulent and ill-affected spirits' who had dominated the Commons, issued a lengthy justification of his policies and his dealings with parliament. In 1624, the last year of his father's reign, Charles insisted, parliament had encouraged the crown to throw England into the war raging in Europe to uphold the Protestant cause, reeling under the assaults of the forces of Catholic Spain, the Holy Roman Empire and Bavaria. But, once committed to military action, Charles discovered that parliament, forgetting 'their ... engagements at the entry into the war', was deeply reluctant to pay for it. The king, unable to mobilise forces on an appropriate scale, was 'disgraced and ruined, for want of timely help'. Worse, parliament 'taking advantage of ... our necessities', sought to use his financial embarrassment to lever him into policies that would seriously weaken the crown – sacrificing his favoured servants and counsellors, abandoning royal prerogatives essential to the government of the state. When he did give way to their blackmail, as he had when he accepted the Petition of Right in June 1628, this merely encouraged the further delay of adequate fiscal provision and more extreme demands.[1]

Many politically well-informed commentators believed that the king, infuriated by the particular insult to his authority on 2 March and the general pattern of opposition and procrastination, had immediately decided to rule without the dubious assistance of parliament in perpetuity. Charles eventually denied any such intention in a proclamation issued on 27 March, but his comments certainly suggested there might be a substantial intermission in parliamentary sessions. He rehearsed the bleak history of his relationship with the Commons and the consequent destruction of his initial 'love to the use of parliament', and he reminded his audience of his absolute prerogative for 'the calling, continuing and dissolving' of that institution. Crucially, he insisted that parliament would only meet again when the circumstances were right, when his people had 'come to a better understanding of us and themselves'.[2]

Charles's determination to rule without parliament for the foreseeable future presented an immediate problem of finance. The interventionist policy in Europe was quickly abandoned, peace treaties being negotiated with France in April and Spain in November 1629. Even without the financial drain of military engagement, however, the sources of income to which Charles had direct access were inadequate for the needs of government. Without parliamentary taxation, Charles had to find new sources of revenue, and his search followed two paths. First, he sought to milk royal rights that had fallen into desuetude. The keeper of the records trawled the documents in the Tower to produce a list of the money-raising schemes attempted by Charles's predecessors. While some of the suggestions that emerged were only of antiquarian interest, two projects based on impeccably dusty medieval precedents – the fining of those eligible gentlemen who had not sought knighthood at the coronation, and those who had breached the long-disused laws governing the royal forests – were resurrected. Significant sums were raised by these expedients, but they were essentially one-shot deals. To secure a more permanent provision of income, Charles had to develop a system of taxation based on more flexible aspects of the royal prerogative than those warranted by the medieval past. Ship money, 'this new old way', first introduced in 1634, had some of the patina of medieval precedent. But its essential justification lay in the doctrine, with which the king had experimented in the war years from 1625 to

1627, that the king had a duty to act for the public good when the safety of the realm was imperilled and he alone could judge when such a state of emergency existed.

In 1629 Charles had determined to rule without parliament; and, in the next five years, he had pieced together the financial means of doing so. Yet, when the Long Parliament first met in November 1640 it is evident that the conditions specified by Charles in his March 1629 proclamation did not appertain. In the course of the next year this parliament hounded and proscribed some who had been the king's most trusted counsellors in the 1630s. It outlawed the innovative fiscal programmes that Charles had developed in that period, and abolished some of the agencies through which he had enforced his will. It began an assault on the king's religious policies. Charles, it seemed, was hostage to a parliament determined to dismantle the regime that he had nurtured in the previous decade. Why had he called a body that was to prove so intransigent?

He had, in fact, little choice. On 28 August the English forces defending the fords of the Tyne and the key city of Newcastle against the army raised against Charles by his Scottish subjects had been outmanoeuvred and then outfought at the battle of Newburn. The English retired to York; the Scots occupied the northern counties. Charles's own troops had to be sustained to halt any prospect of further inroads into English territory, and, from, mid-October, when a temporary cessation of hostilities was negotiated, the king was also committed to paying the Scottish army of occupation £850 a day for their maintenance. Charles's military failure had left him to carry the costs of two armies: the humiliation was as complete as the king's treasury was empty. The majority of the king's intimate advisers, exhausted by their efforts to mount the campaign and demoralised by its defeat, came round to the opinion already canvassed vigorously by other men of influence who stood outside the inner circles of power. A parliament was essential. Only a parliament could possibly levy the taxes required to maintain the two armies, Scots and English, quartered in northern England.

Charles himself was one of the last converts to the policy of calling a parliament. His eventual agreement was predicated on a measure of self-delusion. His counsellors, dispirited and defeatist, could simply see no alternative to a parliament, and with it, uncomfortable but unavoidable, the prospect of a serious interrogation of the king's policies. Charles, slow to accept the necessity for a parliament, finally did so in a naive hope that his subjects would be inspired by a visceral patriotism to defend his and their honour, so deeply compromised by the Scottish invasion and occupation. The king announced his decision in a sabre-rattling speech; the expulsion of the Scots from English soil would be the prime business of the new parliament. In the event, the Houses did not prove so jingoistically pliant, nor should the king have expected it, given his recent dealings with and experience of the mood of his subjects as expressed in that forum.

In the summer of 1637 Charles's revised Prayer Book had been imposed on Scotland, as part of a more general attempt to bring the kirk into line with the discipline, doctrine and ceremonies of the English church. The initial reading was greeted with horror and riot in Edinburgh – 'The Mass is entered among us'; 'Baal is in the church' – and with petitions and formal protests from the country at large.[3] These responses snowballed into a more general challenge to the royal government of his northern kingdom, not least because of the king's intransigence and refusal to negotiate: 'I mean to be obeyed.'[4] Charles resolved to bring the Scots to heel, and by the spring of 1638 both the king and his opponents began military preparations. Many of his English subjects anticipated that Charles would summon a parliament as a prelude to war. This was an occasion on which kings had traditionally called parliaments, both to secure the necessary taxes and to project an image of national unity: 'It is thought ... the King will answer [the Scots] with the voice of the whole kingdom', wrote Sir Thomas Peyton to a fellow Kentish gentleman.[5] One of the king's company commanders made a similar point, 'You go the wrong way to work', he told Charles, 'the only way to prosper is to go back and call a parliament'.[6] But Charles sought neither parliamentary finance nor the ratification of his policies. He determined to go it alone. A substantial war chest was raised by some pretty desperate expedients – loans, anticipation of revenue, pawning the royal jewels. The English fleet blockaded the Firth of Forth, and an army of 16,000 men was painfully raised and marched north. A phoney war of threat and manoeuvre was played out on the Scottish border in May and June 1639, and it was Charles's nerve that failed. There was no general engagement, and the king agreed to a treaty with the Scots, the Pacification of Berwick, on terms of little more than the disbanding of forces by both sides.

Charles's failure to pursue the military option in which he had invested so much is difficult to understand. The king and his advisers were troubled by the failure of the naval blockade and by the fact that no groups had emerged in Scotland to challenge the dominant faction on the king's behalf. The English commanders also overestimated the military strength of the Scots. Most telling may have been the general sense of demoralisation and uncertainty in the English army, 'confusion' in the command, and a fear that the troops – raised with difficulty in the localities, inexperienced, poorly equipped and supplied, under funded – would simply not stand up to the Scots.

The Pacification of Berwick proved only a temporary respite. Negotiations on the substantive issues between the Scots and the king almost immediately broke down in the face of mutual intransigence. Charles insisted on the retention of episcopacy, the Scots were adamant that it must be abolished and went on to deny the king any authority to appoint the major officers of the Scottish state. By the autumn both sides were again preparing for war. And on this occasion Charles's plans incorporated the calling of parliament, but it was to be a parliament, as the French ambassador noted, 'à sa mode'.[7] The king's view of parliament's role was purely instrumental. The Houses should be presented with the estimates of the monies needed for the suppression of the Scottish rebellion, and then vote those sums. If parliament failed to follow the royal agenda, if 'his people should not cheerfully, according to their duties, meet him in that exigent when his kingdom and person are in apparent danger', then he would be freed from all constitutional restraints, 'to use extraordinary means'.[8]

Parliament was summoned on 12 February 1640, and met on the 13 April. At the polls in many constituencies the electorate had displayed their concern for current issues and their disaffection from the king's policies. Any hint of vague association with the court, whether true or not, could be fatal to a candidate's prospects, as could a man's involvement in the enforcement of any of Charles's policies. 'Choose no ship sheriff', began a rhyme circulating in Lincolnshire before the election; 'we'll have no Deputy Lieutenants!' bellowed the 'rude multitude' at the Northamptonshire hustings, 'Take heed of Deputy Lieutenants!

'The Portraiture of the Mighty Monarch Charles I', an etching by
Wenceslaus Hollar, first produced in 1639. This is a supremely ironic
commentary on the disparity between image and reality in the Caroline
period. The commanding king and the disciplined force bear little
relation to the shambles of the campaign against the Scots.
(*Ashmolean Museum, Oxford*)

No Deputy Lieutenants!'[9] Charles's counsellors bleakly noted the defeat of those 'that have relation to the court' and the triumph of 'most refractory persons', and surmised that 'the parliament will not sit long'.[10] It did not. Any hope that loyal subjects would vote money for the Scottish war as a matter of urgency was swept aside by parliament's insistence that priority must be given to discussion and redress of the grievances of the English. A late attempt was made to propose a compromise, whereby Charles would abandon his major fiscal innovation, ship money, in return for parliamentary funding of the war. This failed more narrowly, in part because a number of vocal, committed MPs spoke against it, in part because the king lacked the patience and perhaps the inclination to seek to build a consensus in parliament. Three weeks after its first meeting, parliament – understandably nicknamed 'the Short' – was dissolved.

Charles had now achieved the position foreseen prior to parliament's meeting. He had turned to his subjects for their assistance; they had spurned his request. He was, then, driven by 'unavoidable necessity' to 'use extraordinary means' in his operations against the Scots. The case was put most powerfully by the earl of Strafford, the king's highly effective and energetic viceroy in Ireland, at a council meeting immediately following the dissolution:

> Go on with an offensive war as you first designed, loosed and absolved from all rules of government. Being reduced to extreme necessity, everything is to be done as power will admit, and that you are to do.[11]

High theory was all very well – Archbishop Laud assured the king that in the circumstances he could raise money 'by the law of God' – but practicalities were another matter. 'I can not learn by what means we are certain to get one shilling', wrote one of the king's advisers, 'It grieves my soul to be involved in these counsels.'[12]

What followed in England, as Charles sought to mobilise a new army, was not the revolt feared by some of the king's counsellors, but a torpid and reluctant response to royal demands in the localities. The local governors raised men and money painfully and slowly. Groups of unwilling conscripts were moved to the north, but they were ill paid, and lacked both supplies and equipment, partly because their officers dared not trust them with weapons. They expressed their disaffection en route by large-scale desertion, iconoclasm in churches, poaching, smashing enclosures and attacking their officers. Two of the latter, alleged to be Catholics, were murdered by their men. The position taken by the English at Newburn was poorly chosen, easily swept by the superior Scottish artillery. But the drained spirits of the royal commanders and counsellors, exhausted by the struggle against a dead weight of disaffection throughout the country, were more responsible than a tactical blunder for that defeat.

Charles called the Long Parliament because his army had been beaten, and an empty treasury ensured that he could not embark on any further military operations. The king was bankrupt, his finances and his moral authority exhausted. The Scots had defeated an English king – not a frequent occurrence in the history of the relations of the two countries – and forced him to beg for terms. The English were complicit in the success enjoyed by the Scots. They had refused, formally in the abortive Short Parliament, pragmatically in the disputes and foot-dragging that attended subsequent attempts to raise men and money from the localities, to behave as Charles required. Loyal patriots eager to chastise the Scots for the insults they offered to the honour of the king and to the integrity of the English nation were few in 1640.

The next question is obvious: how had this extraordinary situation come about? The king himself was primarily responsible. His policies in the 1630s demonstrated both tactical mistakes and a more fundamental failure to observe or even understand the structures of society, of government, and of ideology that circumscribed royal authority in England.

F. W. Maitland, the great Victorian analyst of medieval law and society, described the administration of medieval England as 'local self-government by the king's command'. The phrase, with its emphasis on symbiosis and consensus, is equally applicable – perhaps more applicable – to England in the sixteenth and seventeenth centuries. Juridically England was a highly centralised polity. A 'common' law was created and enforced though central mechanisms, and both the law and its institutions derived their force from the king, the apex and focus of the system. Yet this centralised system possessed only the most rudimentary bureaucracy, and its tiny cadre of paid officials at Westminster

was necessarily supplemented by an army of unpaid amateu
localities. Each year leading members of English village commu...
the grassroots units of administration, took their turns in serving as the
king's agents in matters of police, justice, taxation and social welfare.
The majority of those filling middle-management posts, the brokers
channelling orders from Westminster to the localities, and supervising
their enforcement, were also amateurs – local gentlemen commissioned
by the crown.

The Tudor monarchs enhanced the centralisation of the system that
they inherited. Liberties and franchises, semi-autonomous areas where,
technically, the king's law and his power were restricted, were abolished.
Papal authority, and with it the claims of the ecclesiastical hierarchy to
independent status, was renounced, and the crown's role as head of the
church asserted. These changes were accomplished in parliament, which
was finally established as a supreme legislature, universal in its scope and
omnicompetent in its authority. Yet, while developing the scope of the
theoretical pretensions of the centralised state, the Tudors still relied on
the medieval structures for the execution of their policies in the localities. Indeed, they increased the demands, and thus their reliance, upon
those structures. The break with Rome spawned legislation to police
religious dissent. A welter of new regulations designed to mitigate the
adverse social effects of population rise and changes in the structure of
the agricultural economy were disseminated. The backs of local magistrates and officers 'had to bear so many, not loads, but *stacks* of Statutes,
that have been laid upon them' an Elizabethan commentator noted
wryly.[13] More work required more manpower. New offices were created.
Leading gentlemen were invited to assume military responsibilities,
supervising the county militias as deputy lieutenants; villagers now
had to appoint additional officers, the overseers of the poor, to administer the flurry of social legislation at the turn of the century. With
long-established posts the number of men commissioned to act was
simply multiplied – the number of justices of the peace by a factor of
three in most English counties in the period 1500–1640. Generally the
number of unpaid amateurs who acted in some more or less temporary
capacity as royal agents in the localities increased dramatically.

The structure of early-modern English government, in which the centralised creation and direction of policy was combined with localised

enforcement, entails an obvious problem. How did the centre secure conformity to its directives from its local officers? That the indolence or self-aggrandisement of its ostensible agents might deflect government policy was a favoured theme of satirists. Some justices of the peace, quipped an MP in a speech to the 1601 Commons, would 'for half a dozen chickens ... dispense with a whole dozen of the penal statutes'.[14] But this was not a joking matter for the counsellors and law officers of the crown. They recognised the problem, and pursued a double strategy in relation to it: punishment and persuasion.

Punishment, involving fines or imprisonment, or humiliation – dismissal from the bench for JPs, public abasement for village officers – was meted out by or at the instruction of the central government. But the council's ability to police its agents effectively was seriously restricted. Distance was always a problem, and with it a consequent dearth of accurate information concerning events in the periphery. More germane to Charles I's government in the 1630s was another systemic weakness. The council was a small body, lacking any very extensive secretarial back-up or bureaucratic infrastructure; it could not do too many things simultaneously. If its energies became focused on some major matter of policy, its attention to other issues, including the deficiencies and recalcitrance of its local officers, might wane. Such a situation had arisen in the earlier years of Charles's reign. In the autumn of 1626, the king, denied funds in parliament to sustain war with Spain, instructed the local governors to raise a sum equivalent to that denied him by the Commons, ostensibly as a loan. Local objection and resistance to this policy, initially powerful, was swept aside in a flood of conciliar activism, which, as the Venetian ambassador complained, paralysed all other business including vital diplomatic negotiations. Privy counsellors toured the counties to supervise meetings for the assessment of the loan; those gentlemen nominated as local agents who refused to act, or those who failed to pay, were imprisoned in droves. The intimidation of lesser taxpayers included the threat of conscription into the force that Charles was raising to serve on the Continent. Such pressure, a product of the council's single-minded dedication, guaranteed large returns on the loan. But close supervision could not be continued indefinitely. By the summer of 1627 muddle and lack of direction emerged as the council turned its attention to other matters.

Accounts were not properly kept; defaulters were no longer hounded, and their immunity encouraged others, previously compliant, to refuse payment. Many of the gentry who had been coerced into acting as local assessors and collectors by the hard line taken by the council earlier in the year slipped away as the government's attention wavered.

The structural deficiencies of Charles's government, apparent in 1628, were blindingly obvious in 1640. In the period between the dissolution of the Short Parliament and the battle of Newburn the council received a series of bleak reports concerning the enforcement of its policies from all areas of England. Charles needed men and money if his Scottish policy was to succeed. The parish constables, threatened by the deputy lieutenants with their own impressment into the army if they failed, produced their designated quotas of men, though the levies were of very doubtful quality. Charles had hoped that there would be a 'very good choice made of the men out of the trained bands';[15] in the face of a chorus of complaint, substitution was permitted and the conscripts were mostly marginals and misfits. The king's general in the north thought them 'the arch knaves of the kingdom', and that their 'rawness and untowardness' explained the subsequent disaster.[16]

Men of a sort Charles got: money was another matter. After the failure of the Short Parliament, Charles was relying heavily on the local levy of 'coat and conduct money' to pay the initial charges of raising his army, and on ship money for disposable income. Raising a fraction of the anticipated sums from either source proved exceptionally difficult. The collapse of the ship money collection, given its earlier success, is particularly telling. In 1640 the machinery for its collection had failed, leaving the sheriffs of the counties – local gentlemen holding the office for a single year – ultimately responsible for raising the levy. It proved an impossible task. Most were obliged to take on the lengthy and contentious task of assigning each taxpayer's individual contribution, because the parish constables had refused to assess their fellow villagers. The local officers also proved 'remiss and careless' in the task of collecting the money, and most of the sheriffs had then been forced to hire bailiffs or to employ their own servants to act as collectors. The sheriff of Oxfordshire was reduced to touring the county, attempting to make distraints with two of his sons and a household servant. The collectors were faced with a wall of resistance by a host of individual taxpayers.

There was a general refusal to produce the money, and the sheriff and his servants were compelled to seize the goods of the recalcitrant. Those engaged in this time-consuming process faced routine abuse, threats of lawsuits, and occasional violent resistance. A force of half a dozen bailiffs attempting seizures at Melbourn were attacked by a mob, stoned as they sought to retreat, and driven into a ditch 'where some of their horses stuck fast'. An attempt to prosecute the rioters for assault at the Cambridgeshire quarter sessions was simply thrown out of court by the grand jury. Where seizures were made, they often proved unavailing. Sheriffs found themselves stuck with the goods that had been seized 'because there come no buyers'; the sheriff of Bedfordshire believed that prospective bidders had been warned off attending auctions of goods 'that are distresses for ship-money'. In Cornwall the sheriff had been obliged to return the beasts he had distrained because he could not hire sufficient pasture on which to graze them.[17] Threats of punishment accomplished little. The privy council was too busy to give proper attention to local defaulters; even when it did, its rebukes were ineffectual. An Oxfordshire bailiff who had been summoned before the privy council was not galvanised into action by the experience: a month later he had collected only £5 10s. of the more than £400 he had been instructed to levy. The option of imprisoning village officers was obviously counter-productive, because it was on them that the burden of levying the men, money and military supplies to sustain the king's Scottish policy also fell. Indeed, some sheriffs suggested that the constables courted imprisonment as an opportunity to 'avoid all other services'. The Somerset constables who said 'they had rather fall into the hands of His Majesty than into the hands of resolute men' were voicing a common preference.[18]

The administrative failure in 1640 is most apparent at the level of the parish, and in the recalcitrance of the constables. But a reluctance to advance royal policies, shading into a deliberate obstructionism, also marked the behaviour of the gentry 'brokers' in their intermedial roles. A number of sheriffs, in the opinion of the council, failed to make even the most basic response to the local opposition that faced them. The sheriff of Yorkshire was placed under close arrest, and proceedings against eight of his fellow sheriffs were begun in Star Chamber. The office of deputy lieutenant had been the plum post for leading members of the local gentry, recognising and reinforcing their prestige in the shire. By 1639 Charles was refusing to allow men to resign from this once-coveted position. Despite this, a good proportion of the deputy lieutenants in 1640 failed to carry out their responsibilities. Some, like those of Somerset and Wiltshire, raised technical quibbles concerning the validity of their commissions; others simply made themselves scarce, leaving only one or two of their colleagues to shoulder the burdens. The JPs were less directly involved in the execution of the king's policies in 1640, but they often used their authority to hinder them. They refused to assist in the process of ship money assessment, and failed to act against those who violently resisted attempts to seize their goods. In Cheshire the JPs protected those constables whose recalcitrance the sheriff was attempting to punish, and threatened to prosecute the sheriff's bailiffs for irregularities in the process of distraint. In Berkshire the JPs released soldiers imprisoned by the deputy lieutenants for desertion. An incident in Staffordshire is a telling reflection on the confusion and breakdown in local administration in 1640: in August bailiffs employed by the sheriff were seizing goods from the deputy lieutenants for the ship money they had not paid.

Village officers and their gentry supervisors, overwhelmed by an impossible workload, simply downed tools in the summer of 1640. The council, desperately attempting to mobilise for the invasion of Scotland, could not give attention to defaulters, and the numbers of the latter snowballed. A breakdown in the machinery of local government lay at the heart of Charles I predicament, explaining defeat in Scotland and the necessity of again summoning parliament. But the king's inability to comprehend the limits imposed on his government by the structure and mechanics of English local administration was not his only failure. The anger that confronted the constables in their communities, and which made them prefer to risk the threats of the council than those of their neighbours, suggest that Charles's policies aroused more than a passive, visceral aversion to heavy taxation. The king's policies offended the legal and constitutional sensibilities, the political consciousness, of his subjects, not least of those who were both taxpayers and the local executors of those policies.

Ironically, the development of an understanding of political obligation, widely dispersed through the social hierarchy, which was hostile to Charles's fiscal policies, owed much to the efforts of the king's predecessors. The counsellors and law officers of the crown, keenly aware of their limited ability to guarantee local enforcement of policy by an amateur administration by policing and punishment, also sought to educate the local governors in their duty to conform to norms and agendas dictated from the centre. From the mid sixteenth century, proclamations, judgements in key trials, exhortations in various contexts – to parliament, in Star Chamber, at the biannual assizes when the judges of the central courts visited the localities – were employed to inculcate a proper sense of public responsibility. In all these media the same corporatist and legalist themes recur. The local magistrates must put aside self-interest, and devote their energies to active participation in a great cooperative endeavour, the preservation and advancement of the common good. They must internalise their role as trusted deputies. They were agents in a double capacity: of a common law –'the best laws in the whole world' – that defined the rights and duties of all members of the polity; and of a monarch whose vigorous commitment to justice and beneficent rule they must emulate.

The gentry were the prime targets of these messages, which were echoed in the sermons by their favoured ministers and in handbooks designed to provide detailed guidance for them on the technicalities of law enforcement. Such themes were reinforced by their increasingly formal education at university and the Inns of Court, the prime purpose of which, Christopher Wandesford told his son, was 'how to assist in the government of your country'.[19] But the gentry were not the only audience for this language of public duty, of the commonwealth. It was not only the JPs, massed on the bench, who listened to the exhortations of the judges and the godly sermons that were an increasing feature of the assizes, but those who attended in their roles as jurors and constables. And the same rhetoric might be employed at less august gatherings, and more specifically tuned for an audience of village officers 'you that be of the middle sort'. The JPs and the local officers, all appointed by the king 'in our several places', a Hertfordshire sessions jury were told, ought to cooperate to ensure that the laws were 'profitable to the commonwealth for the suppression of sin and vice'. Warwickshire jurors were encouraged to think of themselves as 'the champion of justice, the patron of peace, the father of thy country'. In 1587 a Kentish jury of 'the honest and meaner sort', empanelled to investigate the manipulation of grain

prices by racketeers, were exhorted, 'in these common causes and public services' not to 'be afraid to join with God, her majesty, and the
realm against any few ... whatsoever'.[20]

The rhetoric that emphasised duty to the commonwealth and the
overarching framework of the common law had been developed by government spokesmen eager to educate amateur, part-time, temporary
local agents in their public responsibilities. But these emphases could
prove a two-edged sword. The language might be appropriated and fired
back against royal policies that contravened the norms of the common
law or that appeared to advance private interests over the public good.
Nor was it just the gentry in their roles as MPs and JPs who could dis-
comfit the government by reciting the lessons about the mutual
obligations of ruler and subject mediated through common law that had
been taught them by royal spokesmen. The development of a view of
political obligation that was shared by taxpayers and village officers with
their gentry supervisors and superiors is an important aspect of
Charles's failure in 1640.

The levy of ship money from 1634 was based on the development of
a novel theory of taxation. In normal circumstances, the king should
seek parliamentary approval for levies of money; but, when the safety of
the realm was at stake, he had a duty to act for the public good. Further,
he alone had the authority to determine when such a state of emergency
existed. The judges rubber-stamped this claim in an extrajudicial opinion early 1637, and the majority of the bench affirmed it in the test case
involving John Hampden later that year. In 'cases of necessity', Justice
Berkeley argued, the 'ordinary rules' of law no longer bound the king;
he must be enabled act as he saw fit by his 'regal power' for the 'preservation of the safety of the commonwealth'.[21] These arguments were
profoundly subversive of the traditional constitutional assumptions held
by those who collected and those who paid national taxation.

Charles had first deployed this doctrine early in his reign when he
sought money by way of gifts and loans in 1626 and 1627. The public
justifications of the king's demands emphasised 'unavoidable necessity',
'a case of this extremity', a crisis 'to which no ordinary rules can be
prescribed'. The degree to which these ideas challenged the political consciousness of his subjects is apparent in their initial responses to the
king's projects. The request for a free gift, presented to the taxpayers in

a series of county assemblies in the summer of 1626 by specially commissioned JPs, produced a few utterly derisory sums and a mass of
excuses alleging local poverty. But in some areas the taxpayers were
reported to have offered legal and constitutional objections to the king's
request. The precedent would be dangerous, it was argued; the 'usual
and ancient custom' of a parliamentary grant was preferred. It is tempting to see this as mere ventriloquism. The gentry concealed their own
recalcitrance by foisting responsibility for the scheme's failure onto
a large and largely anonymous group – freeholders, subsidymen, 'the
better sort'. Yet where the evidence allows us to move behind the formal
reports sent up to Westminster, it suggests that the issues had been discussed and conclusions reached independently by social groups below
the level of the gentry. In Bedfordshire the subsidymen refused to recede
from their refusal to give, despite being twice required to reconsider the
matter by the gentry commissioners. They wondered if 'this course now
holden was not against law ... and they feared future danger by such a
precedent'.[22] The response to the forced loan was less coherent not least
because, as we have seen, the council was determined that the project
should succeed, and from the first leaned heavily on the gentry commissioners and the local taxpayers to secure conformity. But in counties
remote from London, and from 'the awe of the council', refusals to act
as commissioners or to pay the levy were more frequent, and might be
justified by reference to the conventions that had been rehearsed in the
summer of 1626. Warned that he risked 'the king's high displeasure',
Sir Thomas Darnell replied that 'he hoped he should have the liberty of
a subject to dispose of his ... estate at his pleasure'.[23] Most men, aware
of the crown's readiness to compel payment, did not court martyrdom.
If they were not enforced to immediate payment, they laid low, disputed
the details of the sums demanded, paid reluctantly. And, as the council's
attention steadily focused on the pressing military and logistical tasks
that confronted it in the summer of 1627 their foot-dragging both saved
their own money and retarded the success of the project as a whole.

The response to ship money resembles that to the forced loan. Initially
major doubts concerning the legality of the tax were expressed. The
sheriff enforcing the first ship money levy in Oxfordshire found that
collection was delayed by the refusal of many village officers to
make assessments; they failed to respond to his warrants and made

themselves scarce when messengers were sent to them. Eventually he extracted an answer from one of the defaulting constables, Francis French of South Newton: he was firmly told that no money would be raised in the parish, 'till such time as you shall make known unto us a law or statute binding us thereunto ... till when we shall remain in suspense and expectation of an answer'.[24] The sheriff promptly impounded the South Newton herd, but the £12 due from the village was still not forthcoming. The villagers refused to redeem their animals, challenged their seizure on legal technicalities, and denied that the sheriff's commission gave him any right to sell their property. In 1636 the council could ultimately crush the opposition of a small village that had the temerity to challenge the legality of the king's demands. Indeed, it could bring a whole county to heel. Essex had proved peculiarly recalcitrant in 1635 and 1636, and by the end of that year it had the largest sum in arrears of any English county. The sheriff was at his wit's end: 'there is no penny paid that is not forced, god help me, amongst the people'.[25] Many of the leading figures in the shire were denying payment, led by the earl of Warwick; and local officers, many of them appointed by Warwick, were also refusing assistance to the sheriff. A petition against the levy was presented by the grand jury, claiming to represent the county. Early in 1637 the earl made a direct appeal to the king to change his policy, withdraw the tax and summon a parliament. His tenants, he said, were old 'and used to the mild rule of Queen Elizabeth and King James'. They were reluctant to be even passively responsible for giving away 'the liberties of the realm'; they wished to bequeath 'the sacred treasure' of the law to their posterity.[26] Charles was unmoved. Legal proceedings were begun against sixty leading refusers, and dismissal from office was threatened against those who remained recalcitrant. A dynamic sheriff was appointed, and given complete support by the council; faced with the refusal of a couple of high constables to act, the sheriff descended upon them with a convoy of wagons, and seized and sold their goods to defray the arrears from the entire hundred. Under this assault resistance to the levy melted away, until the circumstances of 1639 made overt opposition once again a safe option.

The council's vigorous response to opposition to ship money that challenged the king's right to the levy drove such sentiment underground: it did not eradicate it. Public payment might be accompanied by the private expressions of doubt and resentment. The constable of Winfarthing noted in his 1637 account his payment for the sum assessed on the town lands 'for that unlawful tax of ship money'.[27] Sir Simonds D'Ewes, as sheriff of Suffolk in 1640, defended his inability to collect the sum with vague generalities about the poverty of the county and failures of the village officers. Earlier, in the secure privacy of his own journal, he had written that the tax was 'the most deadly and fatal blow ... to the liberty of the subjects of England' in the last five hundred years.[28] The disparity between private opinion and public performance was not, however, total. Few men dared to challenge ship money openly before 1640, but they did engage in covert resistance – delaying assessment, and challenging the rates when they were made; paying slowly or obliging the sheriff to proceed by distraint.

This process was assisted, paradoxically, by the king's insistence that ship money was warranted by law and tradition. The policy of making the county sheriff personally responsible for the levy *was* an innovation, designed to prevent the evasions that were possible in a system of collective responsibility, as had emerged with the commissioners for the forced loan. But no change was made to the length of term for which a sheriff served, or to the traditional way of choosing men to hold this key office. Little attempt was made to ensure that the gentlemen appointed as sheriffs had much administrative experience or were likely to prove conscientious and effective officers. Some sheriffs were newcomers to the counties, with few contacts among the governing elite and little understanding of its administrative structure. The 1640 sheriff of Cambridgeshire was ' a private man ... of very small power, countenance or command in the country ... never before employed in public affairs'.[29] A few were grossly corrupt, more were incompetent: the sheriff of Essex in 1636, up against a coordinated resistance organised by some of the leading figures in the county, was Sir Humphrey Mildmay, a feckless *bon viveur*, happiest in the taverns, gambling joints and brothels of London. Some were men who had criticised Charles's earlier fiscal schemes. The 1635 sheriff of Lincolnshire, Sir Walter Norton (a 'stranger' in the county, keenly attuned to the possibilities of peculation), complained of the opposition he faced from men noted for their 'backwardness and crossness to royal prerogative ... treading a parliament way'.[30] One of these men was Sir Anthony Irby, a forced loan refuser in 1627. In 1637 Irby was chosen sheriff of the county. The council might have foreseen the heavy arrears, the product, they thought, of Irby's deliberate recalcitrance in his office. The annual appointment of sheriffs further ensured that there was little administrative continuity, and, worse, the sheriffs were often in receipt of contradictory instructions from the council. Villages whose assessments varied from year to year chose to suspect, often correctly, that the sheriff was engaged in a little logrolling on behalf of friends and neighbours. The result was a series of complaints about the fairness of the rating process, which the council, insistent that ship money was not an arbitrary mulct, and keen to display its consequent concern for due process and sensitivity to responsible criticism, entertained. Twenty-four times the disputed rate for Tintinhull hundred in Somerset came to the attention of the council: in their efforts to get appropriate information to set a fair rate, they sought assistance from the bishop of Bath, the assize judges and local JPs. A host of busy officials, with better things to do, became enmeshed in this local dispute.

Charles I's insistence on the traditional status of his demand, which partially explains the weakness of the administrative machinery established by the king, had another unintended consequence. It led him to trumpet the legality of ship money in the localities, using the same techniques employed by his predecessors to educate their subjects. This may have been counter-productive, serving not to silence dissent but to focus attention on the legal debate. In the summer of 1635 Lord Keeper Coventry, addressing the judges before they began their peregrinations to the county assizes, provided them with a model of the speeches they were to make at those assemblies. He listed the law enforcement agenda of the government, employing a good deal of traditional commonwealth rhetoric on the impartial enforcement of justice for the public benefit. But he also required them to stress that ship money was 'just and reasonable' and 'for the general good of [the] kingdom'.[31] In February 1637 Coventry made a similar demand. At the assizes the judges were to publicise their answer to the king's letter concerning the legality of ship money, with its acknowledgement that in cases of necessity the monarch must act for the public good, and that he alone was the judge of necessity. The crown refused to allow trials arising from ship money to proceed before its lawyers had set up a test case that would give it the maximum procedural advantage, but occasional opportunities arose for the judges to display their enthusiasm for ship money practically. It emerged in the course of an assault case at the Gloucestershire assizes. The alleged thuggery had been perpetrated by bailiffs distraining the goods of a farmer, Robert Hoblin, who had refused ship money 'because it was not granted by parliament'. The judge told Hoblin 'in great passion' that 'the king was not to call a parliament to give him satisfaction', directed the jury to find for his opponent and imprisoned him.[32]

From 1638 judges were able to refer to the judgement in Hampden's case, affirming the legality of ship money; several of them did so, before, early in 1640 the lord keeper required them to do this in their assize speeches. The crown's case, then, was presented to the gentry and parish officers at the assizes by the judges 'the oracles of the law'. But it did not gain general acceptance; rather it sparked debate. Sir Roger Twysden, after hearing the defence of the judges' extra-judicial opinion by the judge at Maidstone assizes, retired to his library to consult his tomes on law and history. His erudition was no doubt exceptional, but he thought that his fellow gentlemen and 'the common sort' were equally involved in serious and troubled consideration on the constitutional implications of the matter. The judgement in Hampden's case also provoked reflection rather than obedience. It was the opinions of judges Croke and Hutton, who had declared unequivocally against the king, that circulated and were 'plausibly received' in the localities, where they 'have made men more backward than they would have been'.[33]

In almost all counties the sheriffs found it increasingly difficult to collect the tax before the outbreak of the Scottish war placed further burdens on local administration. In so far as taxpayers offered justifications of their recalcitrance, it was in terms of the unfairness of the rating process: individuals, villages, subdivisions of the county all claimed that the sheriff or the local assessors had discriminated against them. Sorting out these complaints took time. Not all complaints of inequitable rating were a cover for a principled opposition to ship money, but many certainly were. The assessment upon Tintinhull hundred was the most contentious in England, shackling and frustrating the sheriffs of Somerset throughout the history of the levy. The challenge was instigated by Sir Robert Phellips, who had opposed the forced loan and the king's arguments from necessity in the parliament of 1628. Magnates and gentlemen who had questioned Charles's policies also lived in other areas almost equally fertile in rating disputes: Rochford hundred in Essex contained the seat of the earl of Warwick and Bloxham hundred in Oxfordshire that of Lord Saye. But elite leadership was not always necessary. Southern Lincolnshire lacked a powerful resident gentry. It actively resisted the initial demand for the forced loan, and then, in response to the council's stricter policing of dissent, turned to delay and technical quibble. By 1637 it was a centre of rating disputes over ship money; in that year a constable from the area expressed a preference that was common in 1640: 'He had rather answer afore the Lords of the Council then distrain his neighbours.'[34]

Tudor governments had sought to secure the enforcement of edicts in the localities by creatively seeking to inculcate a sense of public responsibility in the men who were its local agents. The lesson was learned well, ultimately to the embarrassment of the government. Westminster's schemes were evaluated and found wanting by an articulate, experienced and well-informed group of magistrates and village officers. Their doubts about aspects of the central government's agenda could easily frustrate its local enforcement. The government could silence the direct expression of criticism of the legality of its policies, but this might only divert such sentiments into other, less obviously confrontational channels. Concerns about constitutional propriety that often underlay the disputes over technicalities could still give force to practical opposition to the crown's policies, as successive sheriffs discovered in the late 1630s. And, when in 1640 the strong hand of the privy council wavered, they could burst out to overwhelm the king's policies. Charles's government slowed and seized up in 1640 in the face of such local antipathy and a consequent reluctance to act.

In the Commons on 17 April 1640 the Speaker reported the speeches of Charles and of the lord keeper four days previously on the agenda that they anticipated the parliament would pursue. The 'foul and horrid treason' of the Scots was proved. Military action was unavoidable, and the immediate supply of money for the provision of the army was essential. MPs should 'lay aside all other debate' until taxation had been granted. There would be time enough for a discussion of grievances once the military and fiscal priorities had been addressed. The response to the

Speaker's synopsis was carefully stage-managed. Two lengthy speeches by Francis Rouse and John Pym were followed by the presentation of petitions from three counties by their MPs. All these contributions emphasised grievances, grievances that, in Pym's words, 'disabled us to administer any supply until they be redressed'.[35] The lists of grievances included, of course, the fiscal experiments undertaken by the king in the 1630s, but in each of these performances priority was given to obnoxious features of Charles's religious policies. 'Innovation in religion' headed the Northamptonshire petition;[36] for Pym 'the greatest grievance to be looked into' was religion; and religion, argued Rous, was 'the root of all our grievances'.[37] The king's failure to understand the constraints placed on his freedom of action in fiscal matters by the meld of administrative realities and constitutional assumptions was, it seems, mirrored in a failure to comprehend the religious prejudices of his subjects.

James I had sought to promote a broad, inclusive, ecumenical church that attempted to incorporate the great majority of Protestants, though of divergent shades of theological opinion and of ritual practice. Tests for membership were minimal: ministers had to acknowledge the Royal Supremacy by conforming to the king's intermittent injunctions concerning ceremonies or preaching. James's indulgent approach was reinforced by the lethargy that infected much of local administration in his reign, and created a Church of England that was a patchwork of semi-autonomous parishes, and a mélange of ceremonial and liturgical practice. Worse, in the opinion of many ecclesiastics, the policy had allowed puritan extremists to follow their own inclinations in a way that had led to the subversion of the essential principle of a national church. A group of moderate Essex ministers complained in 1629 of 'most men doing what seemeth good in their own eyes, and few regarding the authority of the church'.[38] Crucially, Charles I agreed with this analysis and shared this concern.

The case of John Vicars, the minister of St Mary's church, Stamford, tried in 1631 before the Ecclesiastical High Commission in London, represented all that Charles found most offensive in puritanism and in the lax regime that had permitted it to flourish unchecked in the localities. Vicars refused to wear the vestments or to employ the liturgy of the Book of Common Prayer, which he dismissed as 'superstitious'. But this was the least of his offences. He was committed to extreme Calvinist theology, and believed that the elect minority, chosen by God for salvation, could be distinguished from the reprobate. Vicars organised those in whom he discerned the signs of saving grace, a group that drew its members from a wide area around Stamford, into an autonomous congregation that met regularly for exhortation, prayer and fasting. This private congregation, 'his own family and children as he calleth them', 'his children begotten in the Lord', entered into a covenant 'to do whatsoever God commandeth'. They insisted on strict sabbatarianism, refused to work for ungodly employers, and practised a restrictive sexual code – Vicars' large female following was derided locally as 'the new nunnery of Stamford'. They also clubbed together to improve their spiritual leader's income. Vicars used his public pulpit to snipe at England's insufficiently zealous foreign policy and, nearer to home, to excoriate the sins of the reprobate of Stamford. 'The arrows of God's vengeance' and 'the thunderbolts of God's wrath' were denounced against drunkards, swearers, usurers, sensualists and those who feasted riotously at Christmas. In his tirades Vicars did not spare the civic elite: their patronage of a visiting company of players was singled out for particular invective. The town worthies – and their wives, characterised on one occasion by Vicars as 'painted Jezebels ... and whorish Dalilahs' – deeply resented this highly divisive ministry.[39]

At Stamford extreme Calvinist doctrine in the hands of a tactless prig had destroyed the corporate life of the parish, polarised the community, and subverted the social order. Charles, in partnership with his trusted religious adviser, William Laud, from 1628 bishop of London and from 1633 archbishop of Canterbury, was determined to reconstruct a church that affirmed, through uniformity of religious practice, the unity of the realm and the harmony of the parish. The mystery of divine election was unfathomable, so ministers must recognise their obligation to the entire Christian community and must serve 'the body of the whole visible church' in charity. Accordingly a declaration issued in 1626, elaborated in 1628 and reinforced in later episcopal mandates proscribed discussion in sermons or pamphlets on the complex mysteries, the 'deep and dark points', the 'points obscure', of free will and predestination, for 'the peace and quiet of the Church of England'.[40] Royal instructions of 1629 sought to establish a uniform liturgical and ceremonial practice within the church, and to ensure that prayer and worship were given as much importance as the sermon in the religious life of the parish. Ministers were enjoined to read the Book of Common Prayer service before preaching, and to read it in the prescribed vestments. The laity should be reverent during the services, bowing at the name of Jesus, and following the directions of the Book of Common Prayer concerning posture and gesture. God, said Bishop Curll of Winchester, was to be 'worshipped not only in holiness, but in the beauty of holiness'.[41]

In 1634 Laud moved further to enforce a uniformity of ceremony in the church, issuing instructions that the communion table should normally be placed behind a rail at the east end of the chancel, and that parishioners should be encouraged to come up to the rails to receive communion. These practices were embodied in the new canons promulgated by Convocation in the spring of 1640. Charles and Laud also endeavoured to restrict those activities that detracted from the parish as the prime focus of religious life. Unbeneficed lecturers were to be carefully policed, as was 'sermon-gadding', the process whereby laymen sought out those ministers whose doctrine and performance they found most inspirational. In 1633 the king published an order that perhaps best indicates his sense of the role of the parish as both a spiritual and social unit. The Book of Sports, originally issued by James in 1618 but largely neglected in the absence of consistent enforcement, permitted people to dance or engage in 'harmless recreation' after Sunday service. It also declared that Morris dancing and May Day celebrations, and parish festivals with the games that accompanied them, were legitimate. For Charles, the festivities were affirmations and reinforcements of the organic harmony and hierarchy of local society, through commensality and charity. As the king further insisted that the Book should be read out in parish churches, the performance of this task became a litmus test of ministers' obedience to royal authority in the church. Those ministers who refused to promulgate the Book were reported, and many of the recalcitrants were temporarily suspended and a few deprived of their livings.

The puritans had, at the cost of some minimal and infrequent gestures of conformity, been able to create enclaves of evangelical religion in the tolerant, ramshackle church of King James. Their strongholds were at risk in the changed ecclesiastical atmosphere of the 1630s, with its emphasis on conformity – and on conformity to novel ceremonial requirements – and its interventionist administration. The immediacy of the threat faced by the godly varied from diocese to diocese, depending on the commitment and efficiency of the bishop. Bishop Wren, at Norwich, went beyond Charles and Laud in his enforcement of the ceremonies; Bishop Williams at Lincoln waged a campaign of suave procrastination against the demands of his hated rival, Laud. But the godly, even if they enjoyed a relative local security, could not doubt the tenor and direction of the policies patronised by the king, and they were keenly aware of their consequences for their 'brethren' when pursued by energetic bishops. A godly gentleman, Walter Yonge, from the relative haven of Exeter diocese, noted in his diary the suppression of Calvinist books in the diocese of York and Laud's campaign against lecturers in the diocese of London. The religious agenda favoured by the godly – the vigorous promulgation of Calvinist theology, powerful preaching, sabbatarianism – were being downgraded, marginalised and suppressed. The godly were appalled by practices that appeared to challenge and abandon the central tenets of the Protestant Reformation. Many fled to the more tolerant Netherlands, or to the 'howling wilderness' of New England. In both these areas, and within anonymous and hard-to-police London, the godly distanced themselves from a church that increasingly appeared to them Antichristian, and set up separatist congregations of the saints. Some of those who remained in England expressed their antipathy to the dominant current of religious practice in fervent prayer 'against wicked bishops and their hierarchy'.[42] The more daring published bitter public invectives. For William Prynne, in a pamphlet of 1636, Wren of Norwich was that 'little pope' and his fellow bishops 'profane, atheistical, graceless persecutors'. For Henry Burton, preaching in the same year, the bishops were 'Antichrist's factors', and their cathedrals 'nests and nurseries of superstition and idolatry where the old beldame of Rome hath nuzzled up her brood of popelings'.[43] When the government responded to such tirades with prosecution and savage punishment – Prynne and Burton were pilloried, branded, mutilated (losing their ears) and exiled by order of Star Chamber – the godly rejoiced in the witness of these 'holy living martyrs'.[44]

Puritan zealots like John Vicars of Stamford did not court popularity. Villagers and townsfolk resented their self-satisfied and pharisaic holiness, their challenge to neighbourly sociability and to social hierarchy, and mocked them in interludes, squibs and lampoons. A song against the 'pure sect' in Nottingham was set to the tune of 'Bonny Nell', and became part of the repertoire of local ballad-singers. A 'railing rhyme' against the 'synagogue of Stratford' catches the tone of many of these productions:

> These men seem of a pure faction,
> But like the devil in dissimulation.
> As smooth as oil outward, in words,
> But within they are full of dissension and discords.[45]

Charles's welcome for the news that one of the leading godly ministers of Norwich was preparing to emigrate, 'Let him go; we are well rid of him', was independently expressed in a number of contemporary ballads. And yet the king's policies, far from creating the unity that he sought, further divided the church and pushed moderate laymen temporarily into the arms of the puritan radicals. The reasons for this involved both the substance and the style of Charles and Laud's policies.

The ceremonial and ritual practises insisted upon by Laud were deeply troubling, and not merely to the puritans. Particular injunctions could be justified by Elizabethan precedent, by pragmatism – dogs were less likely to urinate against or boys sleep upon a railed communion table – and in terms of the obligation of individuals to observe royal mandates in matters that were theologically indifferent but were designed to ensure uniformity of practice. Yet the sum of these demands created a distinctive synthesis that eroded such conformist arguments. Charles and Laud were insisting on conformity to a series of practices, which, taken together, implied theological convictions very different from any shade of Calvinist opinion. Incantation, solemn and reverent ritual and lavish decoration all suggested the peculiar sanctity of the 'House of God', and of the 'Table of the Lord' within it. The mystery of the divine presence in the sacrament of the altar was affirmed, and with it a suggestion that grace was made available to the Christian by participation in the sacraments, particularly the Eucharist. Moderate ministers, who might have welcomed prohibitions against preaching upon tortured points of election and grace, were disturbed by the rigmarole of the Laudian ceremonial programme. When in 1635 a Cheshire vicar saw the new stone altar in Chester Cathedral he wrote in horror to his bishop: the act was, he thought, 'schismatical', dividing the church. It would ensure not only that the puritans would be 'more stiff in standing out against conformity', but that 'we that are conformable shall be the less strong to contest with them'.[46] Robert Sanderson made a similar point in 1640. The new canons of that year both insisted on full ceremonial conformity and required all ministers to swear that they approved 'the doctrine and discipline, or government established in the Church of England, as containing all things necessary to salvation'. Not only the 'preciser sort', Sanderson noted, would refuse this oath, but so would men 'otherwise every way regular and conformable'.[47]

If moderate ministers found the ceremonial aspects of Laud's policies most troubling, laymen had other objections to his programme. Laud sought to reverse the consequences of a century of lay rapacity and contempt on the morale of the clergy. The standing of the clergy was to be enhanced, and laymen taught to know their place. Clerical income was to be improved. Long-established commutations of tithes, whereby payment in kind was replaced by a fixed sum that took no account of the rapid rise in prices, were challenged in the courts. Gentlemen whose ancestors had acquired impropriations, presentations to livings, or long leases to lands in the smash and grab raids on ecclesiastical property in the sixteenth century found their titles subject to a strict interrogation. Those who trumpeted their self-importance by elaborate pews or private chapels within 'their' parish churches – Sir Thomas Gawdy's pew was 'of a monstrous height, curtained like a bedstead' – were ordered to demolish the offending structures. The king supported all these moves, in particular pressuring the common law judges to handle cases involving clerical rights, which had often failed or been delayed on legal technicalities in the past, sympathetically. The king also appointed clerics to secular offices; they became JPs in the localities and privy counsellors at Westminster. Laud's triumph in his coup in securing the appointment of Bishop Juxon as lord treasurer in 1636 catches this aspect of his policy well: 'now if the church will not hold up themselves under God, I can do no more'.[48] But laymen were troubled by such promotions, and by the concomitant sense that clergymen were intruding into matters that properly fell to other authorities. Many of the Somerset magistrates, few of them in any sense puritans, could not comprehend the royal policy embodied in the Book of Sports. For them, the festivals were not symbolic affirmations of organic community, not nymphs and shepherds dancing round the maypole; they were orgies of drunkenness, violence and promiscuity. Their petition requesting the retention of their prohibition against the festivals was airily dismissed by Charles, who preferred the account of the festivals provided by the bishop of Bath and Wells, which was carefully tuned to reinforce the king's assumptions.

Laud sought to boost the morale, the *esprit de corps*, of the clerical order, but self-confidence was not always the impression given by him or his fellow high-ranking ecclesiastical supporters in the enforcement of their policies in the 1630s. Prior to the period of their triumph within the church, when fighting for patronage at the court of James I and subject to the unremitting hostility of Archbishop Abbott, the Laudians developed a defensive, outsider mentality. In the period of their triumph this mind-set, formed in their earlier experiences, often produced an administrative style that seems vindictive and fussy. In 1637, after a case that dragged on for eight years in Star Chamber, Laud broke his old rival, John Williams, bishop of Lincoln. But the animus that envenomed this relentless prosecution, the manifestly tainted 'evidence', and the accusations of fornication, intimidation, bribery, and perjury against high ecclesiastics that were publicly rehearsed during the case, hardly enhanced the moral authority of the church. Prynne's journey to prison in North Wales after his savage punishment by Star Chamber was transformed into a triumphal procession; at Chester the martyr was feted and admirers commissioned a number of portraits from a local painter. Archbishop Neile of York, after 'mature consideration', ordered that the pictures should be publicly burned. When he learned that the authorities had already destroyed the portraits privately, he solemnly insisted on a public bonfire for their frames.

If Laud and his colleagues were bemired in a defensive mentality, the robust clerical self-confidence he sought to inculcate was apparent among the lower echelons of the clergy. Brash young ministers, fresh from university, often demonstrated a total disregard for the doubts, prejudices and traditions of their congregations in their enthusiasm for the archbishop's agenda. Peter Titley, vicar of Grantham, was almost instantly at daggers drawn with his congregation and the town authorities. He refused the lecturers funded by the town the use of his pulpit, and he sought to improve his own maintenance from tithe. He was an extreme ritualist: his genuflexions at the name of Jesus were so elaborate that the service book often dropped from his hands. On one occasion he toppled over. Without consultation, he moved the communion table into the chancel, where he would be invisible and inaudible to the bulk of his congregation in the vast church. After an unseemly tug-of war between the vicar and the churchwardens, the table was replaced in the body of the church. Titley then contemptuously informed the civic leaders that he was not much concerned what they did 'with their old trestle', as he intended to build a stone altar, and would officiate nowhere else in the church. The village of Radwinter experienced the ministry of another bulldozing Laudian, Michael Drake. Drake barred off the chancel with a rich and elaborate wooden screen, carved with cherubim, a Latin inscription and the IHS monogram; with the last also emblazoned on his surplice, he treated his congregation as an excluded audience to his private devotions within his newly-created sacred space. He allowed them admission to the chancel to receive the eucharist, but then only on condition that they sedulously observed his standards of reverence – 'bowing superstitiously', and genuflexion. A parish previously noted for its conformity had become a cockpit of contention; the bitter animosity culminated in the summer of 1640, when a group of Radwinter parishioners persuaded some of the soldiers impressed for the Scottish War to smash up the offensive screen. Yet Drake's diary, written in Latin, breathes only conviction of his own righteousness and utter contempt for the yokels who opposed him.[49] Tempestuous inter-parochial relations were not the hallmark solely of puritans like John Vicars. Communities could be torn apart by the polarising doctrines of experimental Calvinism, but equally by the pretensions of clerics who, encouraged by Laud, asserted the claims of a priestly caste to impose religious practice without respect to the concerns of their congregations.

In the reign of James I, Laud, and those associated with him had argued that the puritans had disingenuously taken advantage of the king's indulgence and, they hinted, lassitude, to shatter the fabric of the Church of England. The practical consequences of high Calvinism with its dualistic theology, its 'titles of distinction' – godly and reprobate; 'saints' and 'men of Belial' – were division in the parish and confusion in the realm. They, by contrast, were the proponents of unity. Laud and Charles believed that once they could isolate and drive out the tiny minority of puritan subversives, they could establish a truly national Church of England, united in worship. But ecumenical charity was not much apparent in the dealings of the Laud and his followers, by turns fussy, vindictive and bumptious, with those they defined as their enemies. Nor was unity promoted by their policies. Laud's ceremonial preferences, taken in conjunction with his aspirations for the clerical order and the tenor of his interventionism, appeared to entail a rejection of the Protestant Reformation. They were far too close to 'popery' for the comfort of moderates, both clerical and lay. In 1636 Sir Henry Slingsby, a pious and serious Yorkshire gentleman, no Calvinist, sought the consecration of his domestic chapel. Archbishop Neile rejected the request on the grounds that there was a general policy to avoid the establishment of extra-parochial sites of worship that could be colonised by puritans. Slingsby was peeved by this interference in his prerogative as a gentleman, and his diary contains a tirade against the clergy – 'covetous, contentious, proud, boasters, ambitious'. But he went further in his attack on the pretensions of the Laudians: he remarked the tendency 'of late' to 'turn devotion into superstition, and place it in the splendour of outward things'; in this, he thought 'we ... draw near to the superstition of the Church of Rome'.[50] Charles himself recognised the degree to which his policies had been misunderstood in his preface to the 1640 canons; clarification was required because his subjects had been 'misled' into a belief that 'the rites and ceremonies now used in the Church of England [are] introductive unto popish superstition'.[51] It is somehow typical of Charles's succession of misjudgements, and of the suspicion in which his government was held by 1640, that the canons had precisely the opposite effect to that intended. Their issue roused fears that further religious innovations were in train and reinforced the dangerous identification of his regime with popery.

Charles was obliged to call parliament in November 1640 because of the spectacular failure of his policies in defeat and bankruptcy. His appeal for a vigorous assertion of national honour and affirmation of his kingship in a triumphant campaign against the rebellious Scots had been answered by a fatal combination of outright rejection, legalistic niggling, and procrastination. Charles was a king obsessed with order and unity in his realm. Yet his fiscal and religious agenda in the 1630s had brought only confusion and division.

In this account, the Scots have been little more than a *deus ex machina*. Their rebellion obliged Charles's government to impose further financial demands upon already overstrained local officers and resentful taxpayers, causing the system ultimately to seize up. But the Scots played a more deliberate and dynamic role than this, and their interactions with England were far closer. They undertook a vigorous propaganda campaign in defence of their actions, and their publications were widely disseminated. In August 1640 the Essex conscripts were reading Scottish pamphlets smuggled to them by a Suffolk clothier. 'Your grievances are ours', they were told, 'the preservation or ruin of liberties is common to both nations; we must now stand or fall together'.[52] This theme, the Scots' desire to unite with the English against 'the wicked counsels of Papists, prelates, and other fire-brands their adherents', was a leitmotif of all their productions. They played on the common Protestant heritage of the two nations, praising England's part in advancing Protestantism in Scotland. Both nations were the targets of an insidious conspiracy by the 'Canterburian' faction whereby 'first Scotland, and then England ... had become in their religion, Romish'. They sought to dissuade Englishmen from supporting Charles's military expedition, and encouraged them to press for a parliament.

It is difficult to judge the general impact of the Scots' propaganda. The government was certainly worried by it, intercepting letters, threatening penalties against those who failed to surrender any pamphlets that came to their hands, and launching dawn raids on the shops of London booksellers thought to be part of a clandestine distribution network. Eventually the king felt obliged to answer the arguments of the Scots in a series of declarations.

By doing so he may only have fuelled debate. The efforts of the vicar of Kilsby, preaching unconditional obedience to the king and against the rebels, were deeply counter-productive, inspiring his parishioners to express their sympathy for the Scots and hostility to government policy. The parish constable offered an unflattering comparison of the king's demands with those of Pharaoh on the Israelites.

The positive impact of the Scots rebellion and of the propaganda that accompanied it is more discernible in relation to a subset of the English nation: the godly. While the Scots manifestos employed a broadly inclusive language, they made a particular appeal to the godly – the 'good Christians', the 'brethren', 'the people of God' – in England. The godly were keenly aware of the parallels, insisted upon in the Scottish tracts, between the Laudian programme in the two countries, while the success of the Scots challenge to religious innovation indicated providential approval for their mutual cause. But the Scots provided more than a galvanising inspiration for the godly. The rebellion encouraged them to reflect on traditional assumptions about political obligation. More practically, it provided an opportunity to embarrass Charles and, potentially, to pressure him to a major change of domestic policy.

In January 1638 four men, the earl of Warwick, lords Saye and Brooke, and Henry Darley seriously considered settling on Providence Island, off the coast of Honduras. A complex web of kinship conjoined these men, as did mutual responsibilities as trustees, guardians and executors, and involvement in other ventures designed to encourage colonial expansion. But their prime unity was a function of religious and constitutional conviction. Warwick had made his principled stand against ship money in a direct appeal to Charles early in 1637. It proved unavailing, and Warwick and his local allies in Essex, under the stern eye of the council, were reduced to the more common tactic of quibbling over rating. Saye pursued a very similar course in northern Oxfordshire. Much of the energies of Warwick and of Brooke in the 1630s went into sustaining and protecting the cohorts of godly ministers they had patronised from Laud and his myrmidons. In 1636 Brooke had very publicly snubbed Charles when he left his seat at Warwick Castle a few days before the king visited the town on progress. The revolt of the Scots gave these men their opportunity: thoughts of emigration were abandoned.

In the summer of 1638 the earl of Warwick's Essex mansion was the venue for radical discussions of resistance theory. Jeremiah Burroughs, a minister silenced in the diocese of Norwich but promoted as Warwick's household chaplain, was inspired by the example of the Scots. He argued that kings derived their authority from the people, and that, in case of 'tyranny', when a king broke the agreements that he had sworn to observe at his coronation, it was lawful 'to defend ourselves and liberties by arms'.[53] Early in 1640 Warwick employed his network of preachers in Essex to ensure the return of godly men to represent the shire. On 28 August, though ignorant of the shattering defeat at Newburn, Warwick and eleven other lords petitioned the king, complaining of religious innovations and demanding the summoning of another parliament. Two of his co-signatories of this appeal were Saye and Brooke, who had already undertaken actions that shaded into the active resistance recommended by Burroughs. In April 1639 both Saye and Brooke refused to provide horse and men for the war effort, or to swear a newly devised oath of allegiance to the king, Brooke insisting that Charles should call a parliament. Brooke, who had welcomed one of the leading Covenanting ministers to his house and local pulpits, had been detected in correspondence with the Scots in 1639. Saye's son, Nathaniel Fiennes, in the immediate aftermath of Newburn, kept the Scots informed on the finances and morale of the English army, and co-ordinated political strategy with them. Henry Darley was also active in the summer of 1640, criticising the king's request for Yorkshire to pay for the billeting of his army, and his plan to deploy the county's trained-bands beyond the county boundaries. Not only was he one of the Yorkshire gentry whose 'murmurings and repinings' ensured that his countrymen behaved 'like men that wanted both heart and will to the business', he also acted as the link between the county and the twelve peers.[54]

Charles called parliament because the rebellious Scots had defeated him. That defeat owed much to the dead weight of hostility to his policies, fiscal, administrative and religious, in the localities. But Charles was also aware of the subversive role of a fifth column within England, galvanised by the Scots' actions both to cooperate with the invaders and to resist openly the king's efforts to bring the Scots to heel. After Newburn, Sir Francis Windebank, one of the secretaries of state, remarked that it would be easy to discover those Englishmen who had colluded with the Scots. The king's cold marginal note, 'It shall not be forgotten', catches his sense of the betrayal of his own and England's honour.[55]

It takes two sides to fight a civil war, and there were not two sides in November 1640. Charles was isolated. Parliament's continuance and political dominance was guaranteed by the need for taxation to fund the two armies marking each other in northern England. The men who had formed the king's inner circle of advisers and administrators were in disarray. Some were almost immediately imprisoned, notably Strafford, Laud and Wren, while the threat of impeachment hung over others. Some, fearing that they might be sacrificed to parliament's vengeance for their activities in the 1630s, effaced themselves, either tamely surrendering their posts, as did Cottington, or fleeing the country as did Secretary Windebank and Lord Keeper Finch. A few were prepared to cooperate with parliament.

Barely two years later, all this had changed. On 23 October 1642 at Edgehill, Charles, with a force of some 24,000 men, fought a drawn battle with the parliamentary field army of approximately similar size. The nation was fundamentally split into royalists and parliamentarians, Cavaliers and Roundheads.

How Did the King Gain Support
in Parliament?

As the axe fell, the huge crowd of spectators on Tower Hill, whose 'madness and fury' had led the lieutenant of the Tower to fear that his prisoner might be lynched before he reached the block, roared their approval. Couriers rode post haste from London – 'His head is off! His head is off!' – and bonfires greeted the welcome news they brought.[1]

Nothing indicates the isolation of Charles I in the face of a popular movement in support of the policies of parliament than the execution of the earl of Strafford on 12 May 1641. The Commons had passed the Act of Attainder declaring Strafford guilty of high treason and sentencing him to death on 21 April. The Lords approved the Act on 8 May; two days later Charles signed it. The crowds that witnessed the execution had played a major part in securing that result. On the 24 April twenty thousand Londoners had signed a petition demanding the earl's execution. More direct action followed on 3 May. Rumours of a military coup against parliament produced an excited response, well caught in the terse language of the report of one of the Scottish commissioners in London to his compatriots. 'In a clap all the city in alarum; shops closed; a world of people in arms run down to Westminster.'[2] Roaring for 'justice', the crowd intercepted and interrogated individual peers, demanding to know how they would vote. The pressure on the Lords was maintained until the Bill was passed. Then, with the legislation awaiting the king's response, the crowd moved to Whitehall, threatening to rush the gates and overwhelm the guards. Charles finally signed the Attainder Bill in a court gripped by utter panic; terrified courtiers hid their jewels and, if Catholic, sought out their confessors and prepared for death.

Wenceslaus Hollar's print of the execution of the earl of Strafford (1641).
A vast concourse of people watched the scene (including the collapse of one of
the stands). (*Ashmolean Museum, Oxford*)

A. Doctor Vſher, Lord Prima-
te of Ireland,
B the Sherifes of London,
C the Earle of Strafford,
D. his kindred and Friends.

In the face of the forces arrayed against him Charles was irresolute and tearful. His immediate entourage was divided, some floating ill-designed schemes to rescue Strafford, others happy to betray them to the parliamentary leaders to save their own skins. The privy council was similarly fractured, only unanimous on 9 May when it advised Charles to accept the Attainder Act. Charles never forgave himself for his surrender of Strafford; it was on his mind when he was brought to the scaffold eight years later. 'An unjust sentence that I suffered to take effect, is punished now by an unjust sentence on me.'[3] But Charles's failure of will in May 1641 is understandable. He was terrified for the safety of his family; he had no organised political support upon which he could rely. The king's political isolation was total.

Seven months later the political climate, if not the enduring sense of crisis, had changed. At two o'clock in the morning on 23 November 1641, after fourteen hours debate, the Commons passed the Grand Remonstrance by 159 to 148 votes. The Remonstrance was a provocative document. It began with a blatantly partisan account of the policies pursued by Charles I since his coronation; the first ninety-nine of its 204 clauses consisted of a lengthy catalogue of specific examples of misgovernment in the 1620s and 1630s. This was designed to prove the existence of a potent conspiracy to subvert 'the fundamental laws and principles of government, upon which the religion and justice of this kingdom are firmly established'. Those plotting this 'malignant and pernicious design' were from three overlapping groups. 'Jesuits and other engineers and factors for Rome' were primarily responsible, but they had been aided by two groups of fellow travellers, bishops and royal counsellors. After detailing these enormities, the Commons spent thirty-six clauses in self-congratulation. They listed their achievements in the face of the extraordinary mess left by the regime, and promised further legislative reform. The Remonstrance then shifted into a bleaker, darker mood: the conspiracy against English liberties was far from defeated. Its agents – the usual suspects – were working covertly, their 'venomous counsels' occasionally revealed when specific plots were uncovered, to break the parliament and ruin its work. The conspiracy's most nefarious attempt was to destroy the reputation of parliament with the king and with the people.[4]

The opponents of the Remonstrance questioned the wisdom of a unilateral declaration that took no account of the sensibilities of the Lords. They may have objected to specific substantive points, although Pym had modified the Remonstrance in committee to accommodate some of these concerns; the clauses attacking the Book of Common Prayer and accusing all the bishops of promoting idolatry were struck out. But the ferocity of the opposition that the Remonstrance faced in the Commons on the 22–23 November stemmed less from its substance than from its intended audience. Ostensibly addressed to the king, in reality the Remonstrance was an appeal to the people. This emerges in the most dramatic scene of that hectic night. After the vote some MPs, physically and emotionally exhausted, left the House, but those who remained then voted by 124 to 101 that the Remonstrance might be published. Immediately, one of the minority asked to register his dissent from the vote formally, and this nearly precipitated violence in the tense, over charged atmosphere of the House. Members chanted, waved their hats, drew their swords: 'I thought we had all sat in the valley of the shadow of death', wrote one MP.[5] The Commons' preferred self-images of unity, of consensus decision-making were shattered irrevocably.

It would be wrong to see parliament nose-diving suddenly from unanimity into polarisation simply over the specific question of the Grand Remonstrance. A number of issues had already divided MPs in the previous year, and some had pitted the two Houses against one another. These cracks had been papered over, or debate and decision on the matters themselves had been delayed to avoid the potential risk of a confrontation within parliament. But this process sparked tension and uneasiness within the Houses, which exploded in the Grand Remonstrance debate. The policies pursued by John Pym, the brilliant leader of the Commons, a man whose skills had been honed in the House in the 1620s in opposition to Charles's fiscal and religious policies and who had worked covertly in the 1630s to challenge ship money and develop ties with the Scots, created growing unease in four areas. Three were the political settlement that was to be established in the aftermath of Charles's experiments in the 1630s; the treatment of the Scots; and the religious settlement. The fourth issue, the key to the fierce debates on the Grand Remonstrance, and to the process of polarisation as a whole, concerned fears that the fabric of society was being undermined by the attacks on royal and ecclesiastical authority.

Settlement entailed both the dismantling of the instruments and institutions of Charles's government in the 1630s, and the establishment of a new framework for political action. Of these two, the work of destruction proved the less contentious. The arrest or threats of proceedings against the 'evil counsellors' and pliable judges were generally favoured, and the fiscal experiments that they had devised or supported were struck down. The abolition of ship money, forest fines and knighthood compositions scarcely occasioned a ripple of debate. The king's dependence upon parliament for the grant of customs revenues was asserted. Those hounded by the regime were publicly vindicated. Burton, Prynne and their fellow martyrs were released from their distant prisons, tumultuously welcomed in London, and voted reparations against their persecutors. The High Commission, which had first prosecuted these men, and the court of Star Chamber, which had so savagely punished them, were abolished, as were the similar jurisdictions exercised by some of the provincial courts, notably the Council of the North. The enactment against Star Chamber faced some criticism in the Lords, but the majority agreed with Saye and Essex that, 'having laboured all this parliament to make themselves freemen and not slaves', the courts must go.[6]

One part of the policy of demolition did rouse violent passions: the execution of the earl of Strafford. In his anguish, Charles was unlikely to take much comfort from this incident, so emblematic of the king's helpless isolation in the spring of 1641. Yet it did provide some evidence that the unanimity of the regime's opponents could be fractured. There was a general sense that Strafford, by far the most visionary, able and energetic of the king's counsellors, must be neutralised. Several of the privy council joined in the attack on the man whose determination to crush the Scots rebellion at all costs after the failure of the Short Parliament had brought them all into danger. Secretary Vane – after a laughable charade designed to extenuate a major breach of confidence – made his notes on the secret discussions in the privy council on 5 May 1640, confirming one of the major charges against the earl, available to the prosecutors. The destruction of Strafford's influence was generally agreed by all save the king; the question of punishment was not. Some parliamentarians, not least Pym and his patron the earl of Bedford, were prepared to consider using Strafford's life as a sweetener in negotiations with the king; others, a 'rigid, strong, and inflexible party', wished to sweep him away as expeditiously as possible.[7] They agreed with the earl of Essex: 'Stone-dead hath no fellow.'[8]

The trial procedure initially favoured by the Commons – impeachment, whereby the lower House acted as prosecutors and the Lords as judges – was designed to secure the maximum publicity for the crimes and the condemnation of Strafford. But the impeachment proceeded slowly, as the earl's skilfully handled defence won support in the Upper House. Strafford argued that the long list minor charges against him, many concerning offences – if they were offences – in his government of Ireland, could not, simply by their number, support a conviction of high treason in English law. As defence council was to argue later in the trial of Laud on a very similarly configured charge, 'I never understood two hundred couple of black rabbits would make a black horse'.[9] Strafford also appealed to the fellow feeling of the Lords as the natural counsellors of the king. If royal advisers were to become subject to the kind of relentless and vindictive scrutiny that had been focused upon him, then the king would find himself without any counsellors on public affairs: 'no man will meddle with them that hath wisdom, ands honour, and fortune to lose'.[10] The patience of those determined to crush Strafford soon wore thin. After the trial had dragged on for three weeks, they hit upon another procedure. A Bill of Attainder, whereby the earl would be condemned and executed without further judicial process, would be 'the safest and speediest way'.[11]

This Bill proved divisive. It finally passed the House of Commons by 204 votes to 59, and, after further debate, the Lords, by 26 to 19. In both Houses a good number of members claimed sickness, failed to turn up, or slipped away during the debates rather than commit themselves on this issue. The passion roused by the discussion emerges in the subsequent printing of the names of the minority in the Commons vote: 'These are the Straffordians, the betrayers of their country'. Later a printed list of Strafford's implacable opponents, 'the Anabaptists, Jews and Brownists of the House of Commons', was also circulated.[12] Strafford's destruction, the nadir of royal authority, revealed divisions among the political elite upon which the king might play.

The destruction or neutralisation of the agents and agencies of Charles I's regime in the 1630s created few divisions, with the significant exception of the trial of Strafford. Parliament made far less headway in devising any new scheme for government in 1640 and 1641. An enactment that was to prove enormously significant, that this parliament should not be dissolved without its own consent, passed in May 1641, should be seen in the first instance as a response to a short-term crisis, the furore over the attainder of Strafford and the concomitant fears of a royal coup. More indicative of the considered constitutional agenda of Pym's circle was the Triennial Act, passed in mid-February, which obliged the monarch to call parliament every three years. Parliament was to be an essential, but not a permanent feature of the political landscape; executive government was to be, as in the past, undertaken by a council. How that council was to be chosen became the major issue of contention in subsequent discussions of the constitutional settlement.

Initially those who had opposed Charles's policies in the 1630s and who had encouraged him to call a parliament, perhaps cooperating with the Scots to that end, sought to colonise the royal executive. In January 1641 it was being confidently reported by those close to the court that the earl of Bedford would be made lord treasurer, with Pym as chancellor of the exchequer and Lord Saye as master of the court of wards. In late January Oliver St John, legal council to Bedford and to Hampden during the ship money trial, was appointed solicitor general. Next month Charles created seven new privy councillors, six of them, including Bedford and Saye, signatories of the August 1640 petition of the twelve peers begging Charles to call parliament. In April Warwick also joined the privy council, and next month Saye finally became master of the wards. Late July 1641 brought further rumours of royal favour for ex-opponents of the regime, with Saye taking the treasurership. Much was hoped of this: 'bringing in of these new men' indicated that the king 'resolves to steer another course', and would 'make up an entire union between the king and his people'.[13]

Despite the enthusiasm, these appointments proved abortive. Bedford's premature death in May removed a key figure in the negotiations, but the scheme was rickety even before this. From the first, some around the king saw the policy of integration merely as window-dressing. Charles seems to have come to this opinion rapidly, if he did not hold it initially. He doubted, with some reason, that those he promoted could guarantee to deliver the votes of their followers in the Houses. Would they save Strafford? Vote new sources of revenue to the crown? Resist radical plans for government of the church? Those invited to serve, who found themselves exercising negligible influence in the king's councils, resented the tokenism. Charles, meanwhile, was taking advice from other, less official sources.

In consequence, parliament began to demand more formal control over the court and council. In June 1641 Pym introduced, in the Ten Propositions, prohibitions on the access of papists to the court and, in particular, from the presence of the queen, who was to accept an entourage appointed 'by advice of parliament'. The document also demanded that the king dismiss those of his own counsellors who endeavoured to 'stir up divisions between him and his people', and to appoint men 'as his people and parliament may have just cause to confide in'.[14] This phrase was repeated verbatim in the Grand Remonstrance, but by November the issue of the control of the executive had become even more urgent. In late October the Irish Catholics, terrified by the anti-popish rhetoric employed in both England and Scotland, had staged a pre-emptive strike. Ireland flamed in revolt, the Anglo-Scottish settlements were devastated, and only a few garrisons, of which crucially Dublin was one, held out. Forces and money had to be raised to suppress the revolt. Pym initially argued that parliament should do nothing until Charles agreed to appoint counsellors and officers acceptable to them. Such naked blackmail in the face of a major crisis provoked anger in the Commons, but on 8 November Pym carried a motion that was as revolutionary in its implication. It was agreed by 151 votes to 110 that, if the king refused to make acceptable appointments, parliament, 'in discharge of the trust which we owe to the state, and to those whom we represent', should act unilaterally to ensure that the finances and forces for Ireland should be disposed to 'such persons of honour and fidelity as we have cause to confide in'.[15] By June 1642 parliament had extended this demand to include the right to choose all members of the privy council, all high-ranking officers of central administration and justice, and all military commanders. Charles was to be a shadow-king.

While parliament upped its demands and the stridency with which it insisted upon them, Charles was successfully broadening the base of support from which he could draw advisers and administrators. Men who had initially cooperated with Pym were drifting away, some to positions of unofficial influence at court and, eventually, to posts within it. The MPs Edward Hyde, Sir John Culpepper and Lord Falkland had actively supported the work of demolition undertaken by the summer of 1641, and believed that the constitutional and legal balance, thrown out of kilter in the 1630s, was now restored. As Hyde said, responding to a motion on 28 October to secure 'a negative voice' for parliament in the appointment of administrators and counsellors, things were now 'in a good posture if we could preserve them as they were'.[16] Charles had shown his commitment to the rule of law with his acceptance of the reforming Bills passed before August 1641; he must now be given the opportunity to govern within the recovered 'ancient constitution'.

Pym's position was simple. Charles could not be trusted to accept the letter or the spirit of the restrictive legislation, or with any significant modicum of power. Further restrictions had to be placed on his free-dom of action. Pym's suspicions of Charles were well grounded. Throughout 1641 the king had been involved, sometimes tangentially, in a series of plots which, had they succeeded, would have freed him from the incubus of parliament. In March and April some officers of the English army in the north, seething under their defeat and the greater attention being paid to the necessities of the Scottish army, planned to pressure parliament either by a petition or, more dramatically, by mov-ing their forces towards London. A very similar scheme, with the same confused objectives, was under discussion in June. Both plans, and the king's tentative encouragement of them, were leaked to Pym. Charles's stay in Scotland for three months from mid-August, ostensibly to settle the government of the country after the treaty was finally signed, was a further cause of mistrust. Covertly, Charles hoped to guarantee the neu-trality of his northern subjects in relation to England, perhaps even to use them as a counter-weight in his dealings with parliament. When these negotiations failed, Charles connived in a plot to seize, and if necessary to assassinate, two of the leading Scottish nobles who were most active in thwarting his project.

Given this record, what is remarkable is not Pym's insistence on fur-ther restriction of the king's authority, but the trust that Hyde and his friends were prepared to place in Charles's constitutional rectitude. Their optimism survived the major example of the king's folly and duplicity. On 2 January 1642 Falkland and Culpepper were given offices and made privy councillors. The next day the king, in a scheme that originated among the queen's entourage and of which his newly enrolled supporters were ignorant, sought to impeach Lord Mandeville and five members of the Commons for treason. On 4 January Charles, with an armed guard, entered the House of Commons, intending to arrest those he had named. He found 'all the birds are flown'; forewarned of his plans they had sought refuge in the City of London. The king's new allies were temporarily thrown by Charles's unexpected resort to violence, but were soon back on side. On 12 January Culpepper sought to encourage the Commons to take action designed to restore good relations with the king. In February and March Hyde was the major draftsman of the king's declarations in his negotiations with parliament. Those who had decided to cooperate with the king, who argued that Charles was a changed man thoroughly committed to the reformist achievements of 1641, had to make an extraordinarily imaginative leap of faith. They were able to achieve this because they were less drawn to Charles than repelled by the policies – and not just the constitutional policies – pursued by Pym and his allies.

The Scots army occupying northern England finally marched home in August 1641. It then became possible to disband the English forces that covered it south of the Tees. Until that date the two armies required £60,000 a month, to be supplied by parliament. This sum rapidly fell into arrears. The necessary taxation was voted, and the sums were subsequently collected, slowly. Loans proved difficult to negotiate in an unstable political climate; those with ready cash to invest moved it into the altogether less risky Dutch capital market. Inadequate pay led to a deterioration of discipline in both armies, which began to live off the countryside where they were quartered. Northern MPs, barraged with dire predictions of anarchy and starvation from their constituents, began to express hostility to the Scots and to question the policies that seemed to delay the negotiations that would rid them of their unwanted guests. But they were not alone in their disgust at the military occupation.

Many MPs believed that the Scots victory and occupation of English soil had dishonoured the nation. This sense of affront was compounded when Pym and his followers agreed to pay reparations to the Scots for the expenses that they incurred in their invasion. In debates on 22 January and 3 February 1641, many MPs protested at the sum – £300,000 – that Pym and his allies were prepared to pay out to the Scots and were scornful of its description as 'Brotherly Assistance'. The Scots' meddling in English politics roused further antipathy. The eighth clause in the Scottish proposals for a treaty was phrased in nebulous terms of greater union between the two kingdoms. This was disliked because of the implied interference in English affairs, more so because the vaguely worded agenda seemed to guarantee lengthy negotiation. But one section of the clause, concerning a common Confession of Faith, took on a frightening precision. In a printed tract the Scots commissioners, resident in London, argued that this entailed a commitment to the abolition of episcopacy. The Scots were surprised at the angry response this drew, many 'taxing us of presumption, as if it were presumption to give directions to reform them and evert their laws'.[17] Pym was able to beat off an attempt to censure the commissioners in the Commons, and then, on 5 March, to defeat a proposal from the Lords immediately to terminate negotiation on the eighth clause by a two to one majority in the Commons, but 107 MPs voted against the Scots on this occasion. Pym and his friends could censure or expel the most vocal anti-Scots, men who spoke openly of 'rebels' or of 'dishonour', from the Commons, but they could not silence a growing body of opinion hostile to the long-continued Scottish occupation, to their fiscal demands and to their interference in English domestic politics. Among these men suspicion festered that the negotiations were being spun out by Pym only to secure a continuing role for the Scots as a powerful lever in English politics.

The reform of the church was high on the agenda of every MP in the early days of the Long Parliament. Laudian excesses would be pared away, and those who had been enthusiastic in enforcing them on their dioceses or parishes censured. But parliament was not just concerned with the novelties of the 1630s. Venerable demands that had exercised the parliaments of Elizabeth and James, for a resident ministry of powerful preachers, well educated and morally upright, were resurrected. 'It would be the greatest glory of his majesty's reign', enthused Sir Simonds

D'Ewes, 'if we could change the greater part of the clergy from brazen, leaden – yea, and blockish – persons, to a golden and primitive condition.'[18] In pursuit of this vision, the Commons actively encouraged petitions against deficient clerics and particular abuses, set up investigating committees and prepared legislation. But a dissonant voice jarred against this initial consensus. On 11 December a petition from London, with 15,000 signatures, was brought to the Commons by 'a world of honest citizens, in their best apparel'.[19] It too dilated on the deficiencies of the church, set out in the blackest colours, and the need for reform – but not the piecemeal reform in which the Commons were engaged. It demanded radical surgery. All the evils in the church, and a great deal more besides – monopolies and the decline of the cloth industry, 'whoredoms and adulteries', and the 'swarming of lascivious, idle and unprofitable books' – were the responsibility of the bishops. Accordingly episcopacy, 'with all its dependencies, roots and branches', was to be abolished.[20]

The presentation of the petition owed much to the cooperation of an influential group of London godly ministers and their colleagues attending on the Scots commissioners. Sympathetic but cautious MPs had requested that the petition be held back until more progress had been made in the proceedings against Strafford, but the Scots-London clerical caucus were impatient and aggressive. The premature appearance of the petition produced, as the cautious had predicted, only division in the Commons – 'there were many against and many for the same'.[21] After a sharp debate, the issue was dropped. A petitioning campaign outside London – between 13 and 30 January thirteen counties backed the Londoners' demands – and the ill-considered publication of the Scots' pamphlet insisting on the abolition of episcopacy resurrected the issue. Another sharp debate on 8 and 9 February concluded in a studied compromise: the 'Root and Branch' petition was forwarded for discussion in a committee, but its central plank, the question of church government, was reserved for future discussion by the House of Commons. On 27 May a Bill for the abolition of episcopacy was presented in the Commons, and, after a vote of 135–108, read a second time. It was discussed again on 11 June, when debate raged from 7 in the morning until 4 p.m. Then the Bill stuck in committee, as an alternative system of church government was thrashed out. Progress was slow, and nothing finalised by August; when the House reassembled in November the Bill was again allowed to languish. Nothing was said about the abolition of episcopacy in the Grand Remonstrance, and clauses criticising the Book of Common Prayer and the bishops, accusing them, for instance, of introducing idolatry, were cut from the final version of the document.

It is clear that throughout 1641 the issue of church government could split the House. In January an MP noted that episcopacy 'hath so many advocates and so strong a party in our house'.[22] In November D'Ewes explained that the language of the Grand Remonstrance was watered down to avoid 'further trouble', because 'we saw that the party for episcopacy was so strong'.[23] But the year had also seen a fixing and hardening of attitudes. In their early speeches, D'Ewes and Sir John Wray had praised 'godly, zealous and preaching bishops', men like Cranmer, Ridley and Latimer, martyred by Queen Mary; such 'rich jewels' were 'fit to be set in the King's own cabinet'. They had reserved their denunciations for the aggressive ceremonialists and anti-Calvinists and for the careerist temporisers who had been promoted by Laud.[24] By November, however, both MPs were committed to the outright abolition of episcopacy. Sir Edward Dering moved in the opposite direction. He revised a version of the London Root and Branch petition from his native Kent, and presented it in mid-January; he moved the legislation against episcopacy in April. But two months later he was speaking in favour of a moderate episcopacy as the optimal government of the church. Men were taking up increasingly polarised and entrenched positions. Consensus on substantive aspects of church government was becoming impossible, and its appearance could only be achieved by ducking the issue altogether. What lay behind the contention over episcopal government and the growing polarisation of parliament?

The defenders of episcopacy and their opponents agreed that the recent record of the bishops was poor. Some enthusiasts, some sycophants, they had defended and enforced the obnoxious innovations promulgated by Laud. But supporters argued that the legally established and historically warranted form of church government should not be demolished because of the weaknesses of deficient individuals. They also doubted that a better replacement could be devised. Their opponents argued that episcopal government was unscriptural and popish in its origins, and that, because it was intrinsically corrupt, it polluted those individuals who were chosen as bishops. Better alternatives were clearly available in the models provided by more thoroughly reformed churches, not least that of Scotland. This controversy ran the gamut of scriptural exegesis, of early church history and that of the post-Reformation period, of comparative politics. But in all the major Commons debates, the speeches of the supporters of episcopacy contain a key subtext: the hierarchical structure of episcopacy mirrored that of the social order; to assail the one, carving away its legal defences, was to risk the other. As Sir John Strangways argued on 9 February, 'if we make a parity in the church, we must come to a parity in the commonwealth'.[25]

In part, this argument was theoretical, comparing episcopacy as an oligarchic, hierarchical, government with the supposedly democratic character of its main rival, the Presbyterian system of the Scots. But the supporters of episcopacy thought they saw a significant conjunction between the substance of the anti-episcopalian message and the way that message was delivered. The leaders of the party opposed to episcopacy were already working out the democratic, even demotic, aspects of their ecclesiological theory as they encouraged popular involvement in their cause.

The passage of the Grand Remonstrance early on 23 November, as we have seen, was the climatic moment of division within the Commons. Its most contentious aspect was its anticipated audience: not the king, to whom it was ostensibly addressed, but the people. Pym's allies had made this intention clear early in the discussions. On 11 November it was suggested that taxation to support the beleaguered Protestants in Ireland should be delayed until the Remonstrance had been passed and 'gone into the Country to satisfy them'. Pym emphasised the point in the debate on 22 November, 'this declaration will bend the people's hearts to us, when they see how we have been used'.[26] The opponents of the Remonstrance were appalled by such populist propaganda. Sir Edward Dering 'did not dream that we should remonstrate downward, tell stories to the people and talk of the king as of a third person'.[27]

The new world of a politics of popular engagement was signalled and symbolised by the publication of the Remonstrance, not initiated by it.

By late 1641 MPs had plenty of experience of Pym's readiness to involve the people in the political process. Strafford's execution, as we have seen, had been achieved by a measure of popular intimidation – the massive crowds who bayed for 'Justice and Execution' as the Lords arrived on 3 May, and who raged around Whitehall a week later.

The occasional eruptions of the Londoners to exert political pressure terrified some MPs, but it was the activities of the extra-parliamentary proponents of radical ecclesiastical reform that represented the most sustained challenge to traditional assumptions about the nature of the political process. In June 1641, after his change of heart on the issue of episcopacy, Sir Edward Dering was challenged and denounced by some of the 'usual black walkers in Westminster Hall'; such 'Parliament-Pressing Ministers' were the front men, the lobbyists, for a pressure group that extended well beyond London.[28] In the localities, their colleagues backed their direct appeals with a barrage of fervent letters to MPs thought to be sympathetic, praising what had been achieved and demanding continued activism. 'All that wish well to Zion here give you many thanks for your zeal and labours … against Antichrist', wrote a Kentish minister, suspended by Laud, to Dering in January 1641: 'let the zeal of God's glory and his house eat you up', wrote another a month later.[29] Together London and local ministers organised the petitions against episcopacy, whose vast rolls of signatures roused the sneering condescension and the alarm of conservatives at such mass intervention, such 'irregular and tumultuous assemblies of people'. 'Can there be a greater presumption than for … a multitude to teach a parliament what and what is not the government according to God's word?' asked Lord Digby in February. In May Waller made the social subtext more explicit, 'if by multiplying hands and petitions they prevail for an equality in things ecclesiastical, the next demand perhaps may be … the like in things temporal'.[30]

We can also see this lobby in action, encouraging participatory politics, in the denunciation of obnoxious ministers. In early December the Commons agreed that MPs should report on the state of the clergy in their shires. This order was almost immediately published in a pirated version and widely disseminated. The tract was prefaced with a tendentious introduction alleging that the Commons would welcome denunciations of pluralist, non-preaching, innovating and scandalous ministers from 'all ingenuous persons in every county'.[31] The order sparked a welter of local petitions, and, more generally, galvanised religious radicals in the localities with a sense of parliament's empathy. Ministers, in particular, protested that their status and influence was undermined by the order, but local gentlemen also complained that 'the monstrous easy receipt of petitions makes authority decline', and that 'orderly government' was at risk from the Commons open-door policy.[32] Local radicals who desired not 'reformation' but 'ruin' were encouraged, it was alleged, by the vacuum that parliament was allowing to develop in relation to the government of the church.

In March an intelligent visitor to London wrote that it was 'a most fearful thing' to see the state of religion in the city. 'We shall shortly have not so much as the face of a true Protestant church, but all will be in confusion.'[33] By the spring and early summer of 1641 MPs could see what the religious radicals were up to in London – iconoclasm, refusal to employ the Prayer Book, argument against any kind of national church. Tradesmen were preaching, as were women: Anne Hempstall, in her prophetic trances, denounced men who wore long hair; more daringly, Joan Barford argued that wives might divorce their husbands.[34] MPs might also receive information concerning local developments from friends in the country. Dering's change of heart on the issue of episcopacy owed much to reports from Kent of incidents of radical zeal, the 'fomenting of popular spirits against laws', and of the consequent clerical demoralisation. 'To have my conscience, credit and pains trampled upon by my people after twenty-four years is an hard task', complained the minister of Cranbrook, 'I beseech you, feel with me'.[35] For six weeks from mid-September, when the Houses adjourned, many MPs returned home, which gave them direct knowledge of local events and, in particular, the concerns of their fellow gentry. They would have seen the divisive consequences in the localities of the Commons' order of 9 September, passed by a narrow majority and promulgated without the approval of the Lords. This enjoined the removal of communion tables from the east end, demolition of altar rails, and the destruction of crucifixes and images. At Chelmsford the authorities removed stained-glass representations of Christ and the Virgin from the east window; this did not satisfy the radicals, who smashed the window to pieces, shattering the 'escutcheons and arms of the ancient nobility and gentry, who had contributed to the building' in the process.[36] At Kidderminster the attempt to demolish a crucifix in the churchyard was halted by 'the drunken riotous party of the town (poor journeymen and servants)'.[37] Not surprisingly, when Dering attended the quarter sessions in October, his fellow JPs questioned him closely concerning the constitutional validity and political wisdom of the Commons' order. MPs must also have been keenly aware of riots stemming from economic and social grievances. In many areas enclosures were assailed; at Colchester hedges were burned and buildings demolished on the day following Strafford's execution. Disafforestation schemes, like that in the Forest of Dean, undertaken by the queen's secretary, the papist Sir John Wintour, and drainage projects in East Anglia, had received powerful backing from Charles I in the 1630s. Both areas were the scenes of a series of major riots in the spring and summer of 1641. In August the Lincolnshire JPs, having described the seizure of crops in the newly drained fens, and the destruction of the engineering works, noted that their authority and the orders of parliament were alike derided and neglected. The situation, they wrote apprehensively, threatened 'further and greater mischief and a more evil consequence ... the endangering of a rebellion'.[38]

From the perspective of men like Dering, the policies of Pym and his friends presented a most serious threat to the social order. Divided counsels at the centre and the failure of executive and police agencies animated those with economic grievances, or with a radical religious agenda, to take direct action. But Pym's policies were not merely passive. The Junto (the name increasingly applied to Pym's supporters) nourished a new kind of political engagement. They cooperated with extra-parliamentary lobbies, particularly religious pressure groups, welcomed petitions, and encouraged grass-roots action. When Digby sneered at the social status of the London petitioners, the radical City MP Isaac Pennington acknowledged that some of the signatories were mean men 'yet if they were honest men there was no reason but their hands should be received'.[39] While many MPs drew back uneasily from the abyss that seemed to open up as the existing government of the church was undermined and popular intervention in the closed world of political action was encouraged, some of Pym's associates appeared to relish the sense of moving into utterly uncharted territory. Men who had begun hoping to achieve a series of piecemeal reforms of the church now demanded a complete demolition of the current ecclesiastical government, and, beyond that, affirmed their readiness to attend upon progressive divine revelation. Lord Brooke expressed his commitment to the unhampered search for new truths in a way that must have terrified his conservative colleagues. Luther's challenge had been a moment of world-historical significance, Brooke conceded, but his vision had been only partial, 'no truth can shine in its perfect lustre at the first: light is darkness when it first appeareth'. Calvin represented an advance on Luther, and yet 'since him God hath raised up a more glorious light', and Brooke praised the religious experiment in New England. But even this was a way station. Brooke concluded his reflections on the development of divine purpose triumphantly:

> Thus light dilating, and enlarging it self seemeth to become more pure, more Light, more Glorious; and yet it seemes not to be Noon. The light still will, must, cannot but increase; why then do we shut our eyes?[40]

From the perspective of Hyde or Dering, this was to embrace anarchy.

3

How Did the King Get an Army?

Charles's abortive attempt to arrest the Five Members raised London against him. Rather than witness the triumphant return of his projected victims to parliament, he hastily withdrew from Whitehall, not to enter it again until, a prisoner, it became the scene of his trial and execution. After sending Henrietta Maria to refuge in France, the king moved north, settling at York, which became his base for the months from mid-March to mid-August 1642. He also endeavoured to seize Hull, a well-supplied magazine and key port for the introduction of any troops and equipment secured from the Continent, but was frustrated by the energy of the local MP, Sir John Hotham. Early in August the London newspapers gloated over the king's limited success. He had raised few volunteers. The Yorkshire militia had also proved reluctant to assist him: 'the King beat up his drums, but none cometh in here; he beats his drums, but not a man'.[1]

Parliament, by contrast, was confident. The enthusiastic and determined popular response in London to the attempt on the Five Members was duplicated, at least verbally, from the shires. On 11 January five thousand Buckinghamshire freeholders rode into Westminster with a petition assuring the Houses of the county's readiness to live and die in defence of the privileges of parliament. By May thirty-six of the remaining thirty-nine English shires, and a good number of towns, had sent up similar statements, often accompanied by 'mighty multitudes'.[2] The clerks of the Commons staggered under the weight of the appended parchment rolls of signatures and marks – Essex, with 30,000 names, hit the jackpot. Essex was also the first shire to execute the Militia Ordinance, organising the county's trained bands under parliamentary control in defiance of a royal proclamation; 'with our hands on our swords, we stand ready at your command'.[3] Before mid-July the local militias of a further ten counties had been mustered under the

lord lieutenant appointed by parliament, and had formally acknowledged the authority of the Houses. Reports of the solemn commitment,
the unanimity and the focused energy displayed at these musters were
trumpeted in the London press.

Reinforced by such popular enthusiasm, parliament was intransigent
in its negotiations with the king. The Nineteen Propositions, in the
opinion of one of those who framed them, could not have been any
more moderate in substance or more respectful in language, given the
political climate at Westminster. Yet these minimum terms were an
ultimatum that reduced the monarch to a shadow, effectively removed
from the process of government. And, as Charles noted, the propositions applied not only to himself but his successors; accepting such
terms would be 'to depose both ourselves and our posterity'.[4] Parliament's confidence also emerges in its handling of any hint of dissent.
Sir Edward Dering was expelled from the Commons when he published
his speeches favouring episcopacy and against the Grand Remonstrance.
Ministers who preached on uncongenial texts or themes, like Edward
Symmons of Rayne who asked sardonically 'if David's heart smote him
for cutting Saul's garment, what would it have done if he had kept away
his castles, towns and ships?', were summoned to Westminster to
answer for their temerity.[5] At the March assizes at Maidstone, a group
of Kentish gentlemen organised a petition expressing their doubts
concerning the Militia Ordinance, their preference for episcopacy,
and their fears of the breakdown of ecclesiastical discipline. Despite its
temperate language and plea that 'good understanding be ... speedily
renewed between his Majesty and ... Parliament', the Commons were
'transcendently incensed' by the petition. It was burned by the common
hangman and its promoters impeached.[6]

'My heart pities a king so fleeting and so friendless', Dering wrote to
his wife in the immediate aftermath of Charles's flight.[7] Charles position
continued to look precarious through the summer of 1642, and was
derided as being so in parliamentary propaganda – not least because an
army of some fifteen thousand men had been mobilised in London.
When the king raised the royal standard at Nottingham on 22 September
as a formal declaration of war he was attended by only eight hundred
cavalry and so few infantrymen that they could not provide a permanent
guard for the flag. A high wind brought the standard down a few days

later. Yet, despite the ill omens and the small numbers who rallied to his initial summons, there were indications that the king enjoyed considerable sympathy in the country at large; and, equally, that the policies pursued by Pym were being seriously questioned.

The unity of parliament had been threatened, as we have seen, by contention over church government from the first appearance of the Root and Branch petition. From the summer of 1641 this issue had spilled over into the provinces. While the attack on episcopacy had sparked a riposte in favour of the hierarchy in only three counties in the first six months of 1641, from November local defenders of episcopacy proved more vocal. Thirteen counties petitioned in favour of the existing hierarchy and liturgy between November 1641 and May 1642; in this last month, Sir Thomas Aston, a Cheshire gentleman, published a collection of several of these petitions with a commentary. Aston had been a vigorous defender of church government by bishops from January 1641, initially almost a lone lay activist in the localities. By December he had organised two pro-episcopacy petitions from Cheshire, and had battled to impress upon parliament that the 'Root and Branch' petition forwarded from that county was a crude fraud that had never been signed or even circulated locally. In May 1641 he published a reasoned account of his support for the institution of episcopacy, the *Remonstrance against Presbytery*, in which the theme of the parallel between ecclesiastical hierarchy and the structures of political and social subordination, expressed in the parliamentary debates, were powerfully developed. 'I consider,' he wrote,

the Nobility and Gentry of this Isle ... situate as the Low Countries in a flat, under the banks and bounds of the laws, secured from the inundations of that Ocean the vulgar, which by the breach of those bounds would quickly overwhelm us and deface all distinctions of degrees or persons.

An attack on bishops, those 'pillars of our state that prop up the regulated fabric of this glorious monarchy', would be to abrogate ancient laws and bury the nation in 'the rubbish of chaos'. Already, Aston argued, the egalitarian ecclesiology of the religious radicals in Cheshire was slipping into the secular sphere, and had led to a 'denial of the right to property in our estates. They would pay no fines, do no boons, no duties to their landlords.'[8] This language formed a ground bass to all subsequent county petitions in favour of episcopacy and the liturgy. The Essex petitioners attacked 'the very ill effects both in the church and civil government' that followed from the weakening of ecclesiastical discipline, and called for the settlement of 'that form of worship which hath been the cement and union of church and state'.[9]

The conjunction of traditional legal and constitutional principles and the maintenance of the social order were also the burden of the king's more secular declarations in the spring and summer of 1642. The talents of Hyde and his friends, who had steadily gravitated to York after the passage of the Militia Ordinance, were employed in the paper war between the king and the Houses. They continued to insist, as they had from the summer of 1641, that Charles was now a paragon of constitutional propriety, a thoroughly trustworthy executor of the system defined and defended by the new legislation. But their major debating tactic was vigorous, sardonic denunciation of the radical novelties in governmental practice and constitutional theory propagated by Pym and his cronies at Westminster. They noted, suavely, that parliament's intention of removing any obstacles that stood in the way of the implementation of its policies now appeared to threaten the known law of the land. They insisted that the traditional representative function of the Commons could not justify its seizure of unilateral authority to legislate or an executive role. They questioned whether the Commons now represented anyone. These arguments proved compelling to some local gentlemen. In Herefordshire, they surface in an exchange of letters between the local magistrates and the two knights of the shire. 'We send you,' the JPs insisted, 'not with the authority to govern us, but with our consent for making ... laws as to his Majesty, the Lords and Commons shall seem good.' Privately, they were more explicit. 'They say the parliament does their own business and not the country's.'[10] The Nottinghamshire gentry lectured their MPs in similar vein: 'We never conceived your only votes should be our law.'[11]

Royal propaganda did not only dilate upon high constitutional theory. The social disruption inherent in parliament's constitutional position and policies, as in its ecclesiology, was also emphasised. Pym's readiness to countenance and encourage popular participation in the political process would lead, it was suggested in the *Answer to the Nineteen Propositions*, to a destruction of 'all rights and properties, all distinctions of families and merit'. In consequence, 'this splendid and excellently distinguished form of government' would end in 'a dark equal chaos of confusion, and the long line of our many noble ancestors in a Jack Cade or a Wat Tyler.' Two weeks later Charles instructed the judges that at the forthcoming assizes they were to insist upon his concern for law and order, both in their formal charges and in their enforcement of legislation against rogues and vagabonds, who, encouraged by the 'distempers of the present times ... dare to make a prey of our good subjects'.[12]

In the summer of 1642 Charles's play on fears of the 'many headed monster' was not merely an academic exercise. Many of the populace apparently shared the view expressed by an Essex poacher, arrested in May 1642, that 'there was no law settled at this time that he knew'.[13] In this 'time of liberty' there were a series of attacks on the deer parks of the upper classes, in a 'rebellious, riotous, devilish way'.[14] The spring of 1642 also saw a major outbreak of rioting in the fens. Traditional rights of common were affirmed in a ritual game, 'throwing out a football, and playing at it drove it against a new house set up in the drained fens, and because it stood in their way, pulled it down ... and so have they pulled down many'. Standing crops and the drainage works themselves received similar treatment. Local juries refused to find verdicts against the rioters, and the efforts of the sheriff and some JPs to restore order resulted only in their own humiliation. Threats of violence forced them to abandon legal proceedings, to surrender the prisoners they had taken, and to retire hastily from Boston in a volley of 'dirt and stones' with the jeers of the fenmen ringing in their ears.[15]

Perhaps more troubling were those riots that were not affirmations of traditional rights but were ostensibly justified by the orders of parliament. In late August Sir John Lucas of Colchester made an attempt to join the king at York with a number of armed servants. His plans were betrayed and he was arrested by the mayor, but garbled rumours spread like wildfire through the town, which was soon in an uproar. The 'rude sort of people' broke into Lucas's house, stripped it, and then, supported by the inhabitants of other Stour valley clothing towns, moved into the countryside to plunder the houses of Catholic gentry and Laudian clergymen. The local governors, keenly aware of unemployment and hunger among the clothworkers, the product of dislocation of the trade in a period of economic uncertainty, were terrified by the violence of the outbreak. Yet the rioters claimed that their actions were warranted by the declarations of parliament, pointing to sermons, approved by the Commons, like Stephen Marshall's *Meroz Cursed*, that insisted on popular activism. 'When the mighty of the world do oppose the *Lord*,' Marshall preached, 'God's *meanest servants* must not be afraid to oppose the *Mighty*.'[16] MPs certainly chose to view the riots as a manifestation of enthusiasm – a little over-ebullient, perhaps – for the cause. They congratulated the 'honest inhabitants' on their 'very acceptable services to the Commonwealth ... such a one as doth express a great zeal to their religion and liberties'.[17] Charles and his supporters were not slow to draw the moral: the demotic language employed by parliament and its propagandists was promoting anarchy.

The effectiveness of the case being presented on Charles's behalf is apparent in the growing distance in the localities from the policies being pursued by Pym. The powerful local affirmation of parliamentary authority apparent in the wave of petitions after the attempt on the Five Members was wavering. While parliament's agenda became increasingly suspect, however, this sentiment did not by any means transmute immediately into a readiness to support Charles in arms. The relentless barrage of royal and parliamentary propaganda combined with fears for the fragility of the social order seemed to indicate that negotiation and reconciliation were imperative. Traditional assumptions about law and constitutional theory, to which both sides appealed, in fact made the choice between the competing orders from York and Westminster an utterly impossible one for moderates. In May 1642 as a Norfolk gentleman, Thomas Knyvett, was sauntering through Westminster he was greeted by one of the local MPs and presented with a commission, signed by the lord lieutenant appointed by parliament, instructing him to take command of an infantry trained-band in the county. A few hours later he read the royal proclamation that denounced the Militia Ordinance, the authority by which his commission was issued. 'Oh! sweetheart,' he wrote to his wife, 'I am now in a great straight what to do.'[18] Knyvett's private dilemma was not uncommon, and found collective expression in a number of counties. A series of local petitions for an accommodation between the two sides sought to establish a pose of studied neutrality, begging both Charles and parliament to recognise the force of the other's contentions, and to make concessions that might restore consensus. Cheshire petitioners reprehended the 'dangerous and disloyal distinction (which rings too loud in our ears) viz. For the king or for the parliament', and insisted that 'king and parliament, being like Hippocrates' twins, they must laugh and cry, live and die together; and both are so rooted in our loyal hearts that we cannot disjoin them'.[19] Twins became a favoured, if incongruous, metaphor. The Devon petition bewailed their 'unhappy condition, made judges in apparent contraries! In how hard a condition are we, whilst a two-fold obedience, like twins in the womb, strives to be born to both!'[20]

Confusion and uncertainty emerged in practice, not merely in rhetorical offerings. In many counties efforts were made to distance, even insulate, the locality from the war efforts of both sides. Lincolnshire, for instance, sought to secure its isolation by raising a force designed to repel the forces of the belligerents. The incident is a telling one. The proximity of Hull ensured that parliament was quick to attempt to gain control of the militia of Lincolnshire. That goal was apparently achieved by the end of June 1642, and achieved with minimal opposition. On 4 July the parliamentary lord lieutenant, Lord Willoughby of Parham, presented a declaration to the Houses from the county, whose signatories, several thousand strong, expressed their enthusiasm in the usual pro-parliamentary catch phrases. Ten days later these rang very hollow. The king had visited Lincoln, where he had received a tumultuous reception attended by the militiamen who had so recently acceded to Willoughby's authority. A petition, subsequently voted 'false, scandalous and seditious' by parliament, was promulgated, and a subscription to raise a force of four hundred cavalry was begun. Royalist commentators were euphoric, but their delight proved premature and their assumptions simplistic. Despite broad hints from Charles, no immediate attempt was made to execute the Commission of Array in the county. And the cavalry force was raised not for the king but to secure 'the peace of the county' against a triple threat of overseas invasion, of the depredations of soldiers from adjacent counties, and of internal insurrection by 'many men of desperate fortunes'. The Lincolnshire men were not 'turncoats' whose allegiance had flipped from parliamentarian to royalist: their actions displayed both a common desire not to appear as 'malignants either against the king or parliament', and a more positive policy designed to protect the county from invasion or riot.[21]

Behaviour akin to that of Lincolnshire – hesitation, apparent ter-giversation, a desire to neutralise the locality – can be found in twenty-two counties in 1642. In some of these local 'third forces' were also proposed. In Staffordshire a specially convened public meeting, three weeks after the battle of Edgehill, warned off both royalist and parliamentarian troops and recruiters, and it was agreed to raise a force of eight hundred infantry and two hundred cavalry to secure the county from any invasion. Other counties might not express their preference for peace in such institutional form, but private negotiations among the gentry indicate the potency of pacific and localist sentiments. In Cornwall in August the 'general desire to quiet this county' was noted.[22] Activists had to proceed circumspectly, struggling against the dead weight of the majority the county elite, who 'sat still as neuters, assist-ing neither'.[23] In Norfolk the rallying cry of the gentry in the summer of 1642 was 'the peace of my county'. Sir John Spelman, who was later to die at Oxford, suppressed a project to execute the royalist commis-sion of array, hoping that thus 'our country would have enjoyed immunity from the common calamity'. 'My country's quiet', was the declared goal of Sir John Potts, MP, who later administered the shire for parliament, 'I labour to preserve peace'.[24]

The proposed local forces were never raised in Lincolnshire or Staffordshire; in both counties men were compelled to take sides and both were engulfed in the war as the belligerents scrambled to control their resources for their respective war efforts. Cornwall and Norfolk were luckier: local peace was achieved, but only by acceding to the administration of the counties by committed partisans, royalist and par-liamentarian respectively. A powerful visceral sentiment, neutralism could not create an ideology designed to insulate localities from the demands of the state. It could not justify policies that seemed 'to call the conclusions of England to the bar of Yorkshire', as Sir John Hotham wrote sardonically of an attempt to create a treaty of neutrality in his native county.[25] The cultural assumptions of localism could not survive the determination of the two competing sides to secure local control.

We now need to come back again to the original question of how the king managed to raise an army. Our analysis suggests that Charles had to overcome or marginalise a body of neutralist, pacific sentiment if he was to undertake effective military preparation and action. This was equally a clog on parliament's war effort. Both sides depended on the efforts of a minority of the committed, men prepared to entertain the unpalatable prospect of war. It is easier to explain the development of militant engagement in the parliamentarian cause – and this explanation is a necessary corollary to any answer to the question of royalist commitment.

Religious conviction was the key to enthusiastic engagement in the parliamentary war effort. Westminster's propaganda emphasised that the king was the dupe of a powerful faction of papists, determined to eradicate Protestantism. The events in Ireland, massacres and atrocities luridly described and overstated in the press, were a dreadful warning. It was a religious duty incumbent on the godly – all the godly – to resist this threat. This was the burden of the sermons of ministers like Marshall, in his much-preached *Meroz Cursed*, or Jeremiah Burroughs, arguing a commission 'from the Lord of Hosts' to 'his people', his 'precious saints,' to defend religion.[26] We catch some of the potency of this in an incident from 1643, the surrender, after a lengthy siege, of Brampton Bryan House in Herefordshire. A royalist minister questioned the garrison soldiers on the motivation for their bold defiance. They replied that

> all the true godly divines in England (amongst whom they named in special M. Marshall) were of their opinion, that Antichrist was here in England as well as in Rome, and that the bishops were Antichrist, and that all that did endeavour to support them were popishly affected, Babilonish and Antichristian too ... and therefore they thought they were bound in conscience to fight ... and in doing so they did but help God against his enemies. I urged them to show by what call or warrant they had to do so, being not authorised by the king, they seemed to infer a three fold call or warrant. 1. The command of parliament. 2. The example of all godly and powerful ministers, leading, encouraging, and stirring them thereunto and 3. The motion of God's spirit in all God's people, provoking them all with one mind, to undertake the same business.[27]

In certain areas local power brokers who supported the parliamentary cause focused and deployed such sentiments to mobilise their areas for the war effort. In Essex the machine, a cooperative cadre of godly ministers and sympathetic gentlemen that the godly earl of Warwick had employed to secure victory in the 1640 elections, was equally adept at swiftly promoting huge anti-episcopal and pro-parliamentary petitions in 1641 and early 1642. By the summer it was gathering financial support for the cause and raising men. The leaders at Westminster and London journalists waxed lyrical in their praise of the county's commitment, and Warwick's godly influence. Essex was the 'place of most life of religion in the land' wrote a leading supporter of Pym's; the county raised volunteers, reported a newsbook, 'to show their zeal to parliament and love to the earl of Warwick'.[28] The zealous Lord Brooke played a similar role in Warwickshire. In both counties the role of these peers was to focus and canalise pre-existing pro-parliamentary sentiment. Neither employed seigneurial mechanisms to raise forces; both relied on an ideological appeal, particularly from their associated ministers. Neither sought to raise men from their own tenants, or appealed solely to the county elite. Brooke, in particular sought his assistants and officers from men below the gentry rank, men who shared his own uncompromisingly radical religious views.

In Essex and Warwickshire, the zeal of the godly was given focus and direction by powerful magnates. Leading gentlemen played similar, if less decisive, roles in other counties: Sir Nathaniel Barnardiston in Suffolk; Sir William Brereton in Cheshire; Sir Robert Harley in Herefordshire. But in the absence of such elite figures the militant godly were perfectly prepared to act unilaterally. By June 1642 those of the Wellingborough area had organised an armed force of volunteers, who displayed their commitments and practised their military skills raiding neighbouring villages and destroying wayside crosses and other ecclesiastical paraphernalia they considered 'superstitious'.[29] The situation in Lancashire was similar; Salford Hundred and particularly Manchester were active in organising pro-parliamentary volunteer companies, recruited from 'men of the best affection for religion'. Again, their zeal was initially demonstrated and honed by destroying copies of the Book of Common Prayer, surplices, organs and decorated fonts.[30]

Preaching the responsibility of *all* men to oppose the popish conspiracy, arming the godly, officering the newly-raised forces with men from outside the charmed circle of the traditional rulers looked very dangerous. But the godly could, as it were, see through the immediate danger to a higher purpose. So a Yorkshire minister, Thomas Stockdale, contemplated the potential breakdown of order in early 1642 with some confidence.

> The insurrections ... (as all ungoverned multitudes) are of very dangerous consequence; but God, who works miracles, can, out of such violent actions, bring comfortable effects ... Unjust and irreligious pretences [the king's policies] seem to give warrant and precedent to an opposite irregularity of the same nature, which is for just and religious ends in this kingdom.[31]

Nerved by a powerful sense of the shaping role of divine providence in the crisis, the belief that God was involved, directly and actively, in 'those wars that concern his people',[32] the godly could contemplate a shaking of the social system with some equanimity. The godly raised voluntary contributions to support the war effort; they worked to secure their localities for the parliamentarian interest; they officered the volunteer regiments, and many served in their ranks. As in any army there were recruits motivated by 'base ends', pay and plunder in a period of economic dislocation, but the typical figure is Sergeant Nehemiah Wharton, who reported the activities of such 'goddame blades' among his fellow soldiers with abhorrence. Wharton, on the march from Aylesbury to Worcester in the late summer of 1642, revelled in hearing sermons, in all-night marathons of psalm singing, in acts of iconoclasm. He and his companions were, he wrote, determined to 'valiantly fight the Lord's Battle', confident that 'the Lord of Hosts will in the end triumph gloriously over these horses and all their cursed riders'.[33]

So who became committed royalists? Two analytically distinct questions need to be answered here. First, who funded, administered and officered the king's armies? Secondly, who volunteered to serve in them? Those from the elite who joined with the king usually justified their commitment, at the time or afterwards, by reference to 'the punctilio of honour'. 'Honour and loyalty' motivated the earl of Newcastle, who 'thought it his duty rather to hazard all, than to neglect the commands of his Sovereign'. Sir Edmund Verney, who carried the royal standard into battle at Edgehill and died there, 'did not like the quarrel'; but 'my conscience is ... concerned in honour and gratitude to follow my master'.[34] In a few cases motives for the choice of royalism are more fully documented. Sir Thomas Salusbury's justification for joining the king at York included his reflections on constitutional law, on contemporary history and, above all, on scripture. The Book of Proverbs had taught him to 'fear God and the king, and meddle not with those that are given to change'. The second clause of this injunction was obviously deeply important to Salusbury. The policies pursued by parliament, particularly its religious policies, were encouraging a 'multitude of schisms' that threatened social as well as religious and political breakdown. 'Filthy dreamers' had arisen who 'despise dominion and speak evil of dignities'.[35] Early in 1641 Sir William Courtenay had enthused over parliament's reforms; by late 1642 he was an officer in the royalist army. It was accounts of religious factionalism and iconoclasm that seem to have most troubled him; 'the honour of the state is engaged to see these foul disorders punished or else greater oppression will certainly follow on men of the best ranks', he wrote.[36] Concerns of this kind are the subtext of the rhetoric and actions of many royalists. A prime motivation was to defend the traditional social order against the prospect of subversion so extreme as to threaten anarchy.

This conservative concern for traditional order was at the heart of royalist conviction. It also informs the answers of contemporary royalist commentators and historians to a subsidiary question that must concern us: the recruiting of the king's army. For royalists, it was axiomatic that loyal peers and gentlemen encouraged their deferential social subordinates, their tenants and dependants, to volunteer. Long after the event, Edward Hyde, who had played such a major role in defining Charles's cause in 1642, recalled how,

> The earl of Lindsey was a man of very noble extraction and inherited a great fortune from his ancestors … [He had] a very great interest in his country … the several companies of his own regiment of foot being commanded by the principal knights of Lincolnshire, who engaged themselves in the service principally out of their personal affection to him … Sir Gervase Scroope … an old gentleman of great fortune in Lincolnshire, had raised a foot company amongst his tenants, and brought them to the earl of Lindsey's regiment, out of devotion and respect to his lordship as well as duty to the king.[37]

This is political and social theory masquerading as history. In some areas of Britain mechanisms akin to those described by Clarendon provided the king with men. James Stanley, earl of Derby, who brought three infantry regiments to Charles at Shrewsbury in October 1642, boasted that he enjoyed 'the general applause of my neighbours, as one they would like to follow, as they did my ancestors before me'. But, as with Derby's retainers and tenants from northern Lancashire, social deference was strongest in peripheral, economically backward areas – Wales, the northern border counties, Cornwall – where older cultural assumptions about social and tenurial relations had survived.

Even in these areas the mechanisms that depended upon invoking traditional patterns of deference were often less effective than those who sought to use them anticipated. Many of Sir Bevill Grenville's tenants appeared at the first Cornish muster summoned by the royalists, their pikes decorated with his family's colours of white and blue, but, as he complained, others of his 'neighbours' refused the summons and 'came not out'. A good number of Derby's tenants also failed him, some, to his chagrin, joining the parliamentarians; 'the baser sort thought it a fine thing to set up against the great ones', he complained bitterly.[38] In other parts of England it is easier to list the failures of attempts to raise tenants on behalf of the king than the successes. In the east midlands a royalist reported Charles's disappointment that 'the gentry of these counties do not draw after them such numbers of commons as his majesty presumed upon'.[39] Similar failures were reported in southern Yorkshire, in Northamptonshire, in Devon, in Gloucestershire and in Somerset. In Cheshire the royalist squire, William Davenport, attempted a little recruiting amongst his tenants. The response was a letter signed by twenty-four of them, begging him

> not to repute us ill-affected or false hearted tenants in refusing to venture our lives in causes that our hearts and consciences do persuade us is not good or lawful, nor such as we dare ... with good consciences to defend you in ... we dare not lift up our hands against that honourable assembly of parliament.

Davenport said that he would answer their letter shortly, but his tenants 'not ... caring much for me or my answer ... listed themselves ... to become soldiers for the parliament'.[40]

The bulk of the royal army at Edgehill did not consist of forelock-tugging tenants, loyally serving under the personal banners of landlords and local magnates. Basically officers with commissions from the king had to rely on volunteers. Their recruiting sergeants, like those of Fitzwilliam Coningsby in Herefordshire, toured towns and villages 'beating my drums' and offering the usual incentives to military service – cash, alcohol, comradeship. It worked. Despite the tepid and jealous attitude of the nominally royalist Lord Scudamore, 'the prince in quality in that county', Coningsby mustered 685 soldiers in January 1643.[41] Parliamentarian journalists were scathing in their descriptions of those who enlisted in the royal armies: barefoot Welshmen; 'desperate ruffians'; 'such for condition that I think the earth affords not worse'; 'abundance of the rascality of the country'.[42] Recalling 1642 long after the event, the godly minister of Kidderminster, Richard Baxter, took a similar line concerning the royal forces. His ministry was reviled and his congregation terrorised by the violence and menaces – 'we shall take an order with these Puritans ere long' – of 'the debauched rabble', 'the beggarly drunken rout'. He noted smugly, however, that 'almost all these drunkards went into the king's army and were quickly killed so that scarce a man of them came home again'.[43] But Baxter's language and that of the contemporary journalists, for all its venomous hostility, indicates that popular royalism was not just a matter of mindless, proletarian violence. Those 'poor journeymen and servants' who chanted 'down with the Roundheads' were roused to action by the iconoclasm of Baxter's supporters; they were patrons of the stage plays, wakes and other traditional festivities so abhorred by the godly. No less than those of the elite who committed themselves to the king's cause, lower-class royalists sought to defend a traditional world from the threats posed by interventionist puritan zeal. We get a nice sense of the cultural divergences in the motivations of the forces of the belligerents in two incidents from the war in Lancashire. After the royalists abandoned the siege of Manchester, 'the saints sung the song of Moses' in the church and the streets outside it, and the soldiers 'with a loud voice and one consent, clapping their hands apace ... reported God fearful in praises, working wonders'.[44] At Lathom House, the capture of the parliamentarians' main siege mortar was greeted by the common soldiers with 'shouting and rejoicing as merrily as they used to do with their ale and bagpipes'.[45]

Royalist commitment at all social levels was rooted in a fear of the subversive consequences of militant puritanism. This explains why the king had difficulty raising an army initially; why his troops were raised *after* the parliamentarian forces were mobilised. For the man troubled by the threats to social order or local community that appeared to inhere in the direction of Pym's policies, 1642 posed a formidable quandary. Would the feared spiral into religious and social breakdown be more enhanced by the enforcement of those policies as interpreted by local cadres of the godly, or by the outbreak of war itself? In this sense, royalism and neutralism, as expressed by Thomas Knyvett or temporarily institutionalised in Lincolnshire, were very closely related.

What then drove a man from uneasy neutralism to commitment to the king's cause? Charles's immediate presence in an area could play a role. So, too, could direct experience of pro-parliamentary enthusiasm in a locality, as zealots organised and armed, and as their troops undertook unofficial but violent acts of iconoclasm. A small group of committed royalists attempted to mobilise men and resources for the king in Worcestershire in August and early September; their efforts were undermined by local uncertainty and suspicion, even indifference. They were far more successful in the winter after the county had experienced the reformist zeal of the earl of Essex's army. Large-scale iconoclasm and plunder marked Essex's occupation; his men treated the locals as benighted aliens. For Sergeant Wharton, the shire was 'base, papistical and atheistical ... it resembles Sodom, and is the very emblem of Gomorrah.'[46]

Once the king's partisans had taken control of a shire, previously neutral conservatives would gravitate into royal military forces and local administration. Men who feared social breakdown would, once the royalists were in control, see their administration as the guarantor of local security. But this latter mechanism also worked on the parliamentarian side. In Kent a large group of gentlemen had organised a petition expressing their doubts concerning the Militia Ordinance, their strong preference for episcopacy, and their fears of the subversive consequences of the breakdown of ecclesiastical discipline. Their priority was that a 'good understanding be ... speedily renewed between his Majesty and both Houses of parliament'.[47] But once the dispatch of forces from London brought Kent firmly under parliamentary control, the elite conformed and many of the signatories sidled into their traditional posts in local administration.

4

Why Did Parliament Win the Civil War?

The first major action of the Civil War, on Sunday 23 October 1642 at Edgehill, traumatic and bloody as it was, ended in anti-climax. Neither side won an outright victory. There was to be no swift end to the war, no clear providential judgement on the merits of the two causes. After Edgehill, the king moved south to Oxford, which became his capital for the remainder of the struggle. Essex retired to Warwick, and then marched back to London in time to halt a royalist thrust against the city at Turnham Green on the 13 November.

In the first eight months of 1643 the forces of the king and Essex skirmished with mixed fortunes in the Thames Valley and the Chilterns, while the north and west became the major theatres of the war, and of royalist victory. In the west the king's early tenuous foothold in Cornwall was steadily expanded up the peninsula by the skilled generalship of Sir Ralph Hopton and the valour of his troops. In late July Bristol fell to the royalists, and Hopton's front line was pushed through Wiltshire and Dorset into Hampshire. In the same period the earl of Newcastle, Charles's commander in the north, though a far less able general than Hopton, had beaten the Yorkshire parliamentarians at Adwalton Moor, and forced them to take refuge in Hull. The bulk of his army laid siege to the town, while detachments sallied out to capture Gainsborough and Lincoln, and raid deep into the Lincolnshire fens. The summer of 1643 was the high-water mark of the king's military effort. In the remainder of the year the parliamentarians, partly as a consequence of military reorganisation, recovered lost ground. In September Essex relieved the siege of Gloucester, which had been valiantly defended since the fall of Bristol, and forced aside the king's army, which sought to block his march back to London, at the battle of Newbury. In October the garrison of Hull broke Newcastle's desultory siege, and the earl's forces were also driven from Lincolnshire. Only Hopton, in the south extended the territory under royalist control, receiving the surrender of Arundel Castle on the 9 December.

The military balance had swung against Charles in the last months of 1643, and this trend continued in 1644. Hopton's eastern outposts had proved vulnerable to counter-attack in the winter of 1643–44, and then he was defeated at Cheriton on 29 March; the western army was extricated, but its brilliant record of victories and territorial expansion was at an end, and its morale was battered. The king's position in the north was eroded in January by the victory of Sir Thomas Fairfax at Nantwich over Lord Byron's mixed force of local Cavaliers and five regiments that had been part of the English army in Ireland that had been shipped to Chester. Far worse was to follow. Under pressure from parliament's new Scottish allies whose regiments had crossed the border on 19 January, the resurgent Yorkshire forces, and those of the Eastern Association which had cleared Lincolnshire, Newcastle's army was steadily forced onto the defensive. By midsummer the bulk of the northern royalists were holed up in Newcastle and York. Prince Rupert relieved York in a series of brilliant manoeuvres, but his insistence on immediately fighting the armies that had besieged it led to total defeat at Marston Moor on 2 July and the loss of the north, with the exception of a few scattered garrisons, for the king.

Charles enjoyed some successes in 1644. Essex's wilful and misadvised attempt to invade the king's western heartland, to cut off his recruits and supplies, had led to the humiliating surrender of the parliamentarian infantry, cornered at Fowey, on 2 September. In late October the parliamentary armies, in their turn, trapped the king's army at Newbury. But divisions, distrust and jealousies among the commanders, and the exhaustion of their poorly supplied troops, enabled the king to extricate his force and his artillery from what seemed an impossible position triumphantly.

It was his last military success. Parliament's anger at the inadequate military leadership apparent in the Fowey débâcle, and then the failure to destroy the royalist army at Newbury, resulted, in the winter of 1644–45, in the reorganisation of their forces as the New Model Army, and the establishment of a new structure of command, under Sir Thomas Fairfax. The new system proved its worth in the summer of 1645: on 14 June, Charles himself was routed at Naseby; on 10 July the royalist army in the west, under Goring, was shattered at Langport; on 10 September the defences of Bristol were carried by storm, and Rupert forced to surrender the city. After these triumphs the royalist cause was doomed, but the war dragged on in a series of sieges and skirmishes. Finally on 27 April 1646 Charles escaped from Oxford, then under siege, and surrendered himself to the Scottish forces that were besieging the other major garrison still in royalist hands, Newark. Parliament had won the civil war.

If asked why parliament won the war, many would answer, 'because it won the key battles', which is unexceptional if unhelpful. This suggestion is often offered in tandem with the argument that it was a close run thing, and combined with a good deal of 'what if?' history: What if the king had moved directly on London after Edgehill? What if Rupert had not insisted on immediately engaging the armies that besieged York, but had allowed their demoralisation and divided command structure to dissipate the threat that they posed? In this kind of analysis, the parliamentarian victory seems a matter of contingency and chance. In fact, parliament enjoyed a number of key advantages that rendered its ultimate victory almost certain – as certain as that of the North's in the American Civil War. As with the North, the parliamentarians had to neutralise the initial advantages held by their opponents, but, once the early defeats had been absorbed, the royalist cause was doomed. Of its nature, this is a statement incapable of proof, but compare the effects of the defeat of the forces of Rupert and Newcastle at Marston Moor in July 1644 with those following the king's victory at Fowey and the subsequent surrender of Essex's army two months later. The latter was humiliating to the parliamentarians and their Lord General, but it had only a marginal impact on the outcome of the war. Marston Moor destroyed the royalist cause in the north.

The combination of elements that guaranteed Roundhead victory was complex. The parliamentarians' control of the navy and of London were vitally important, as was their greater success in negotiating effective alliances. Parliament ultimately proved more adept in mobilising resources for war, and in developing an effective command structure. Finally, the morale and commitment of a leaven among the parliamentarians was better able to sustain a prolonged conflict. The last three factors – morale, command and the mobilisation of resources – are both closely interwoven and crucial for an understanding of post-war developments. They, in particular, will be the focus here. But first the initial advantages enjoyed by the cavaliers, apparent in the catalogue of victories early in 1643, must be considered.

In April 1657 Cromwell, addressing the second Protectorate Parliament, recalled a conversation with John Hampden fifteen years before, probably in the aftermath of Edgehill. His analysis of the initial cavalry superiority enjoyed by the royalists is convincing. 'Your troopers', he told his cousin, fellow MP and parliamentary officer,

> are most of them old decayed serving-men and tapsters, and such kind of fellows; and their troopers are gentlemen's sons, younger sons and persons of quality: do you think that the spirits of such base and mean fellows will ever be able to encounter gentlemen that have honour and courage and resolution in them? ... You must get men of a spirit: and take it not ill what I say, – I know you will not, – of a spirit that is likely to go on as far as gentlemen will go, or else I am sure you will be beaten still.[1]

The dash and élan of the Cavalier cavalry, wholly lacking in their parliamentarian opposites, had already been demonstrated at Powicke Bridge. Hampden, whose response to Cromwell's analysis was sceptical, was to discover its accuracy at Chalgrove Field in June 1643. Rupert, retreating towards Oxford from a raid on Essex's quarters, turned on the pursuing parliamentary horse, drove it in rout and left Hampden himself mortally wounded. Again at Roundway Down, a month later, the parliamentary cavalry commanded by Sir William Waller were driven like sheep.

Cromwell's analysis of the initial disparity in the cavalry of the two sides can be extended to the generals. The spirit of the royalist cavalry in the early months of the war was replicated in the aggressive tactics pursued by the best of the royalist commanders. The parliamentarian leaders were, by contrast, cautious and defensive, not least because they doubted that their horse would stand up to the Cavaliers.

Cromwell's remedy for the deficiencies of the parliamentary army needed time for its implementation. Time was made available by the advantages that the parliamentarians enjoyed. From the first, their control of the seas and of London made it difficult for the royalists to take full advantage of their victories.

In 1642 the impressive product of Charles's ship money turned against its creator. When in July 1642 the king ordered the navy to accept the authority of his nominee as admiral, only five of the ships' captains attempted to obey his order. The remainder, and the bulk of the seamen, who had associated themselves with the London populace in its protests and demonstrations from the outset of the Long Parliament, preferred the earl of Warwick. Warwick, a puritan and an active opponent of Charles's policies in the 1630s, had been involved in colonial, commercial and privateering ventures since 1614, all informed by a hostility to Spain, and was in consequence a popular figure in the fleet. The control of the navy, which parliament retained until the naval revolt of 1648, was a vital strategic asset. In 1644 Lord Digby, one of the king's closest advisers, acknowledged that parliament's mastery of the seas 'is a most uncomfortable thing to us in all relations ... It hazards our best hopes'.[2] First, it made it difficult for the king to secure men or supplies from the Continent or from Ireland. Some equipment and reinforcements were received, but never in substantial amounts or numbers. After the cessation negotiated with the Irish rebels, elements of the Irish royal army were landed at Chester and the Somerset ports, but in dribs and drabs. In May 1644 Captain Swanley intercepted a troopship and threw all the native Irish overboard. After this incident, Ormond, the king's deputy in Ireland, noted that – unsurprisingly – Irish troops were reluctant to embark for service in England. 'Until these seas be cleared,' Ormond continued, '[you] can expect little (indeed no) succour from Ireland.'[3]

Secondly, the navy enabled parliament to support and supply key garrisons, including Hull, Plymouth and Lyme Regis, the survival of which diverted royalist troops from the main field army and wasted resources in tedious and debilitating sieges. A journal of the two months' siege of Lyme by one of the garrison is punctuated by the regular arrival by sea of men, ordnance, munitions and 'all manner of provisions'; its writer also reports royalist frustration – the 'grief of the enemy who saw such carrying and recarrying to and fro the ships'.[4] Conversely, the navy could cooperate with the army in the sieges of royalist towns, cutting off supplies and bombarding the fortifications: in the spring of 1644 the murderously efficient Swanley, in a neat amphibious operation with General Laugharne, had secured the main coastal strong points in Pembrokeshire.

Control of London gave parliament both the largest port for the importation of foreign munitions, and the country's major industrial centre for the provision of arms, clothing and shoes. The city was a reservoir of manpower, volunteer or conscript, and its well organised militia made a series of invaluable supplementary interventions on behalf of the parliamentary war effort. The London trained bands joined the parliamentary field army to block the king at Turnham Green in November 1642; in September 1643 they reinforced Essex when he relieved Gloucester and beat off Charles's prime troops at Newbury on their march home. When money was needed expeditiously, loans, secured against receipts of future taxation, could be raised from the London authorities, from the livery companies and from individual citizen investors: £80,000 was raised to equip the New Model Army early in 1645; £200,000 to pay off the Scots two years later. In 1656, responding to complaints about the arrears owed on the assessment, the City governors acidly reminded the government of the vast sums it had 'lent ... to the state in the late troubles', much of which had never been repaid.[5] Finally, London and Westminster were the apex of the administrative infrastructure of the nation state. Charles had nothing comparable, and had to undertake the slow, piecemeal development of new administrative and fiscal mechanisms in Oxford.

From the outset of the war, parliament enjoyed the strategic advantage of control of the seas and of London. As the war dragged into 1643, both sides sought to secure reinforcements from beyond England. Again, the parliamentarians got the better deal. Charles's representatives negotiated a truce with the Catholic rebels in Ireland in 1643. In consequence the king was able to redeploy elements, some eight thousand men in all, of the royal army in Ireland that had been built up by Strafford. Many of the native English troops in the Irish army were not, however, enthusiastic supporters of Charles's cause. The royalist generals Byron and Hopton, whose armies included detachments from Ireland, found them unreliable; 'very cold in this service', 'not to be trusted in this war', 'very mutinous and shrewdly infected with the rebellious humour of England', easily seduced by parliamentary propaganda.[6] After the defeat at Nantwich more than half the prisoners from the Irish regiments, some eight hundred men, immediately took service with Fairfax. Byron preferred to recruit Irish natives, but Charles was never able to use troops from his Irish army, of whatever nationality, in sufficient strength to make a decisive military difference. A more ambitious – or naive – agenda, of securing military assistance from the Confederates, made no real headway in the face of the labyrinthine machinations of the various Irish parties. Worse, both attempts were undoubtedly politically counter-productive. The proposed employment of Irish troops, particularly Catholics associated with the massacres of 1641, fitted exactly with parliamentary propaganda that depicted Charles as the dupe of an extensive 'popish plot' to subvert England's religion and liberties.

Parliament was more fortunate in its major alliance. By the terms of the Solemn League and Covenant, parliament and the Scots promised mutual military assistance, and agreed to establish a religious uniformity, 'according to the Word of God' – a phrase that the Scots understood to entail the establishment of Presbyterianism – in all three kingdoms. In the winter of 1643/4 a Scottish army of 21,000 men crossed the border to assist their English 'brethren' in the cause of Protestant Reformation. Militarily, the Scottish army proved a damp squib. It became bogged down in a tedious siege of Newcastle. Scottish forces were involved at Marston Moor, but then found that the victory was credited in England entirely to Oliver Cromwell, 'with his unspeakable valorous regiments'.[7] The priority which the Scots accorded to compelling their English allies to accede to a Presbyterian church settlement resulted in growing tension, which was compounded by their own lack of success, by their financial demands, and by their plunder of the areas in which their forces, poorly supplied and paid, operated. The Scots became the butt of the hostility and ridicule of elements of the London press. Yet they provided a formidable force that obliged the king's commander-in-chief in the north to tie up units to halt their advance. In the summer of 1643 the earl of Newcastle's forces had captured Lincoln and were raiding deep into the east midlands. In the spring of 1644 the northern royalist army was bottled up in Newcastle and York; both cities were forced to surrender after Marston Moor.

Control of the navy and of London and the ability to negotiate an effective alliance, were important elements in parliament's victory. Beyond these were three crucial and closely interwoven issues: the morale of the two parties; their structures of command; and their ability to mobilise resources for their war machines. Each of these is related to the issues already discussed, on the choice of sides and the raising of forces. The intrinsic *conservatism* of royalism represented a formidable barrier to the necessary changes demanded by war. Parliament too suffered from a similar problem. Zealots had given the parliamentary cause its initial dynamic, but their influence was soon diluted by men who chose to act as parliament's local agents in an effort to shore up a tottering social and political structure. Such traditionalists, reluctant converts from uncertainty and neutralism, had no enthusiasm for total war. So parliament also had to overcome serious barriers to the fullest exploitation of its resources that would enable it to win the war. And it won because it did so far more effectively.

The conservative desire to uphold traditional values, which we have argued was at the heart of royalism, was not the best generator of enthusiastic engagement or zealous commitment. After the defeat at Marston Moor, the earl of Newcastle, the king's commander-in-chief of the north, and Prince Rupert met in York. Newcastle announced his intention of fleeing to exile on the Continent. When Rupert challenged this decision, Newcastle set out his motive in terms of a value system of personal honour and reputation: 'I will not endure the laughter of the Court.'[8] By the winter of 1645 the king's general in Lancashire, the earl of Derby, his great house at Lathom captured and demolished, had also abandoned the struggle and sought refuge in the Isle of Man. There he meditated on the failure of the royalist cause. The text he focused upon, Job 30: 1, is equally revealing of a man who conceptualised his commitment in terms of traditional authority: 'My enemies have me in derision, whose fathers I would have disdained to set with the dogs of my flock.'[9] Such attitudes were not just the prerogative of great magnates. Two gentlemen caught in the twisting political machinations of the royalist party in Herefordshire, and accused of betraying the king's cause, defended themselves against slurs to their *family's* honour. They sought to maintain the reputations of 'my house and posterity' and of 'the blood of ancient gentry and of an untainted family'.[10]

Conversely, the zeal of the godly, the key force in the initial raising of the parliamentary army, induced the vigour and tenacity that royalists recognised and respected. By late Sept 1642 the earl of Derby had gained

Dauentry

Brimidgham

The moſt Illuſtrious and High borne PRINCE RUPERT, PRINCE ELECTOR, Second Son to FREDERICK KING of BOHEMIA, GENERALL of the HORSE of Hs MAJESTIES ARMY, KNIGHT of the Noble Order of the GARTER.

Prince Rupert. Parliamentarian propaganda depicted the royalists as devoted to rapine and atrocity. Here Rupert rides into battle, plundered Birmingham burning behind him. He is attended by his dog 'Boy', which took on almost demonic status in the popular press. (*Ashmolean Museum, Oxford*) control of most of Lancashire for the king but Manchester refused to surrender. All accounts stress the sense of crusade that galvanised the town's defenders as they contemplated resistance in the face of unequal odds. The garrison – God's 'precious servants', 'a poor and praying people', 'religious honest men' – were fervent in 'piety and devotion, in prayers and singing of psalms'. The failure of Derby's assault, and the hasty and humiliating retreat of his troops, produced a euphoric outpouring of spiritual exaltation: 'Encouragement rested only in the breasts of a company of poor despised Christians, who with our town, our poor Manchester, engaged themselves against the great mighty ones of our county.'[11] A similar spirit galvanised the clothing towns of the West Riding of Yorkshire. In December 1642 the royalists approached Bradford. At the news the wealthy fled, leaving 'not a gentleman to command us', but 'some religious persons' resolved to defend the town. Word of the threatened attack spread among the puritan congregations of the area, at Bingley, Coley and Halifax, and detachments of the godly, armed with clubs and scythes moved into Bradford: 'many of us put our hands to the plough with much resolution'.[12] As at Manchester, the royalists were routed.

The godly townsmen of the West Riding became the backbone of the parliamentary cause in Yorkshire. They were the prime source of money, and of men, who were often led into battle by their ministers. At the capture of Leeds, the minister of Croston led a storming party, Bible in hand, singing the sixty-eighth psalm, 'Let God arise, let his enemies be scattered'.[13] Their zeal often outran that of their appointed leaders, forcing the latter to undertake a more vigorous prosecution of the war than was intended. In January 1643 Sir Thomas Fairfax wrote of the cloth towns as 'very impatient of our delays' and asked his father, the nominal commander of the regional forces, 'to give me the power to join with the readiness of the people'.[14] In late June 1643 Fairfax and the West Riding forces were defeated by Newcastle at Adwalton Moor; Fairfax fled to the garrison of Hull, and the victorious royalists mopped up the cloth towns. But the godly were not cowed. Many crossed the Pennines to regroup in Lancashire; new forces were raised, using the puritan congregations as the recruiting units: by autumn the towns were triumphantly recovered. Even in the midst of their enemies, the godly remained actively committed. In royalist Shrewsbury Francis

Burie and his wife sought to suborn and discourage the garrison soldiers – questioning whether they had 'a good cause or no'; vouching 'places of scripture to dissuade' their auditors.[15] The contrast between the very different worlds inhabited by Newcastle or Derby, with their conceptualisation of the war in terms of personal honour and traditional loyalties, and of the godly emerges starkly in an exchange between Robert Blake, governor of the beleaguered and isolated outpost of Taunton, and his royalist besiegers. Blake rejected their suave invitations to surrender with contempt: what was 'the honour and reputation of a gentleman' to him? His trust was in 'the goodness and power of an Almighty Saviour'.[16]

In the winter of 1644–45 parliament undertook a major reorganisation of its military machine. The New Model Army, consisting of twelve regiments of infantry, eleven of cavalry and one of dragoons, in all 22,000 men, and funded by taxation of more than £50,000 a month, was established. It replaced the three major parliamentary field armies, underfunded and battered, of the earl of Essex, Sir William Waller and the Eastern Association. Their poor record in the autumn of 1644, particularly the failure to destroy the king's forces at Newbury, was the obvious inspiration for the change. All the existing armies were top-heavy, their expensive cadre of officers intact but commanding skeleton forces. The New Model involved the selection of a new officer corps, and this choice was subject to the requirements of the Self-Denying Ordinance, passed at the same time. By that enactment, all army officers who were MPs, whether Lords or Commons, were displaced (except, significantly, Oliver Cromwell). The stated intention of these changes was to rationalise the war effort, previously hindered by the competition between the various parliamentary forces for resources and by the personal rivalries of their respective generals. But there was an important unstated subtext. Parliament suspected that the lack of success enjoyed by its forces stemmed as much from their commanders' reluctance to fight the war to a victorious conclusion as from the obvious logistical problems. Manchester, after Marston Moor, displayed 'a continuous backwardness to all action ... neglecting of opportunities and declining to take or pursue advantages upon the enemy'. Why? Cromwell believed that his superior's backwardness 'was not merely from dullness ... but from some principle of unwillingness ... to have this war prosecuted unto a full victory, and a design ... to have it ended by an accommodation, and that on some such terms to which it might be disadvantageous to bring the King too low'.[17] Similar suspicions were held of Essex. Accordingly, all generals from the traditional leadership caste, the lords, and many of their clients and nominees among the junior officers, were displaced. This represented an ideological revolution as much as a shift in military administration. At the outbreak of war, lords had taken military command by virtue of their status and the respect that they enjoyed in society. In the 1645 New Model Army officers were chosen for their professional skills, proven military competence and enthusiasm for the cause for which they fought.

January 1645 represented the culmination of an extended process whereby ineffective leaders – ineffective as defined by the win-the-war party in the Commons – were displaced both in the central and in local forces. With respect to the major parliamentary field army, the combination of the earl of Essex's ambitious pretensions and his reluctance to pursue an active strategy had already led to a substantial limitation of his authority in 1643 and 1644. The foundation of the Committee of Both Kingdoms had whittled his directive power, while resources had been diverted to other armies led by more committed generals, such as Manchester and Waller. The radicals were prepared to jettison these men, too, when their commitment seemed to waver.

In the localities, the creation of a machine designed to secure total victory had a number of dimensions. First, it entailed the displacement of commanders whose loyalty and energy was suspect. In the west midlands, the commander-in-chief, the earl of Denbigh, was an incompetent leader, and his associates were denounced as covert royalist sympathisers. A campaign by the godly Sir William Brereton, vigorously supported by the activists on the Warwickshire committee, secured his dismissal. In January 1644 Lord Willoughby of Parham, militarily unsuccessful and with his troops demoralised and undisciplined, was removed from the command in Lincolnshire that he had held since the summer of 1642. Lincolnshire was summarily incorporated into the Eastern Association, and its garrisons and troops given to officers appointed by the earl of Manchester. In a letter to Denbigh, Lord Willoughby drew a moral that picks up the radical dimensions of this policy: 'here we are all hasting to an early ruin. Nobility and gentry are going down apace ... I thought it a crime to be a nobleman.'[18]

There was also a shift in the quality and credentials of lower-level military officers. Some parliamentary leaders, like Lord Brooke, had from the first sought to give commands to men committed to the cause. But in many areas regiments were officered by scions of elite families, whose strategic concerns focused more on matters of the defence of the area from which their troops were levied than on the broader aims of the parliamentary war effort. In the spring of 1643, Sir John Palgrave daringly advanced his Norfolk regiment to Wisbech, but nothing could make him move deeper into the debatable lands of Holland and the soke of Peterborough. He put up a barrage of excuses – lack of provisions, the indiscipline of his men, the need to police local royalists. But his real motive was the fear that, if he moved forward, royalist forces might assail Norfolk. His blinkered pusillanimity and that of many of his fellow officers from the local gentry drove Cromwell to distraction in the spring and summer of 1643: 'Is this any way to save a kingdom? ... It's no longer disputing but out all you can.'[19] A few officers were employed for their previous military experience, but such men often displayed classic mercenary attitudes – like Colonel Mazeres, who loudly complained of the absence of the usual military recreations of dice, cards, drink and women when he was commissioned into the army of the Eastern Association. Mazeres did not last long in his new command: as the war progressed, committed leaders like Fairfax, Brereton and Cromwell adopted Brooke's policies, ousting both tepid localists and mercenaries. They were replaced with zealous activists. It is in this context, debating with the Suffolk local administrators on the qualifications of a yeoman, Ralph Margery, to captain a cavalry troop, that Oliver Cromwell enunciated the principle of promotion that was to dominate the choice of officers for the army of the Eastern Association, and then the New Model: 'I had rather have a plain russet-coated captain that knows what he fights for and loves what he knows, than that which you call a gentleman, and is nothing else.'[20] In the face of such an affirmation, Lord Willoughby's horrified sense that 'nobility and gentry are going down apace' is understandable.

Finally, the process of gearing up the parliamentary war effort in the localities entailed changes in the structure of the organisation of civil administration, and in the status of those who were employed as its agents. Each new piece of legislation raising money or conscripts, or the enforcement of other aspects of parliamentary policy, gave local men responsibility for its execution. These men, or those of them who chose to act, formed local committees, which increasingly monopolised authority in counties under the control of parliament. Initially those named were from the elite, the traditional rulers of the shires; and many of such men chose to serve less from enthusiasm for the cause than as a bulwark against the social breakdown that they feared. The history of the committees – though the speed and completeness of the process varied from county to county – is one of the displacement, either voluntarily or through purges, of the inefficient or uncommitted. Their places were taken by activists, men often drawn from outside the traditional governing class.

By 1645 Kent was being administered by a group of minor gentry, led by the county boss, Sir Anthony Weldon. The traditional rulers had either resigned because of their objections to Weldon's manipulation of government in his own interests or had been dismissed by parliament for challenging his authority. Weldon's followers were an amalgam of petty officials and time-servers leavened with a hard core of godly zealots, such as Sir William Springate, who reproved some of his colleagues for 'their carnal wisdom in managing of things, and told them it was the cause of God and they should trust God in it'.[21] In Hertfordshire the purge of traditional rulers was even more extreme. In 1643 the committee, dominated by moderate gentlemen, which had protested against parliament's ever-increasing tax demands, proved reluctant to seize the estates of their royalist relatives and friends and to disarm those who refused to affirm their loyalty to the parliamentary cause. In consequence in December they were summarily dismissed and parliament voted control of the county to a new committee, consisting not of 'the principal gentlemen of the county' but of 'persons of mean condition', religious radicals of 'anabaptistical and Independent opinions'.[22] Similar complaints echoed throughout the country. Traditionalists sneered at the 'men of inconsiderable fortunes ... of little or no estate, and strangers in our county', the 'tradesmen committees', upon whom local administration had devolved.[23] But while these men lacked social status and traditional prestige, they were willing executors of parliamentary policy.

The structure of command, both military and civil, among the parliamentarians moved away from traditional principles of authority. 'Natural rulers' with their conservative attitudes to military priorities and local taxation, and their preference for a negotiated settlement, were dismissed and replaced by activists. Those conservatives who had gravitated into the parliamentary camp in 1642 when parliament seized control of their localities were steadily levered from the positions of authority that they had undertaken reluctantly and exercised without conviction.

So parliament restructured its chain of command and administration in its efforts to win the war. It was much more difficult for the king to pursue a similar policy, given his claim as the defender of hierarchy and tradition. Early in 1643 Charles appointed six lieutenants general with local responsibilities. Five of these, men like Newcastle in the north east and Derby in Lancashire, were the greatest magnates in the areas committed to them. Their garrison and field commanders were drawn from the local gentry, as were the civilian administrators with whom they cooperated, the commissioners of array. Of the six, four were from the first disasters as military commanders. Sometimes this was a matter of character, as with Derby, whose weakness and irresolution paralysed all his actions, but it was more often because of their localist and traditionalist priorities. When one of Charles's professional commanders complained that the marquis of Worcester was not raising sufficient forces and supplies from his area, he received a lecture on *noblesse oblige*. His critic might be a better soldier than he was, the marquis remarked sniffily,

> but still to be a soldier of fortune, here today and God knows where tomorrow, and therefore needed not to care for the love of the people, but though I were killed myself I should leave my posterity behind me, towards whom I would not leave a grudge in the people.[24]

County commissioners were equally prone to give priority to local defence and the protection of local resources. After describing the flat refusal by the Shropshire commissioners to provide men and recruits for his forces, one of Rupert's subordinates wrote of these 'insulting people ... from which power good Lord deliver me'. Another, complaining of substandard infantry officered by 'ignorant Welch gentlemen', argued that as long as 'the cursed Commission of Array ... have any power, the king must expect no good out of north Wales'.[25] The local military commanders appointed by the magnates often showed little sense of fighting for a national cause. When the king sought to dismiss the hopeless Lord Capel, the officers of his forces, men of major gentry status in Cheshire and the Welsh border, threatened a strike. Capel was their paladin 'under whose banner we have made our choice to serve the king'.[26] When Charles commissioned Lord Hopton to lead the royalist forces in Somerset, Edmund Wyndham refused to serve under him, demanding an independent command, and threatened that otherwise his forces would disband: 'I cannot ... place the affection of all my friends where he [the king] will dispose of them.'[27]

In consequence many of the professional soldiers in Charles's camp, particularly Rupert, sought to follow the direction of parliamentary policy, displacing local magnates and their gentry associates with men of proven commitment and professionals. Attempts to do this were resented, as in the case of Lord Capel. Royalist gentlemen bitterly complained of policies that would make them 'slaves to the Generalissimo', that promoted 'sharks and children of fortune' to high command.[28] But a major problem was that such policies were not consistently pursued: Charles found it impossible consistently to affirm a policy that would undercut the keystone of his propaganda – his defence of the social order against subversion. In consequence, the king got the worst of both worlds. There was no consistent policy, and factional struggles developed in his court at Oxford between those, like Rupert and Digby, who insisted that military efficiency must be the priority, and those, like Hyde, who claimed that the king must cooperate with the traditional rulers of the shires.

The king's muddled attitudes to the structure of command were duplicated with respect to the mobilisation of local resources for the war effort. Charles certainly did not secure as much from the localities as his opponents. In part, this was a product of the fact that the king never enjoyed the total command of an intrinsically wealthy area, insulated from the war. Parliament's control of London and East Anglia was scarcely disturbed. The royalist heartlands of 1642, Wales and the north, were poorer, and royalist commanders and administrators found their control challenged by hostile bastions – Plymouth, Lyme, Gloucester, Manchester – whose garrisons dislocated local efforts to raise supplies. But the conservative attitudes that typified royal administration were equally counter-productive.

Early in the war both sides relied on volunteers to man their armies, and voluntary contributions, supplemented by loans, to fund their operations. This quickly proved inadequate, and from the spring of 1643 parliament moved to a system of compulsion. Men were impressed to recruit the army. Taxes were levied to support the war effort. These took several forms – the assessment on profits and property; the excise, a tax on consumption; and sequestration, the seizure of the personal property and the revenues of the regime's opponents – and were of unprecedented magnitude. In 1639 the inhabitants of Suffolk had resisted the collection of the ship money demand for £8000, arguing that so exorbitant a sum would ruin them; in 1644 the assessment alone was designed to raise £90,000. In late 1643 (when the assessment was 'only' £5000 a month) the Suffolk committee argued that 45 per cent of every man's income was being siphoned by taxation. Impressment and the regressive excise duty were massively unpopular at the village level. Those enforcing them were regularly the targets of abuse and threats, lawsuits, assault and riot. The constables of Upwell were rash or desperate enough to impress the son of a notorious local witch; they paid for their temerity in dead stock and blasted crops.

The county committees were the local executors of these policies. They were empowered by parliament's legislative authority and had local forces at their disposal to compel obedience. They were often uncomfortable with the role thrust upon them. They worried about the effects of high taxation and impressment on the local economy: in February 1645 the Kent committee argued that the quota of men they were required to raise for the New Model would oblige them 'to press from the plough's handle' and seriously dislocate agricultural production already 'much behindhand ... by reason of the long and tedious frost'.[29] County committees might also try to ensure that they had the first claim on the men and money that they raised. This was the burden of Cromwell's complaints in the summer and autumn of 1643. Money was being diverted to build local fortifications; troops were wasted in holding defensive positions that were irrelevant to anything save the imagined security of the county that raised them. But, as has been shown, the local committees were steadily being educated into a new sense of their national responsibilities, to understand that they were primarily the agents of parliament not the spokesmen of local communities, and remodelled when they failed to learn this lesson.

This is very apparent in the most contentious aspect of resource mobilisation from the perspective of the local governors – the sequestration of the estates of royalists. From June 1643 the goods of those who had settled in the king's quarters were to be seized and employed for the maintenance of the parliamentary cause; their lands were to be leased out and the rents used for the same purpose. Many of the moderate gentry serving on the committees were appalled. This was a flagrant attack on property; it was a policy, as one of the Norfolk committee complained, that would oblige him to act against men 'to whom I have the nearest relations of blood and obligation of friendship ... I could as easily perish ... as perform this office against those to whom I have so great obligations'.[30] Yet, despite the chorus of complaint, the sequestration legislation was executed, often, as in Hertfordshire, after major purges of those who refused to act. In some counties the task was devolved upon a subcommittee; this took the burden from the consciences of the moderates, but it also empowered men from outside the magic circle of traditional authority. 'Indigent and mean persons' were employed in Norfolk; 'persons of low and mean condition' in Cambridgeshire, after 'the gentlemen would not or durst not act'.[31]

In the areas under control of parliament effective machines of local administration were steadily constructed. This development entailed attacks on previously sacrosanct values, the inculcation of novel attitudes towards administration, and an influx of new men into local administration.

What about the royalists? It proved much more difficult for the king to erect an effective machinery to extract men, material and money from the localities. Charles introduced impressment and taxation – a land tax, an excise duty and sequestration – that mirrored the parliamentary schemes. But in each of these cases the king *followed* parliament's innovation. And it proved difficult for the king, as the upholder of traditional forms of government, to justify such experiments and novelties. Charles was particularly slow to provide a formal sanction for the practice of sequestration, and the language in which he did so was awkward and apologetic. He subsequently intervened in local cases in the interests of humanity – suggesting that the sequestration of half an estate's revenue would suffice; seeking to persuade local administrators to allow old tenants to continue to hold lands at substantially undervalued rents. The king simply could not be seen aggressively assailing rights of property. In terms of assessment and impressment, Charles sought to establish mechanisms that would give the localities a voice in the scale of the levies and their local distribution. The commission of array in royalist counties were instructed to consult with the justices of the peace in quarter sessions or with local grand juries, conceived of as the representative body of the county, and to negotiate targets with them.

The king looked at the problem of local administration through the lenses of his traditionalist, conservative ideology. In consequence, local attempts to divert resources to local ends, typical of the early history of parliamentarian local administration, or even the simpler reluctance to pay, were given a strong justification. In the winter of 1644–45, as parliament was restructuring its military machinery, Charles was negotiating with the gentry commissioners of array and yeomen grand jurors in the local communities under his control to raise a new force – the 'One and All' or 'Association' project. They promised a huge force, committed to bringing parliament to negotiate a peace treaty with the king. But the promised manpower came at a price. 'As near as the necessity of the times can admit, our ancient laws shall be observed in force and reputation.'[32] In detail, this entailed the command of the new forces by local officers, the siphoning of money from existing royalist forces for their support, and a greater measure of control over all forces in their localities vested in the county administrators. This was deeply suspect to the military clique surrounding Rupert. Prince Maurice warned his brother that the scheme was a ploy designed by 'cunning men' to secure 'the destruction of military power and discipline'. Another of Rupert's aides was more direct: the locals intended 'to thrust out the soldier'. A garrison commander directly contrasted parliament's vigour and readiness to ride roughshod over the traditional conventions of local government with the 'One and All' policies that 'tie his Majesty to make his provision of war only by the rules of peaceable government'.[33]

These different agendas, and the hostility that festered in consequence, characterised royalist local administration throughout the war. Again and again professional soldiers, intimates of Rupert, complained that they were 'made useless by insulting people who tell us of their power' and damned 'that cursed commission of array'.[34]

Charles, his policies deeply sensitive to local concerns and traditional values, never developed as efficient a system for mobilising resources as his parliamentarian opponents. But as the war turned against the royalists, the military group's argument, that the king could not afford the luxury of consensual practices and a humane attitude to the estates and persons of his enemies, became more insistent. The provinces would have to be terrorised and squeezed into providing the materials without with which the war simply could not be continued. Nothing, the king's council in the west declared in April 1645, could be expected from the 'flatness, peremptoriness and unactivity of the gentlemen of Somerset'; the county must be 'driven and compelled to do what was necessary'.[35] The same theme was echoed in royalist Wales. In May Prince Maurice learned that the fortifications that he had ordered at Beaumaris Castle had not been completed; he inquired why this was of Lord Bulkeley, the resident magnate, who replied that the local gentry had been slow to contribute money to the project, and that he was unwilling to coerce his friends and neighbours. Maurice was incandescent: he sent one of his professional officers as an emissary to complete the fortifications, with orders to hang anybody who obstructed the project.

Such policies, so different from Charles's stated positions on local cooperation, brought their own backlash: the rising of the Clubmen. In February 1645 a royalist force commanded by George Goring was living off the land in Dorset and Wiltshire. His men were predatory and ill disciplined, perpetrating 'horrid outrages and barbarities'. A foraging party raided Godmanstone, clashed with the enraged villagers, and lost a couple of men. When Goring threatened retribution, he was confronted with a massive rising of armed peasants and townsmen, which steadily spread through the south west and into the west midlands and southern Wales. The Clubman movements were a visceral protest against the plunder and rapine undertaken by unsupplied royalist garrisons and commanders. But they had a broader agenda and a more systematic ideology. They hoped to bring the belligerents to a mediated settlement – the Clubmen of western Somerset and Devon called themselves 'the peace making army'. And their justification for organising, and for challenging the soldiery, was an appeal to Charles's own stated ideals, enshrined in his propaganda, the values for which he was ostensibly fighting. The Wiltshire Clubmen complained that 'our ancient laws and liberties, contrary to the great Charter of England and the Petition of Right, are altogether swallowed up in the arbitrary power of the sword'. In Worcestershire, in a statement issued from the mechanisms of local government employed by Charles – the commissioners of array and the grand jury – a local mobilisation was agreed 'to preserve and uphold ... the known laws of the kingdom against all arbitrary government'.[36]

Parliament enjoyed significant advantages over the king in the fighting of the war. Its hold over London and the wealthy eastern part of England was largely uncontested. Royalist regions were poorer, and Charles's control was weakened by the presence of parliamentary garrisons whose raids interrupted the smooth administration of the neighbouring localities. Blockades or sieges tied up royalist resources, and were often rendered abortive by parliament's control of the seas. The advent of the Scots army restricted the freedom of action of the royal forces raised in northern England, even before their destruction at Marston Moor. Charles's Irish reinforcements made no such contribution to his cause. But crucially, in relation to the command structure of his forces and the mobilisation of resources, the king was hampered by his stated policies of upholding the traditional order against social subversion. His hands were tied by his own ideological commitments – and by the fact that his supporters were prepared to fight for him because of their concerns for those values. Parliament, its armies increasingly officered and its administration staffed by committed zealots, was under no such compunctions. Reflecting on Charles's defeat in the First Civil War, Hyde wrote

> They who inclined to the parliament left nothing unperformed that might advance the cause and were incredibly vigilant and industrious to cross and hinder whatsoever might promote the king's; whereas they who wished well to him thought they had performed their duty in doing so and they had done enough for him in that they had done nothing against him.[37]

This was an embittered view, self-serving and heavily dependent upon hindsight, but other royalists, writing at the time of the war, agreed with the basic contention. The king had lost because there was no clear structure of command in the localities; because the gentry would not 'endure' ceding local control to outsiders; because 'laziness ... and indifference to the cause' too often typified the behaviour of Charles's supporters.[38] There is much overstatement in these accounts, of course. Some of the king's supporters saw the need for a more vigorous prosecution of the war – local gentlemen 'turned feral' in Professor Hutton's nice phrase. Some royalist units, like Newcastle's crack Whitecoat regiment or the Cornish foot, who believed 'no men their equals', developed a powerful esprit de corps.[39] But, as an answer to the main question, the contrast between 'incredibly vigilant and industrious' parliamentarians and the 'laziness ... and indifference' of the Royalists, contains a significant insight.

Why Was the King Executed?

On 30 January 1649 Charles I stepped through a window of the Banqueting House, that icon of Stuart monarchical pretension, onto the scaffold. Before the axe fell, Charles addressed the knot of men who surrounded him. His speech, inaudible to the vast crowd behind the ring of cavalry but taken by the short-hand writers and published, was a model of Christian charity and forbearance. He forgave those responsible for his death, and prayed that their rule might secure 'the peace of the kingdom'. He acknowledged the providential justice in his fate; his craven betrayal of Strafford in 1641 was now punished by an equally 'unjust sentence' against himself. But he insisted on his innocence of the specific charges against him. He was no 'tyrant, traitor, murderer and implacable enemy' to the people of England. Rather he was condemned for his refusal to abandon those laws by which Englishmen's lives and their property 'may be most their own'. He sacrificed himself to uphold the laws, and was thus 'the martyr of the people'.[1]

This was a self-presentation that Charles had outlined and had sought, unavailingly, to develop in the course of his trial from 20 to 24 January. His refusal to acknowledge the legitimacy of the court, or to answer the charges against him until its authority was justified, ensured that the king was silenced and convicted without having the opportunity to plead. The court could not admit such a fundamental challenge; in response, Charles insisted, as on the scaffold, 'I do stand ... for the liberty of my people'.[2]

Charles arguments were masterly, designed to cause maximum embarrassment to his judges and those who controlled the state. To bring the king to trial the army had been forced to purge parliament, and a 'Rump' of MPs had passed the enabling legislation, simply side-stepping the constitutional role of the Upper House when the Lords refused to approve their Act. That document named one hundred and thirty-five commissioners to act as judges: only eighty of them ever sat, and twenty-one of these failed to sign the death warrant. There was some outright principled refusal, some convenient tactical illness, more silent defection. Many of those who sat and even signed were frightened, muddled and insecure; some later claimed their participation was designed to secure Charles's release. The king's performance clearly impressed many of his judges, and they were reluctant to condemn him without allowing a full hearing.

But they were not the majority, and they lacked both a common policy and political backbone. The court also contained a hard core of men determined to go through with the trial. Men relentlessly determined to secure the desired outcome against a king who had placed his 'personal interest' and ambition above 'the public interest, common right, liberty, justice and peace of the people of this nation', and who was responsible for 'all the treasons, murders, rapines, burnings, spoils, desolations, damages and mischiefs to this nation, acted and committed in the ... Wars, or occasioned thereby'.[3]

The process by which this party committed to the king's trial and execution was formed began on 5 May 1646, when Charles, who had fled in disguise from his beleaguered capital at Oxford, having instructed his remaining garrison commanders to surrender on the best possible terms, presented himself to the commanders of the Scots army besieging Newark. To understand what happened between the king's surrender and his execution, it is necessary to analyse the motives and actions of the key individuals, institutions and groups. As a prelude, it is useful to sketch in the key incidents of the extraordinarily complex narrative history of these months, not least to identify the leading actors.

For nine months from May 1646 Charles was held by the Scots, who had fallen back to Newcastle with their dangerous prisoner. They sought to broker a treaty between themselves, their allies in the English parliament – the Presbyterian party – and the king. Its key terms were that Charles should agree to the abolition of episcopacy and the establishment of a restructuring of the church in accordance with the Covenant, which he was obliged to take. Parliament was to control the militia for twenty years, and have the nomination of all the major offices of state in perpetuity. The king's supporters were treated savagely. Many were

The Explanation of the EMBLEME.

Ponderibus *genus omne mali, probrisq; gravatus*,
(*Vixq; ferenda ferens. Palma ut Depressa, resurgo.*)

Though clogg'd with weights of miseries
Palm-like Depress'd, I higher rise .

Ac, velut undarum Fluctus Ventiq; furorem
Irati Populi Rupes immota repello .
Clarior è tenebris, cœlestis stella, corusco.
(*Victor et æternùm-felici pace triumpho.*)

And as th'unmoved Rock out-brave's
The boistrous Windes and raging waves :
So triumph I. And shine more bright
In sad Affliction's Darksom night .

Auro Fulgentem rutilo gemmisq; micantem ,
At curis Gravidam spernendo calco Coronam.

That Splendid, but yet toilsom Crown
Regardlessly I trample down .

Spinosam, at ferri facilem, quo Spes mea, Christi
Auxilio, Nobis non est tractare molestum .

With joie I take this Crown of thorn ,
Though sharp, yet easie to be born .

Æternam, fixis fidei, semperq;-beatam
In Cœlos oculis Specto, Nobisq; paratam.

That heav'nlie Crown, already mine ,
I View with eies of Faith divine .

Quod Vanum est, sperno; quod Christi Gratia præbet
Amplecti studium est: Virtutis Gloria merces .

I slight vain things ; and do embrace
Glorie, the just reward of Grace .

G.D.

Τὸ Χρῐ οὐδὲν ἠδίκησε τὴν πόλιν, ἀδ' ὃ Καῖσσα .

Title page of *Eikon Basilike.* This work, first published a few days after the
execution, had gone into forty editions in English by the end of 1649.
Ghost written by John Gauden, a clergymen, from notes provided by Charles,
the work emphasised the king's faith, piety, patience and resignation. It
created a powerful image of Charles as a Christlike figure (note the crown
of thorns), a martyr sacrificed for his church and his people.

absolutely proscribed, their estates confiscated and themselves denied any prospect of pardon; most were excluded from any public office and obliged to pay heavy fines. The Scots finally tired of the king's stonewalling responses to the proposals and his attempts to broaden the fissures among his captors, and, in return for a substantial sum to meet the expenses of their involvement in the war, marched from England in February 1647. They handed the king over to commissioners from Westminster, who moved him to Holdenby House in Northamptonshire, where negotiations on the offer made at Newcastle continued to make little progress.

In June 1647 Charles was removed from Holdenby by a party of cavalry under Cornet Joyce, and taken to Cambridgeshire, where the headquarters of the New Model Army, which had refused to disband according to the orders of its parliamentary paymasters, was located. He remained effectively in army custody until his execution. In the next month the army leaders, with a group of their sympathisers from the Lords and Commons, offered the king an alternative settlement to the Newcastle Propositions, the Heads of the Proposals, and discussion of these continued until the end of the year. The Heads displayed some sympathy to Charles's critique of the Newcastle Propositions; the king was not obliged to preside over the destruction of his friends, nor to abandon his religious preferences. Episcopal government and the rituals of the church were not proscribed in the Heads, though the established church lost coercive power to compel attendance or to police dissent. In the course of this period of negotiation the army leaders had to suppress attacks on their dominance of the political scene and the details of their scheme for peace from two divergent directions. In August they occupied London after an attempted coup by some of the Presbyterian party and their allies – city oligarchs, clergy, apprentices, and disbanded soldiers – in the capital. In November they crushed a mutiny in the ranks of the New Model Army, engineered by the Levellers, who had sought to organise the soldiery in support of a more radical political settlement.

While Charles was discussing the Heads of the Proposals with the army leaders and their parliamentary allies, he was also once again haggling with the Scottish commissioners. In December these negotiations bore fruit: the Engagement was signed committing the Scots to deploying forces to secure the king's authority. The promised army did not materialise until July, by which time a series of uncoordinated risings on the king's behalf in England, involving an unstable amalgam of disaffected military units, old cavaliers, and countrymen antagonised by high taxes and puritan repression, had been crushed or contained. Cromwell smashed the Scottish army in a running battle that began on Preston Moor on 17 August and ended with the surrender of its general, the duke of Hamilton, and his remaining cavalry on the 25th at Stafford.

The majority in parliament, despite the king's obvious complicity in the Second Civil War, again sought to negotiate. Discussions of parliament's terms, a modified version of the Newcastle propositions, began at Newport on the Isle of Wight in mid-September, but the New Model's patience with the king was now exhausted. On the 2 December the army entered London. On the 6th, Colonel Pride and a detachment policed the doorway of the Parliament House: forty-five MPs were arrested, others were forcibly kept from entering the House. Most of the remaining MPs, angry and frightened by the military coup, simply refused to take their seats. A 'Rump' of about seventy MPs cooperated with the army in orchestrating the subsequent trial and execution of the king.

This narrative, the distillation of a complex story, suggests the need to focus upon four key participants: Charles himself; the Scots; the Presbyterian party in parliament; and the army.

Charles's motives are the easiest to delineate. Despite the defeat of his forces and his personal surrender into the hands of his enemies, the king believed that he was far from helpless. His advisers – not least the queen – could see that that the disunity among the victors gave Charles every opportunity to negotiate the best possible settlement. But Charles aimed higher than this. He hoped, if he delayed and procrastinated during negotiations, and haggled with one group and then another, that the tensions and fissures between the various elements of the coalition against him might result in renewed hostilities, to the extent of providing him with the opportunity to revive his cause on the battlefield. It was a policy he outlined before his flight to the Scots. In March 1646 he contemplated escape from Oxford to London, hoping 'that I will be able to draw either the Presbyterians or the Independents to side with me for extirpating one the other, that I shall really be king again'.[4] The flight to the Scots itself was undertaken because he believed that they might back his restoration with military force. The Scots disappointed him on this occasion, but in much of his assessment he was right. From the summer of 1646, when the official proposals for a settlement were first presented to him at Newcastle by the Scots, through the winter of 1647–48, Charles received a series of offers – from the majority in parliament; from the army and its coterie of radical MPs; and from the Scots again – each proffering more favourable terms for the framing of a constitutional and religious settlement. The auction concluded with the Engagement agreed between the King and the Scots at the end of 1647. Charles would have immediate control of the militia; his power of veto over legislation would be retained; and the only concession that he made was to allow a three-year experiment with the Presbyterian church, pending further discussion on the ultimate form of an ecclesiastical settlement. Such an offer could only be realised by military intervention: this followed in the summer of 1648, and went down to bloody defeat at Preston. Charles's attitude in 1647, and his confidence in the strength of his position, is nicely caught in a remark he made to the army commanders during negotiations on the Heads of the Proposals. 'You cannot be without me,' he told them, 'you will fall in ruin if I do not sustain you.'[5]

Even after the defeat of the Scots at Preston in mid-August 1648, and the mopping up of the series of local insurrections that were the Second Civil War, parliament, though keenly aware of the king's complicity in the Scots invasion, could do nothing more imaginative than offer Charles virtually the same terms as the basis of a future settlement that had been offered at Newcastle eighteen months before. Early in the discussions at Newport Charles assumed, understandably, that his prospects were bleak: he was helpless in the face of non-negotiable demands. Parliament intended to 'to make me no King ... at best a Perpetual Prisoner'; his 'too great' concessions were solely designed to lull his captors prior to an escape attempt.[6] But, to his surprise, the negotiators proved malleable. They were desperate to secure some agreement with him, recognising that the alternative was total breakdown of the political system. One of the negotiators at Newport wrote to a colleague in the Commons: 'We shall use our utmost endeavours here to bring the king nearer the Houses, and you will do good service at London in persuading the Houses to come nearer the king ...

No man knows what will become of religion and the parliament if we have not peace.'[7] Charles, discovering that he still had room for manoeuvre, swiftly reverted to his old behaviour. He spun out the negotiations – twice the deadline for agreement was extended by parliament. A further measure of their desperation was their vote to accede to the king's request to return to London as soon as the treaty was completed. Charles was not just time wasting; his answers were designed to enhance the divisions within parliament and to create a confusion from which he might benefit.

By 1646 the Scots had become profoundly frustrated by their treatment by their English 'brethren'. The Scots had had a bad war. Their army had never enjoyed the military success that they and their allies at Westminster had anticipated when they crossed the border late in 1643. In 1645 and 1646 the Scots engaged in a series of minor skirmishes and sieges while the New Model pursued its triumphant course. Their contribution to the campaign was weakened by the need to detach units to halt the remarkable progress of Montrose and his Highlanders, whose victories further damaged their morale and reputation. The Scots believed that their contribution to the war effort was consistently underestimated, and this was used to justify the English failure to fund or supply them properly. Worse, the press and parliament then spent much time rooting into what seemed, from a Scottish perspective, minor and indeed understandable peccadilloes by the unprovided Scottish army – a little pillage; some commandeering of supplies. All of this was designed to weaken the credibility of the Scots, and undermine their role in English politics. Godly activists who had initially welcomed the advent of the Scots increasingly viewed their allies as locusts, devouring the fat of England.

In parliament, the English sought to water down the terms of the Solemn League and Covenant, on which crusading principle the Scots had committed themselves to the war. Nobody, it seemed, chose to view the extreme clericist and theocratic Presbyterian ecclesiology favoured by the Scots as being a necessary consequence of an unprejudiced reading of scripture. The Independent party, MPs who objected to any kind of intolerant national church or who resented Scots meddling in English affairs, were powerful in both Houses. Even those MPs who shared

the Scottish predilection for religious persecution did so only if the
power of the clergy in the church was severely circumscribed. They preferred 'to have but a lame Erastian presbytery', as one of the Scottish
clergy wrote bitterly.[8] Parliament was the fountain of ecclesiastical
authority and the final court of appeal; religious offences were to be
judged by lay commissioners. In addition to defying Scottish pressure
for religious uniformity between the two nations, parliament also
increasingly froze out the Scots from discussion of the progress of the
war, and – more significantly – of peace proposals. In April 1646
the Scots sense of isolation was expressed in the publication of papers
assailing the slow progress of the desired settlement with the king. The
Commons, in reply, contemptuously ordered the work burned by
the common hangman.

By mid-1646 the directors of policy in Scotland, the clerics of the
General Assembly and a number of godly laymen headed by the marquis
of Argyle and his fellow-Campbell, the earl of Loudoun, were wholly
disillusioned by and distrustful of the English parliament and the New
Model Army. It was a belief that such distrust could be transmuted into
military assistance that led the king to surrender to the Scots. Fortu-
nately for the English, the Scottish leaders were equally suspicious of the
king. And Charles's behaviour when in their hands – his intransigence
in relation to the central plank of their policy, the establishment of a
Presbyterian church in England, and the insincerity with which he conducted negotiations – enhanced their mistrust. In January 1647 Argyle
and his allies, tiring of a fruitless negotiation and in return for a substantial tranche of the money owed them, agreed to turn Charles over
to parliament. The decision made sense. It gave them cash in hand and
an opportunity to reorganise their internal affairs without the presence
of a dangerous and duplicitous player. It avoided the hostility that Scottish retention of the king would have occasioned in England. The
London citizen, Thomas Juxon, who had reported accounts of Scottish
pillage in his diary and cynically remarked their reluctance to abandon
England to return to 'oatmeal and water', praised the 'sweet concur-
rence' they displayed in January 1647.[9] But the decision provoked a great
wave of revulsion in Scotland against the Judases in their government
who had sold their king.

Anti-English feeling, fed by insults and marginalisation in 1645 and

1646 and by the sense of the betrayal of the king in February 1647, was enhanced by the increased role claimed by the hated New Model Army in the settlement of the kingdom in the following months. The Scots believed that their king should not be abandoned in the maelstrom of competing parties in England. The growing sentiment favouring a further intervention in English affairs was deployed by a party in Scotland, headed by the king's cousin, the duke of Hamilton, to elbow aside Argyle and the kirk party. It was this group who negotiated the December 1647 Engagement and committed the Scots to another military expedition into England. But while Hamilton could displace Argyle and his clerical allies, and dominate the Scottish parliament and council, he could not deliver a united Scottish nation. The concerns of those who opposed his policy were both pragmatic – that Charles was totally untrustworthy – and principled: Scotland could not go to war on behalf of a king whose antipathy for Presbyterianism was so evident, and who had resisted every importunity to take the Covenant. Opposition fomented by the clergy obliged Hamilton to remodel the officer corps of the Scots army, and ultimately to employ force against those who refused to serve in or pay for the new invasion. This explains the fatal delay in the mobilisation of the Scottish army until after the New Model had suppressed the risings in Wales and England.

The 'Presbyterian' party is an awkward title, but one warranted by contemporary usage. From a Scottish perspective the Presbyterians were no such thing. Basically, they were conservatives wedded to a moderate constitutional settlement, a national church with authority to crush the more extreme forms of religious sectarianism, and a traditionalist social policy. In parliament, they developed an increasingly tight party discipline. But they also instituted an organisation outside Westminster, focused on a knot of clergy in London with ties into the localities. Using this network, information was collected – on the nefarious doings of religious zealots; on the depredations of the New Model Army – and petitions dispersed for the collection of signatures, to be forwarded to the centre.

In 1644 and 1645 the radical win-the-war group were in the ascendant in parliament. It was they who kicked out local administrators and military commanders who were insufficiently zealous in their com-

mitment to the furtherance of the war effort, replacing them with
'persons of mean condition'. Lord Willoughby of Parham's dire pre-
diction in January 1644 that 'Nobility and gentry are going down
apace ... I thought it a crime to be a nobleman', seemed proved when
a year later the Houses passed the Self-Denying Ordinance that oblit-
erated the traditional role of the nobility as military leaders. When the
House of Lords contemplated stonewalling the passage of that legislation, they were bluntly told that, if they continued to oppose what was
for 'the apparent good of the kingdom', the Commons would go ahead
without them. A similar threat of unicameral legislation had been made
in 1644 when the Upper House opposed the establishment of the Committee of Both Kingdoms. But by 1646 the balance of forces at
Westminster had shifted; the radicals who had dominated proceedings
in 1644–45 now found themselves in the minority, outvoted in both
Houses by moderates of the Presbyterian party, led by Denzil Holles.
How had this come about?

   The army believed that a minority faction had gained control of the
Commons by their single-minded employment of improper influence
and procedural tricks. The cabal's leaders met secretly to plan strategy
in advance of the sessions. They called for crucial votes when the House
was thin; Walter Long acted as their whip: 'He hath used much tam-
pering and violence to such of his party as would go out of the House,
and hath persuaded them to stay there for their votes.'[10] They had
sought to rig the elections for new MPs. Party organisation was certainly on the increase in parliament, but it was equally typical of all
groups, and it cannot explain the growing dominance of the
conservatives. In July 1646 the Presbyterian leadership was severely
weakened. The eleven MPs the army found most obnoxious as faction
leaders were pressured into removing themselves from the House.
Other committed Presbyterians were compromised by their involvement with the violent interruption of parliament by disbanded soldiers
and London apprentices in late July 1647 and thereafter kept a low
profile. Yet, despite the loss of their leaders, the conservatives remained
strong in parliament: in September draconian legislation against heresy
and blasphemy was discussed. After the outbreak of the Second Civil
War, they once again became the dominant group at Westminster
and returned to action: the Heresy Ordinance was passed, and the Pres-

byterian leaders ousted and exiled in the previous summer again took their seats.

The sea change in the political complexion of Parliament has two major explanations, though both were products of a common sentiment from 1646. First, many MPs who had supported efforts to win the war became increasingly aware of the costs of that policy once the war was won. Men who had recognised the need to take any action to secure victory, and the opportunity to negotiate from strength, were troubled by the continuation of the wartime excesses after the king's surrender. Parliament had moved far from the grounds on which it had justified the resort to arms in 1642. The principles of the Ancient Constitution and concepts of due legal process, the traditional forms and the personnel of administration, had all been abandoned or changed beyond recognition in the single-minded pursuit of victory. Claims of necessity were no longer compelling from the summer of 1646, and MPs sought a swift return to pre-war normality, to the traditional culture, forms and personnel of government.

So the MPs who had resisted the win-the-war policies, who had opposed the Committee of Both Kingdoms or the Self-Denying Ordinance, and who had backed the delusory schemes for peace in the early months of 1643 and 1645, were joined in 1646 by many of their opponents in those debates. They were also reinforced by newly-elected MPs. In September 1645 the Commons began to issue writs for elections to replace those MPs who had died or been expelled, and by 1648 more than half of the MPs were newcomers. The army claimed that the factional leaders of the Presbyterians had rigged the Cornish elections; their opponents replied that the agents and friends of the soldiers had fixed those in Devon. In the elections for the smaller borough seats traditional clientage and patronage won the day. But in most of the larger, open constituencies men who symbolised or voiced the demand for a return to normality were returned by a war-weary electorate. In Warwickshire the local committee, who had the sheriff in their pocket, imprisoned their most active opponents and mobilised their troops to intimidate the voters. But their efforts were in vain: their candidate, 'no gentleman by birth, a man of mean fortune',[11] was defeated by men running on an anti-military, anti-committee ticket.

The Presbyterian majority in parliament reflected and tapped a strong conservative sentiment in the country at large, which was suspicious and resentful of developments associated with the war years. That sentiment was rooted, first, in the sense that the traditional culture, structures and personnel of government had been sacrificed to the demands of the war-machine. Such concerns are most apparent in the debates from 1645 on over the government of the localities by committees – the structure on which parliament's successful mobilisation of resources had been based. From November 1645 a London newspaper, the *Scottish Dove*, allied to the parliamentary and City Presbyterians, waged a vigorous campaign against the county committees, providing details of peculation and malversation, of injustice and cruelty: 'Committeemen would be as Kings, or rather tyrants.'[12] The project was taken up by moderates in the House of Lords, and culminated in a solemn denunciation in April 1647. Committees, the Lords emphasised, had brought 'great odium' on parliament; they asked the Commons to consider 'How far it may alien-ate the hearts of the generality of the kingdom from them, if such an arbitrary power shall be still continued; from which the hope of being delivered hath been one of the chiefest motives for the engaging of their lives and fortunes in this dangerous and expensive war'.[13]

The kinds of issues that concerned the Lords emerged in a particu-larly venomous conflict in Lincolnshire. In the autumn of 1646, Colonel Edward King – no crypto-royalist but a man who had commanded a parliamentary detachment during the war – publicly challenged the committee concerning its enforcement of central edicts. King claimed that the committee showed no sympathy for the difficulties faced by tax-payers: areas that were still subject to royalist raids or where parliamentary troops were subsisting on free quarter were obliged to pay the full sums assessed upon them. In their zeal to extract the last penny, the committee neglected the terms of the enacting legislation concern-ing assessment and appeal, and denied any semblance of due process. Those who challenged unfair assessment or sought to explain delays in full payment could expect nothing but 'the Justice of only "Take him, Provost-marshal"' and arbitrary imprisonment.[14] Worse, the committee took upon itself the determination of civil disputes concerning property or contract that were delaying the payment of taxes, and reversed deci-sions on such matters decided in the proper courts. The committee, 'our Egyptian taskmasters', had breached all the traditional safeguards of the liberty of Englishmen; they had spurned Magna Carta and the Petition of Right. King's denunciation, made first in the traditional public forum of an address to the grand jury at quarter sessions and repeated in pamphlets, focused the smouldering resentment in the county against an alien institution. The Lincolnshire taxpayers went on strike.

King was not content to excoriate the Lincolnshire committee's fiscal mismanagement and legal innovations; he also labelled them as patrons of religious extremists. Such concerns were another aspect of the conservative agenda by 1646. Paradoxically, while the localities had been subjected to vastly increased interference in relation to the finance and supply of the soldiery, the machinery of church government had fallen into desuetude. After 1642 Laudian clerics had been prosecuted and ousted from their livings, and the agencies of Laudian government dismantled, but no alternative system had been instituted. The consequence was a wave of religious experimentation, which blossomed into a cocktail of anarchic and subversive incidents.

At Whatfield in Suffolk the newly-founded Baptist church, headed by a shoemaker and a tailor, was riven by scandal. A young woman, Ann Wells, joined the church. Her ecstatic pronouncements, speaking in tongues, and self-proclaimed knowledge of Hebrew led to her recognition as a prophetess by the ministers. Her revelations became increasingly bizarre. One of these led to her marriage to one of the ministers. In a second revelation, Ann declared that she was a type of the church of the Jews, her new husband a type of the church of the gentiles, and the other minister a type of Israel. This, by some arcane theology, led to the establishment of a *ménage à trois*, with prophecies of the birth of a child after three months' gestation who would speak in tongues and prophesy. The three extracted large sums of money from their disciples. Some went to clothe Ann's brother in an extravagant suit because he was revealed as one appointed to pour out a vial of wrath, in accordance with the Book of Revelations. Some funded a trip to Holland, on the grounds that the threesome were ordered (by revelation) to go there to convert the Jews.[15] This kind of story was lavishly reported and embellished in the Presbyterian press, most famously in the great encyclopaedia of such horror-stories compiled by Thomas Edwards, *Gangraena*. The swift return to pre-war patterns that was at the heart of the policies of the Presbyterians incorporated a restructured national church, with power, crucially, to police outlandish and subversive belief and behaviour.

Both planks of the agenda of the parliamentary Presbyterian party – the abolition of the wartime administrative structures and the prosecution religious deviance – also incorporated a social concern. Conservatives objected to local government falling into the hands of obscure individuals, 'the blue-new-made-gentlemen mounted',[16] who were seduced by their novel status and by the opportunities for peculation and logrolling it provided. Equally, they objected to the religious radicals because of the social subversion that inhered in their doctrines. Edwards spun his stories of the depravity of the sectaries to emphasise their rejection of hierarchy and gender roles; of taxation, of tithe, of rents – 'the Saints are a free people and should do what they did voluntarily'.[17]

The Presbyterians, then, sought a swift return to the traditional structures of government and society. They favoured a monarchical settlement, and so negotiated with Charles even in the face of his duplicity that had triggered the renewal of war. They wanted to prosecute religious deviants through a redrawn, intolerant national church. They hoped to run down the alien systems of massive taxation and local government that had proliferated during the war, reverting to structures hallowed by tradition. The final aspect of their conservative agenda ultimately proved fatal to it, and to Charles I. They sought to disband the New Model Army as swiftly as possible.

The Presbyterians' hostility to the army dovetailed with two other aspects of their policy. First, and most obviously, it was the pay and supply of the army that had generated the entire apparatus of taxation and local administration to which the conservatives objected. Disbandment of the army was a *sine qua non* for the longed for return to traditional forms of local government. Secondly, the army was powerfully associated with the religious deviance they sought to check. Edwards, in *Gangraena*, sedulously retailed a series of accounts of sectarian behaviour among the soldiers and officer corps of the New Model. Soldiers had torn up the Bible, illegally taken over pulpits and preached heretical nonsense; they had prevented ministers from preaching, and venomously abused them – the minister of Steeple Aston was denounced as a 'black frog of the Revelation'. Whilst quartered at

Yaxley, Captain Beaumont's men, to show their derisive contempt for infant baptism, pissed in the font and baptised a horse. When informed of this prank, the captain, who had preached in the church, and his officers 'all gloried in it'.[18] Of all the wartime excrescences to which the conservatives objected, the army was the chief. It must go.

The New Model Army became a key political force from the spring of 1647. In June, with the Solemn Engagement, it laid claim to a political role and organised itself accordingly; it had asserted that claim practically with the kidnapping of Charles from his Presbyterian entourage at Holdenby. In August it seized control of London and issued its own scheme, the Heads of the Proposals, for a constitutional settlement with Charles. In November 1648, after its victories in the Second Civil War, it assailed parliament for continuing to negotiate with a king tainted with blood-guilt and conducted a purge of the Commons in December. Intriguingly one could argue that the politicisation, if not the political education, of the New Model was initially the work of Denzil Holles and his Presbyterian majority in parliament.

In the spring of 1647 the Presbyterians sought to rid themselves of the New Model, embodying some of the men as a force to be sent to Ireland under a new cadre of handpicked officers and disbanding the rest. But Holles's ability to accomplish this successfully was severely constricted by his inability to meet the New Model's material grievances. Some of these concerned money: the soldiers' pay was substantially in arrears by the spring of 1647. Between April 1645 and June 1647 the infantry had received 76 per cent of the money due to them, the cavalry 58 per cent: the total debt was approximately three million pounds. Holles, having paid off the Scots, with money coming in increasingly slowly from the provinces, and finding it difficult to raise loans in a City of London that was profoundly hostile to the army, could only offer a derisory sum in immediate payment. Men already disbanded, those disabled in war and war widows had already experienced the difficulties – enhanced by a complex bureaucracy – of collecting arrears and pensions. The army therefore required more money up-front and cast-iron guarantees before it would disband. Some of the army's concerns involved the terms on which they would re-enter civilian life: would apprentices who had joined up be subject to a strict reading of their indentures and denied the right to practise their trades? Would soldiers be liable for prosecution for acts undertaken in war conditions? Alarming stories circulated in the army of what had happened to soldiers already disbanded: they had been sued, imprisoned, even executed, by hostile local magistrates and juries, usually for the requisitioning of supplies.

In many ways Holles's policies with respect to the disbanding of the army look suicidal. He seemed to go out of his way to be offensive to the soldiers, to feed their suspicions, to invite their revolt. Certainly his response to their initial campaign in late March was hugely impolitic. Learning of the circulation of a petition in the army against disbandment without adequate financial and legal guarantees, Holles persuaded the Commons to vote its organisers 'enemies of the state and disturbers of the public peace'. This slur to the New Model's collective honour, combined with publication by the Presbyterians of pamphlets and local petitions in which the soldiers were 'mocked, scorned and derided',[19] hardened the suspicion and hostility that festered in the army over their material grievances. They were being sold down the river. Holles must bear much personal responsibility for the eventual cataclysm, yet in many ways his political options were circumscribed. He headed a party that required an immediate return to normal conditions. He could not screw further taxes from the localities to raise the sums necessary to pay off the army. He also could not easily promote legislation that would overthrow the processes of local courts in order to protect the soldiers against those who believed they had legitimate grievances against them.

On 4 June 1647 six cavalry and seven infantry regiments of the New Model marched to Newmarket, in defiance of the direct votes of the Commons on 25 May which had established a timetable for their disbandment. At the rendezvous, the soldiers formalised and justified their revolt. By the *Solemn Engagement* the army collectively affirmed its unity, and insisted that it would not disband until its grievances had been met. The document also established machinery, a General Council, consisting of the staff officers, and two officers and two soldiers elected by each of the regiments, to secure these goals. This integrated the 'Agitators' – junior officers, non commissioned officers and some troopers who had led and coordinated the initial resistance to Holles's policies, and who had organised the seizure of the king a couple of days before the rendezvous – with the central command structure.

None of this was wholly unprecedented; unpaid continental armies had banded together, established bodies to secure collective action, hounded unsympathetic officers, and seized hostages. What was novel was the soldiers' claim to a *right* to political action, a legitimate role as political actors. In the *Solemn Engagement* they expressed their intention to secure not only their demands, but to ensure that 'other the free-born people of England ... shall not remain subject to the like oppression, injury and abuse'. Nine days later the army published a fuller account of their perceived political role. 'We were not,' they claimed, 'a mere mercenary army hired to serve an arbitrary power of a state, but called forth and conjured by the several declarations of parliament to the defence of our own and the people's just rights and liberties.' It was not sufficient merely to purge Holles and his friends from parliament; more fundamental reform was required to secure the institution from any corrupt or self-seeking faction in the future. They insisted that the Long Parliament should be dissolved soon, and a succession of parliaments, each sitting for a fixed term, should be established. They demanded a reapportionment of seats in the Commons and the disenfranchising of 'decayed or inconsiderable towns': this would 'render the parliament a more equal representative of the whole'. They asserted the right of the people to petition parliament, and sought to check the pretensions of the Lords and Commons to assert an unchecked judicial authority. Once parliament was properly structured, and authority was put on a new footing, then the king's powers should be considered and settled – provided they were consistent with 'the rights and freedom of the subject'.[20]

The conceptual underpinning of this claim to a political voice for citizen-soldiers deserves analysis. As the 14 June *Representation* implied, the army's constitutional ideas derived ultimately from parliament's justifications, set out in its declarations and the pamphlet debates, which had persuaded men to enlist at the beginning of the war. As parliament moved into uncharted constitutional territory in 1642, it increasingly abandoned claims that its actions were founded in legal precedent or even that, as the highest court in the land it could thus declare what was law. Its defence came to rest on the claim that the people were the origin of political authority, that it represented the people, and therefore could declare what was for the common good. This analysis was the foundation of the army's diagnosis of their mistreatment, and of their

The manner of His Excellency Sir *Thomas Fairfax*, and the Officers of His Armie sitting in COVNCELL.

Sir Thomas Fairfax, presiding over the discussions of the Council of the Army, from the title page *A Declaration of the Engagements, Remonstrances, Desires and Resolutions from Sir Thomas Fairfax and the Generall Councel of the Army* (1647). (*Bodleian Library*)

A DECLARATION
OF THE
Engagements, Remonstrances, Representations, Proposals, Desires and Resolutions
from His Excellency Sir *Tho: Fairfax*, and the generall Councel of the Army. For setling of His Majesty in His just Rights, the Parliament in their just Priviledges, and the Subjects in their
LIBERTIES and FREEDOMES.

With papers of Overtures, of the Army with the Kings Majesty, the Parliament, the Citie, and with the Souldiery amongst themselves.

Also Representations of the grievances of the Kingdome, and remedies propounded, for removing the present pressures whereby the Subjects are burthened.

And the resolutions of the Army; for the establishment of a firme and lasting Peace in Church and KINGDOME.

Die Lunæ, 27. *Septembris*, 1647.

WHereas Math: Simmons *hath beene at great charges in Printing the Declarations and Papers from the Army in one Volume. It is ordered by the Lords in Parliament Assembled, that the said Math: Simmons shall have the Printing and publishing thereof for the space of one whole yeare from the date hereof. And that none other shall re-print the same during that time.* John Brown, Cler. Parliamentorum.

LONDON,

Printed by *Math: Simmons* for *George Whittington*, and are to be sold at the sign of the Blew Anchor in *Cornehil*, 1647.

proposed remedies. Parliament was manifestly *not* acting for the common good: it had been captured by Holles and his faction, who employed its authority to behave with an arbitrary disregard for its representative function – rejecting petitions, abusing and imprisoning those who presented them. How had Holles been able to subvert parliament? Because, the army concluded, it was not sufficiently representative. The connection between the people and their ostensible representatives was tenuous: it must be strengthened. Parliament must meet frequently and regularly, and MPs must be elected on a uniform franchise in new equal constituencies. Without this 'the House of Commons is of very little concernment to the interest of the Commons of England'.

The position advanced in June was reasserted in all the key army documents, all penned largely by the Commissary General, Henry Ireton, that were issued in the next eighteenth months: the Heads of the Proposals (August 1647), the *Remonstrance of the Army* (November 1648), and the Agreement of the People (January 1649). Parliament must be restructured: regular, frequent elections must be held (biennially in the Agreement, with parliament in session for not less than 120 days, and not more than 240); reapportionment must be undertaken to create equal constituencies; a uniform franchise (all adult males paying taxes for poor relief in the Agreement) must be established. But while many of the army demands remained the same throughout the period, in other respects there was a major shift. The Heads of the Proposals had offered Charles terms for his reintegration into the political structure that were generous, and, in particular, sympathetic to his objections over the treatment of his supporters and his church in the Newcastle propositions. The Heads also assumed a hereditary House of Lords sharing coordinate powers in relation to legislation and the choice of the executive with the Commons. Fifteen months later, the *Remonstrance* envisioned a figurehead monarch, but only of the people's election and with no veto powers. The Agreement left no room for either a monarch or the House of Lords. It envisaged the establishment of a system based on a unicameral representative assembly, which appointed the executive and to which the latter answered.

We can attribute Ireton and the army's foray into unknown constitutional territory to practical considerations: the king's intransigence and proven perfidy, and the readiness of the majority in Lords and Commons to negotiate with him. But their pilgrimage also reflects their relationship, fertile and fraught by turns, with the Leveller movement.

The Levellers were a London-based civilian movement, brought together initially by the issue of religious persecution. In 1646 parliament had reacted to their noisy representations and demotic pamphlets by burning their petitions and imprisoning their leaders. This experience – very similar to that of the army early in 1647 – had led them to question parliament's credentials as a body representing the people and dedicated to the common good. But their thinking took a more radical direction than that of Ireton. Royalist commentators in 1642–43 had pointed out a danger in parliament's developing ideology. Parliamentary sovereignty rested on its status as a representative body. Could the people recover their intrinsic power if their representatives abused their trust? Some pro-parliamentary pamphleteers were prepared to embrace this position, and the Levellers developed these ideas in 1646 and 1647. Nothing should stand in the way of parliament's representative function, particularly not the independent authority of an unelected House of Lords. Parliament should be restructured to emphasise its representative role and a wholesale reform of the political system should be affirmed and symbolised by a formal agreement among the political nation.

In the spring of 1647 individuals among the Agitator activists in the army and the Levellers began to cooperate. The two groups shared common experiences – prosecution and denunciation by Holles and the Presbyterians – and common interests, particularly religious toleration. A London-based network of fellowship and neighbourhood connected many soldiers, members of the gathered churches and Leveller campaigners. Yet the alliance seems, in retrospect, intrinsically unstable. The army's demand for the payment of its arrears was hardly compatible with Leveller concerns about the grinding of the poor by high and regressive taxation. The Levellers were deeply suspicious of the kinds of central and local administrative agencies spawned by the war, but which remained essential if the army was to be paid and guaranteed indemnity from prosecution in local courts. But, if only temporarily, the sufferings of the Leveller leaders at the hands of the Presbyterians and their powerful rhetoric struck a chord in the army. As the soldiers

marched to the outskirts of London, pressuring the Presbyterians in parliament, many of the Agitators reinforced their contacts with the
Levellers. They met regularly with the Leveller leader, John Lilburne, in
his cell in the Tower of London. Leveller language, 'settling ... all the
free-born people of England in the enjoyment of their just rights',[21] was
deployed fluently in public declarations of their intentions.

The Levellers growing influence among elements in the army posed a
serious threat to the generals, particularly Cromwell and Ireton, who
hoped to broker a settlement with the king. The nickname they and their
allies among the officers acquired in this the period, the 'grandees',
catches nicely the growing atmosphere of resentment and suspicion. As
Cromwell and Ireton undertook the delicate negotiations with Charles,
and with their anti-Presbyterian friends from the Lords and the Commons as they sought to build up a new consensus in parliament after the
withdrawal of Holles and his faction, so they seemed increasingly to distance themselves from the sentiments that had been affirmed collectively
at the cathartic moment at Newmarket. Rumours of a sell-out festered
in the army. These were enhanced by reports of Charles's intransigence,
and were promoted by civilian Levellers and by royalists committed to
the king's policy of exploiting divisions among his enemies.

From 9 October until 15 November the grandees had to fight off a
serious challenge to their control of the army from the Levellers. *The
Case of the Army Truly Stated* was published on the 9th. It purported to
be the work of Agitators newly elected by five of the cavalry regiments,
disturbed by the torpid compliance of their originally nominated agents
in the face of the devious schemes of the senior officers. Whether the
'new agents' had any mandate is questionable, but they were certainly
in contact with the Leveller leadership in London. The tract was a
trenchant indictment of the policies pursued by the grandees. *Nothing*
that the army had banded together to secure in the heady June days had
been achieved. Its arrears remained unpaid and were growing, forcing
the soldiers to take free quarter and face the popular hostility that it fos-
tered. Indemnity was still not properly guaranteed. The army's honour
was aspersed daily in the insinuations of the press. There had been no
decisive purge of Holles's supporters, and nothing had been done to
reform the structure of parliament. The grandees, haggling with the
king, trying to keep the Lords on side by retaining their powers and

privileges, cooperating with the remnants of the Holles gang, had broken and perverted the *Solemn Engagement.*

Throughout 1647 Cromwell and Ireton had recognised that the unity of the army was essential if it was to play a determining political role; divided, it gave every opportunity for others – Charles, Scots and Presbyterians – to act decisively. That unity was ultimately reasserted, but it took time and it came at a price. The first attempt to renew army consensus, the discussion of the *Case* with its proponents at Putney, ended disastrously in further and deeper division. The new agents of the five regiments brought their Leveller allies to the meeting, and the Levellers presented a fresh document, The Agreement of the People, for discussion. It was a clear exposition of the arguments for popular sovereignty and the proper structure and limitation of any representative body, arguments that were forcefully developed by the Levellers in the debates, and which were vigorously answered by Ireton. His conservative stance, both concerning the range of constitutional options open to the army and the basis of political authority in the possession of landed property, seemed to deny the 'first principles whereupon we all engaged' which he had penned in June. The two sides continued their discussions at Putney for more than a week, and a few compromise proposals, on the franchise, for instance, were hammered out. But both grandees and Levellers prepared for a showdown. The Levellers and new agents dispersed copies of the Agreement and tendentious accounts of the ongoing debates at Putney among the soldiery. On the 8 November the grandees, ostensibly responding to reports of a series of disturbances in the army encouraged by this propaganda, ordered the agitators to return to their regiments, and summoned the army to a series of rendezvous. The Levellers sought to persuade the troops of the need for a single general rendezvous, paralleling that at Newmarket in June, where a mass demonstration in favour of the Agreement could be staged. On 15 November the first of the rendezvous ordered by Fairfax was held at Ware. Leveller sympathisers sought to present a copy of the Agreement to Fairfax, but were arrested. Two regiments appeared contrary to Fairfax's orders, with copies of the offending document stuck in their hats: harangued by the field officers and subject to a show of force, their mutiny collapsed. Discipline was imposed by the swift trial of several of the leading mutineers and the execution of one of them.

Military discipline was restored and the Levellers' coup frustrated without massive bloodletting or a purge. But this did not strengthen the hand of the grandees or restore their full freedom of action in reaction to the policies they had sought to pursue in the Heads. It had emerged at Putney that while few there subscribed to the suspicions of the motives of Cromwell and Ireton directly asserted by the Levellers – Lilburne wrote of the 'selfishness and timorousness'[22] of the grandees – and implied in the *Case*, many were troubled by the consequences of their negotiations with the king. It was these approaches, and Charles's manipulative responses to them, that were responsible for dividing the soldiers. Army unity could be restored at minimal cost, but only by the abandonment – perhaps temporary – of the grandees' independent attempts to negotiate with the king. The growing awareness that Charles was once again involved in discussion with the Scots can only have reinforced this determination in Cromwell and Ireton. In late December the officers indulged in a well-publicised meeting affirming their unity. At a solemn fast, with Cromwell and Ireton leading the prayers 'very fervently and pathetically', those who had argued fiercely apologised to one another and, in 'sweet harmony', affirmed their status as 'Brethren'.[23]

The outbreak of the Second Civil War removed the army from direct involvement in the political scene. With its conclusion, and parliament's renewed attempts to achieve a reconciliation with the king, the soldiers again swung into political action – an engagement that ended with decisive military intervention and the execution of Charles I. In this period, despite the suspicions and hostility engendered by their struggle for control of the army at the end of 1647, the grandees and the Levellers again cooperated. The army's *Remonstrance* of 20 November 1648, initially penned by Ireton, was revised in the light of Leveller concerns with its language and emphases. The Agreement of the People, presented to Parliament on 20 January 1649 from the army, was initially drafted by a committee in which the Levellers played a major role. In a bitter tirade published in June 1649, with a 'mock-parliament', the Rump, asserting its legitimacy and the Agreement seemingly a dead letter, John Lilburne argued that the army leaders, particularly Ireton, 'that cunningest of Machiavellians', had duped the Levellers. They had been side-tracked into pointless constitutional discussions and drafting to keep them off the streets while the 'grand-jugglers' of the army executed their self-serving coup.[24] This account is unconvincing. Ireton would hardly have wasted days in the Council of Officers in December and January, even after the Levellers had withdrawn from the discussions, debating and modifying the details of the Agreement if the whole exercise had been a charade. Ireton doubted the viability of certain aspects of the Leveller agenda, but he had come to subscribe to their basic demand for a written constitution. Most significantly, he accepted the constitutional theory that the Levellers had asserted at Putney, of which he had then been the most articulate opponent. The *Remonstrance* begins with the premise that political authority originates in the people, and must be exercised for their benefit. No citizen is obliged by oaths or claims of prescription to accept a government that does not conform to this basic test. The current structure of government must be replaced by a parliament, constituted in a manner designed to ensure its representative function, and with clear legislative authority, and to which the executive is responsible. Monarchy remained a possibility in this constitutional sketch, but the king would have no veto and would be recognised as a trustee, answerable for the exercise of his powers. All this should be established by 'by a general contract or agreement of the people'.[25] It should also be established by bringing Charles to trial. He had broken his trust by asserting his arbitrary power in defiance of the known rights and liberties of his people, in consequence 'he is guilty of the highest treason against law among men'; tyrants must be punished to assert the principle of the due exercise of authority.

Ireton had moved far from the position he had taken in the Heads and in the debates at Putney. He was now prepared to use Leveller theories of popular sovereignty to demand justice against the king. But the *Remonstrance* also deployed another strand of opinion for the same purpose, one that owed less to abstract ideas on the fiduciary nature of authority, and more to sentiment within the army. Ireton emphasised Charles's bloodguilt, and the religious imperative of vengeance.

In 1650 the English forces, invading Scotland, produced a justification of their proceedings: its language is millenarian, apocalyptic. The Second Civil War was

> a second testimony given from heaven to justify the proceedings of his poor servants against that bloody Antichristian brood, though with the loss of

many precious Saints – we were then powerfully convinced that the Lord's purpose was to deal with the late King as a man of blood. And being persuaded in our consciences that he and his monarchy was one of the ten horns of the Beast (spoken of, Rev. 17.12–15), and being witnesses to so much of the innocent blood of the Saints that he had shed in supporting the Beast, and considering the loud cries of the souls of the Saints under the altar, we were extraordinarily carried forth to desire justice upon the King, that man of blood.[26]

This sentiment is not just an ex post facto rationalisation. The sense that the New Model Army was an army of Saints, charged by God to act as his agents in the pursuit of his providential purposes, and assured of their righteous performance of that role by their victories, was apparent from 1645. The Saints, marked out by divinely appointed victories, seeking God in fervent prayer and by a charismatic reading of Scripture, could know his will and should execute it. This sense became politically powerful after the army revolt in summer of 1647, and decisive in late 1648. At Putney on 1 November Cromwell invited those present at the council to testify the answers that God had given them to their prayers. Captain George Bishop responded:

After many inquiries in my spirit I find this answer, and the answer which is to many Christians besides amongst us. I say [it is] a compliance to preserve that Man of Blood, and those principles of tyranny which God from Heaven by his many successes has manifestly declared against, and which I am confident may be our destruction.[27]

Several others at the council used the same arguments, despite Cromwell's attempt to rein in the discussion.

The language was resurrected at the great army prayer meeting at Windsor at the end of April 1648. The soldiers met in a chastened mood, a 'low, weak, divided, perplexed condition'. Recent news of the Scottish preparations for invasion was followed by the report of the defeat of the parliamentary force in South Wales and the general insurrection of the region. They reflected on God's promises in scripture, with 'tears, weepings, groanings'. Their spiritual exercises resulted in a cathartic moment of reassertion of their mission. The army rejected 'those cursed carnal conferences our own wisdom, fears, lack of faith had prompted us ... to entertain with the king'. They agreed that it was their duty to fight, and 'if ever the Lord brought us back in peace, to call Charles Stuart, that man of blood, to an account for the blood he had shed'.[28] This language dominated the petitions that flooded in from the regiments in November 1648, as Ireton prepared the army for decisive action. The soldiers demanded impartial justice to silence 'the hideous cry of innocent blood crying for vengeance to Heaven'; impartial justice against those 'whose lives the Lord requires to appease his wrath'.[29]

The grandees had questioned this kind of analysis at Putney. Cromwell, in particular, had sniped at the scriptural exegesis of those who argued for an end to negotiation with a 'man of blood', and reminded them how easy it was to claim divine sanction for their own 'imaginary' opinions. God, Cromwell reminded his colleagues, 'is not the author of contradictions', and the disagreements that had emerged in the debates self-evidently suggested that God had not yet declared himself.[30] By November 1648, flushed with victory in the Second Civil War, Cromwell was increasingly sure that God's purposes were clear. This emerges powerfully in two letters to a colleague, Colonel Hammond, who was troubled by the direction of army policy, and wavering in his commitment to it. For Cromwell, the *consistency* of God's providential dispensations revealed that the army was 'a lawful power, called by God to oppose and fight against the king'. Increasing unity of purpose among the 'Saints', the 'disposing the hearts of so many of God's people ... especially in this poor army' to challenge the negotiations proceeding at Newport, gave a clear sense God's purpose. Charles was a pariah: 'this man, against whom the Lord hath witnessed'.[31]

After his defeat in the first Civil War, Charles had played a difficult hand with some skill. Believing that he was indispensable to any settlement and recognising the serious divisions among those who had defeated him, he had refused to surrender his friends or his church, or to agree to any serious curtailment of monarchical authority. The competitive auction over which he then presided had enabled him to extract surprisingly good terms. But this was not his prime intention. Rather, he sought to play off the parties with whom he negotiated, to widen the differences between them, in order to provoke a second war in which, with his old supporters, he might reverse the verdict of the first. The abject failure of that policy in the summer of 1648 did not chasten the king. Charles responded to the desperate attempt of the conservatives in

parliament to negotiate a settlement at Newport with further procrastination and manipulation.

Those who negotiated with Charles became increasingly frustrated
with his intransigence and suspicious of his duplicity: 'from Devils and
Kings, Good Lord deliver me', an MP exploded after Charles rejected
another proposal.[32] Anger and a pragmatic sense that Charles was more
trouble than he was worth did not, in themselves, result in his execution. Ultimately, by rejecting the opportunity to settle on the terms of
the Heads of the Proposals and by inviting the Scottish invasion, Charles
was faced with men who had developed powerful, if not wholly compatible, justifications for extreme action. The radical constitutionalism
that Ireton borrowed from the Levellers demanded a restructuring of
the state on first principles, a settlement to which monarchy was irrelevant; it visualised executive authorities as trustees answerable to the
people, and sought to symbolise this principle by legal proceedings
against Charles. The army also alleged a providential mandate. An army
of Saints, justified as such by brilliant victories, had rejected the 'unbe-
lief, base fear of men, carnal consultations with our own wisdoms and
not with the Word of the Lord' that had led them into slippery negotiations in 1647. They demanded vengeance on 'that Man of Blood'
because God categorically required it. 'You cannot do without me',
Charles had claimed in 1647: a year later that was no longer the case.

6

Why Was the Rump Parliament Dissolved?

On 20 April 1653 Cromwell rose to speak in the Commons. After some perfunctory praise of the parliament's record, he began to rebuke the MPs for their collective faults, chiefly their concern for their private interests and the delays of justice, and then proceeded to barbed personal denunciation of individual members – whoremasters and drunkards. Finally, he exploded: 'You are no parliament, I say you are no parliament; I will put an end to your sitting', and he summoned the musketeers he had waiting in the lobby.[1] The members were escorted out; the mace carried off; the house locked up. The Rump, spawned by military interference in December 1648, had collapsed in a similar military coup.

The basic outline of Cromwell and the army's objections to the government of the Rump in 1653 are clear. Very specifically, Cromwell believed that the MPs had reneged on a deal that he had brokered the previous evening, concerning the timetable and arrangements for the Rump's dissolution. More generally, the need to dissolve the Rump, whether by its own authority or, as became the case when MPs sought to weasel out of their commitments, by military intervention, was also a common assumption in the army. As Cromwell told the officers before setting out for parliament:

> Reformation could not be expected from the present parliament ... the burdens are continued still on the people, injustice aboundeth, the law is not regulated; they intend nothing but to seek themselves, and to perpetuate themselves to the great hurt and danger of the nation.[2]

In the localities the godly congratulated Cromwell on his intervention, and expressed their very similar analysis of the deficiencies of the Rump. They rejoiced at his scattering of such hypocrites, whose rule had been marked by 'sad oppressions' and 'insufferable grievances' to the Saints.[3]

The soldiers lost patience with its legislative lethargy and failure to reform, and the Rump succumbed to armed intervention. Ironically, it had had its origin in a similar military coup. On 6 December, with New Model regiments occupying the entrances to Westminster Hall and patrolling the neighbouring streets, Colonel Thomas Pride had weeded out those MPs who were still prepared to negotiate with the perfidious king on the terms of the treaty of Newport. About 130 MPs were refused admittance to the House; forty-five of that number were imprisoned. Horrified by the purge and the policies that it presaged, another two hundred and sixty MPs, many of whom would also have been denied admission had they come to the parliament, refused to attend the House. Government devolved upon a tiny cadre of about seventy MPs, a 'Rump' of committed radicals. These were the men who set up the High Court of Justice that tried Charles I and who abolished the 'useless and dangerous' House of Lords. The ultimate justification for both these revolutionary actions was the proposition the people were the sole origin of properly constituted authority. These were the men who boasted of the restoration of ancient liberty: their great seal was inscribed 'In the first year of freedom by God's Blessing Restored'; legal process ran in the sonorous name of 'the keepers of the liberties of England'.

Given its radical origins, how had the Rump become the slough of legislative torpor and vested interest excoriated by Cromwell? And there is another related question that must be answered. Given the Rump's assertions about the nature of political authority, why was an institution summoned by the king in 1640 and transformed by army intervention in 1648 still holding the reins of power in 1653? On 20 January 1649, the officers had presented their version of the Agreement of the People to the Commons; in the document they attributed the 'oppressions and not-yet-ended troubles' under which the nation reeled to the 'undue or unequal constitution' of parliament.[4] The Rump remained clearly susceptible to precisely the same critique. Not only was its four-year tenure in defiance of the specific requirement that the House dissolve itself before 30 April following, but much of the proposed constitutional structure in the Agreement was contradicted by the personnel and pro-

The Great Seal of the Rump (1651). The initial seal of 1649 was similar,
save that it announced 'The First Year of Freedome by God's Blessing
Restored'. Both show a far from typical crowded session of the Parliament.
(*Bodleian Library*)

cedures of the Rump. Parliament was to be 'Representative of the whole nation': elected every two years, it was to sit for no longer than six months. Diurnal executive authority was vested in a virtually distinct Council of State, which was answerable to parliament for the exercise of its authority. Military officers and civil administrators were to be excluded from the House, and its judicial authority was limited to the censure of salaried public officials. The Rump defied, often flagrantly, *all* these provisions. Clearly any answer to a question on the Rump's dissolution also entails a discussion of why it survived so long.

The Rump's retention of power until the summer of 1651 is easily comprehensible. After the execution of the king the first order of business was to shore up an extremely fragile regime. Within England, the Rump was condemned by conservatives and radicals alike. The royalist press, which had developed a bawdy demotic style after the king's surrender, spat out scabrous satires. The Presbyterians wrestled to understand the execution within their own providential reading, and prayed for Charles II. On the left, the Levellers voiced their growing suspicions of an oligarchic regime that had shamefully betrayed the promises inherent in its radical language. The Levellers still enjoyed support in the army, and, as in October 1647, they sought to strengthen these ties by emphasising their concern for the bread and butter grievances of the common soldiers.

Externally, England was the butt of international opprobrium and was wide open to assault from British and foreign enemies. The execution had united the competing factions in Ireland. Ormond, the king's lord deputy, was promised a force of 15,000 men by the Confederate Catholics to bolster his own army. The Scots, bitterly resentful at the execution of their king, swiftly proclaimed Charles II, and began negotiations for his return to his northern kingdom. English royalists controlled the Isle of Man, the Scilly Isles and Jersey, and these were used as bases by a powerful fleet. In the Second Civil War a large part of the navy had revolted against parliament. These ships, now commanded by Prince Rupert, sought to assist Ormond by threatening the supply lines of the few parliamentary forces remaining in Ireland, and, with more enthusiasm and success, plundered and disrupted English commerce.

On the Continent the situation looked equally black. Charles II was welcomed to the United Provinces by his brother-in-law, William II of Orange; the government refused to grant the agents of the Rump an audience, and made little effort to track down the royalist thugs who murdered the leader of the English delegation. The tsar expelled British merchants; the king of Portugal offered Lisbon as a base for Rupert's pirates. In France, the regency government banned all trade with England, connived at the royalist depredations against English shipping, and promised to raise a substantial force for Charles II.

The Rump's policies, at least until September 1651, were very largely dictated by the variety of international and domestic threats. Resources and energies were dedicated to ensuring the security of the regime. In this respect the Rump was supremely successful. On 3 September 1651 Cromwell blessed God for the 'crowning mercy', the annihilation of the Scots–royalist alliance at the battle of Worcester. By that date all the British threats to the regime had been met. On the Continent, the governments that had greeted the Rump with horrified opprobrium now sought alliances with the formidable military and naval power that had emerged. How was this extraordinary resolution achieved?

In some respects the Rump was lucky. The ongoing struggle between France and Spain left neither power with interest or resources to intervene in England, and subject to internal rebellions provoked by the insatiable demands of war. The death of William II of Orange, a smallpox victim, removed a major supporter of Charles II's cause on the international stage; the MP, John Moyle praised God for His 'very great mercy to this Commonwealth' in William's premature death.[5] Divisions among their opponents, internal and external, also aided the Rump's survival. At home, the Levellers, as the most powerful exponents of religious toleration, had drawn much support from the gathered churches in 1646–48. But the leaders of the London sectarian congregations, a 'pack of fawning ... knaves' in Lilburne's jaundiced view,[6] reckoned that their freedom of worship was sufficiently protected by the regime, courted the Rump and distanced themselves from their old allies. The divorce was lubricated by a campaign of propaganda against the Levellers promoted by the Rump's defenders, characterising them promiscuously as communists, anarchists, atheists, Jesuits and crypto-royalists. More significant were the divisions among the regime's opponents in Ireland and Scotland. The denunciation of the alliance between Ormond and the Confederate Catholics by the papal nuncio ensured that significant elements in the Catholic army refused to collaborate with the king's representative. Conversely, many Protestant supporters of Charles II were deeply uneasy about their new Catholic allies, and there were a steady stream of desertions from Ormond's motley coalition; when the Confederation appointed a Catholic bishop to command the forces cooperating with the Scots in Ulster, General Monro and his men joined the English army.

In Scotland, too, the Rump's task was eased by its enemies' divisions. The high Presbyterians dominated the national government after the defeat of Hamilton's forces in 1648. They sought to resurrect Scotland's total commitment to God's cause, by, for instance, instigating a savage persecution of witches, and also to purge those who had been tainted by involvement in the Hamilton adventure. They were deeply, and properly, distrustful of Charles II's credentials as a Covenanted king, and equally of those who rallied to him when he arrived in Scotland. They sought to surround him in court and camp with those who shared their theocratic agenda, and to dismiss servants and soldiers who lacked kirk-approved credentials. The morale of the Scots army was hardly enhanced when, a few weeks before the crushing defeat it suffered at Dunbar, eighty officers and four thousand soldiers were purged from its ranks. That defeat gave Charles a greater freedom of action, as the more moderate Presbyterians recognised that they could no longer afford the luxury of a one-party state, and must cooperate with the Scottish royalists if the English were to be expelled. But a splinter faction of the kirk party provided a different diagnosis of Dunbar. The defeat was God's punishment for their *failure* to secure Charles's proper repentance or to wean him sufficiently from ungodly associates. The moderates triumphed in the Scots parliament, but the extremists refused to assist the king, raised their own independent force, and ensured that the army Charles led to destruction at Worcester was deprived of recruits and supplies from their heartland in south-western Scotland.

The triumph of the Rump regime was, however, not simply fortuitous. The Rump had to ensure that it had sufficient military force to defend itself and deter aggressors. This it achieved by diligent and focused application to the organisation and supply of the army and the navy. The latter was in poor shape early in 1649. Many of the sailors had revolted in the Second Civil War and taken their ships to form Rupert's force. Many of the remaining officers were suspect, naval administration was in disarray, and the vessels themselves in disrepair. The Rump acted with great energy. A new administrative structure, headed by committees answering to parliament and the council of state, and dominated by Sir Henry Vane, was established. Suspect officers were weeded out, and new admirals and captains, often experienced merchant marine officers, appointed. The salaries of the officers were increased and the men given a greater slice of prize money. The size of the fleet was doubled by a programme of shipbuilding and by the purchase and refitting of merchantmen. By 1651 the reorganised fleet had proved its worth. The royalist-held islands had been forced to submit; Rupert's navy had been worsted and scattered; and English expeditionary forces had been supported and supplied in the invasions of Ireland and Scotland. Naval action had obliged Portugal and France to abandon their encouragement of Rupert and of privateers preying on Channel commerce. Maritime strength had forced the continental powers to recognise the republic, to offer favourable trade treaties, and to enter a competitive auction for military alliances.

The Rump also had to give immediate attention to the organisation and morale of the army. Early in 1649 its condition was less ramshackle than that of the navy, but the Rump's control was seriously compromised by the efforts of the Levellers and their supporters among the soldiers.

The Leveller leaders had been troubled by the army council's modifications of the Agreement of the People in the winter of 1648–49, and by the army's forcible purging of the Long Parliament, rather than compelling its dissolution. Their resentment was fuelled by the Rump's actions in January and February. The attempt to silence the press, using the military police as the enforcers of the licensing legislation; the denial of jury trial to those tried in its new high court of justice; the arbitrary power apparently invested in its executive arm, the council of state: all were anathema to the Levellers. Behind the poodle parliament stood the grandees of the army, and the Levellers savaged their self-serving ambition, and the nauseating hypocrisy of their suave and manipulative rapprochement with the Levellers in December 1648. Petitions and pamphlets denounced the army commanders and the Rump in tones that ranged from Lilburne's righteous indignation to Overton's bitter sarcasm:

> Did ever men pretend an higher degree of holiness, religion and zeal to God and their country than these? These preach, these fast, these pray, these have nothing more frequent than the sentences of sacred scripture, the name of God and Christ in their mouths. You shall scarce speak to Cromwell about anything, but he will lay his hand on his breast, elevate his eyes, and call to God to record; he will weep, howl and repent, even while he doth smite you under the first rib.[7]

The government could imprison the London-based Leveller leaders, whose position was weakened by their breach with their old supporters in the gathered churches. Of far greater concern was Leveller agitation in the army. The soldiers had two employment-related grievances in early 1649: money; and the organisation of the projected expeditionary force to Ireland. They were not in regular receipt of their pay, and the sums that were advanced to them often did not cover the costs of their accommodation and food, which were exceptionally high in a period of fierce dearth. Many of the regiments had to commandeer 'free quarter' from the populace and bear the resentment that this invariably created. The choice of certain regiments to serve in Ireland was also a fraught issue. How were the regiments to be selected? Even after it was decided that a lottery was the fairest procedure, there was a prevalent suspicion that the draw had been fixed. Would individuals in the chosen regiments be allowed the option of refusing to serve? If such men were disbanded would they be discriminated against? What portion of their outstanding pay would be given them, and what security for the provision of the remaining arrears owed to them?

The echoes of the concerns that had energised the New Model in the spring of 1647 were obvious to, and developed by, radicals within the army and the civilian Levellers. The officers sought to contain discontent over military grievances by insisting that the soldiers might only petition Fairfax, who would forward their concerns to parliament, and threatened civilians who encouraged disaffection within the army with punishment under martial law. In response, the Levellers were quick to draw the parallels with the behaviour of Holles and the Presbyterian party in 1647, and to deride Cromwell and Ireton's altered stance. Presumably, Overton jibed, the grandees had 'condemned the imprisoning petitioners and burning petitions' in 1647 'because they were not the imprisoners and burners themselves'.[8] The Levellers transformed the funeral of a trooper executed for his role in a mutiny over pay into a public demonstration against martial law and those who enforced it. They encouraged the soldiers to demand not only the redress of their pocketbook grievances, but, reminding them of the language of the *Solemn Engagement*, the resurrection of regimental agitators, the reconvening of the general council of the army and the election of new officers. They invited the soldiers to think of themselves as citizens and to join their challenge to the arbitrary rule of the Rump and the council of state. Waves of petitions from some regiments, and by May of mutinies, were the measure of the success of their propaganda.

The mutinies were forcibly suppressed by the energetic action of Fairfax and Cromwell. More important was their and the Rump's recognition that the army had legitimate grievances over their conditions of service, and by their readiness to take remedial action. Resentment at the process of selection of the regiments to serve in Ireland led the officers in late April to propose that selection should be by lot. On 9 May Cromwell assured the troops that those who wished to leave the army could do so without prejudice: they would be given a mixture of cash and audited certificates for their arrears on the same basis as those who agreed to serve. On the 11 May Fairfax issued a declaration repeating these promises, and emphasising that parliament was engaged in securing the army's arrears against the sale of the king's lands. The defeat of the mutineers did not result in the abandonment of these promises. Chivvied by the generals, the Rump was sedulous in its attention to the needs of the soldiers – an increasing number of soldiers, as garrisons were established in Ireland and Scotland. Between 1649 and 1651 the army establishment increased from 45,000 to 70,000 men. The pay of the regiments serving in England was fully and regularly provided; the expeditionary forces to Ireland and Scotland, if less reliably paid, were well supplied. Arrears totalling £1,300,000 were paid off by the sale of the royal estates. The only specifically military grievances expressed in the army's petition to the Rump of August 1652 concerned bottlenecks in the process of auditing accounts, and the reluctance of some corporate towns to allow disbanded soldiers to practise their trades.

In its pursuit of security from internal subversion and external intervention, the Rump built up an efficient military machine and the administrative and fiscal infrastructure to support it. This imperative could crowd out a great deal: it was not until February 1651 that the Rump remembered to order the destruction of the royal arms in churches, and removed them from the glass and hangings in Whitehall. Yet the pursuit of security was not the whole story. From the first, radicals within parliament believed that the Rump's obligations went further than mere survival. It must pursue a domestic agenda focused on social and administrative improvement. To that end the radical MP, Henry Marten, introduced a raft of reforming measures in June 1649. Such views were even more fiercely expressed outside parliament among radical religious congregations and, more particularly, in the army.

The battle of Dunbar (3 September 1650) was a decisive moment in the creation of the army's self-image, and its subsequent political agenda. It was a brilliant victory against a superior force which occupied a more advantageous position and was better supplied. Both armies had dedicated themselves to God before the battle; their watch-words – 'the Covenant' for the Scots; 'the Lord of Hosts' for the English – indicated their common convictions. In these circumstances, the total victory, 'the enemy made by the Lord of Hosts as stubble to our swords', had to be understood as an irresistible providential mandate in favour of the English. But God's signal favour created obligations, duties set out in Cromwell's letter to the Rump describing the army's triumph. The English governors must dedicate themselves to God by making a firm commitment to a reforming agenda. 'Relieve the oppressed', he adjured them, 'hear the groans of poor prisoners in England; be pleased to reform the abuses of all professions, and if there be any one that makes many poor to make few rich, that suits not a Commonwealth.'[9]

The Rump's failure to act on these initiatives and injunctions cannot be attributed to an agenda that focused exclusively on defence. They suggest more fundamental weaknesses in the regime, weaknesses that appeared more starkly in the continued drought of reformist legislation *after* the security of the regime was assured at Worcester. The Rump's intermittent and abortive gestures towards the reform of the legal system throughout its four-year tenure provide a particularly telling instance.

The existing legal system creaked; it was dilatory and expensive, and substantive justice could be lost in a welter of arcane technicalities. The Rump intermittently discussed sweeping proposals of reform: in the summer of 1649, in the following winter and again after Dunbar. There were periods of lengthy discussion, but with negligible achievement. Marten's June 1649 initiative contained a number of specific proposals, and the Rump responded with a sonorous statement of its commitment to 'regulating … the proceedings in law … for preventing the tediousness of suits and abuses burdensome to the people'.[10] An Act to limit imprisonment for debt (which proved unworkable) was all that reached the statute book. A couple of procedural technicalities that generated only expense for litigants were abolished in the spring of 1650. And (in tepid response to Cromwell's great post-Dunbar exhortation) it was decided to use English not Latin in legal proceedings, and ordinary handwriting, not the traditional arcane and antique scripts, for the keeping of court records.

In December 1651, under renewed pressure from the army, the Rump again took up the issue of law reform. To meet the objection that issues easily got lost and forgotten in the welter of business in the House and its committees, it appointed an extra-parliamentary body, chaired by a brilliant young lawyer, Matthew Hale, to draw up and forward proposals that would then be considered as the basis for legislation. The large and diverse membership – practising lawyers, bureaucrats, London merchants, military men, a few radicals, and not least the fiery preacher Hugh Peter – may have been intended to ensure deadlock and delay. But the committee, though divided on several issues, took their task seriously. 'We are', they insisted, 'to look after moral justice and public interest of the Commonwealth.'[11] They worked hard and cooperatively, and by July 1652 had come up with sixteen draft Bills, forming a comprehensive, solid and sensible programme of piecemeal reform, that were forwarded to the Rump. The press was delighted with the progress made by the committee in 'that glorious work': 'the parliament, council and army are very unanimous, in bringing it to a happy period'.[12] But thereafter nothing emerged from parliament, where the proposals were stalled and then talked to death. One of the Bills proposed the establishment of a land registry; it stated that land to be registered should not 'be subject to any encumbrances'. This was 'so managed by the lawyers' that, as Cromwell later wryly recalled, 'we were more than three months and could not get over the word *encumbrances*'.[13]

Proposals for law reform were retarded, in part by deliberate filibustering and obfuscation over arcane technicalities, by lawyer MPs attempting to defend their profitable monopoly. But the identity of these lawyers provides further material for reflection on the Rump's impoverished record of social reform. In the summer of 1649 an anonymous, but well-informed, author vented his frustration at the limited progress made on the furtherance of Marten's scheme to relieve those imprisoned for debt. When the matter was in the hands of Marten, or of Alexander Rigby, then the proposed legislation had made significant progress, he reported. When Nicholas Lechmere, Robert Reynolds or Bulstrode Whitelocke took a hand, objections and delays were multiplied, and those seeking to promote the Bill were fobbed off with 'promises and repromises, protractions and rejoinders'.[14] Rigby and Marten were regicides: the three foot-dragging lawyers had all returned to the Rump *after* the execution of the king.

This brings us to another aspect of the Rump's initial priority: security. Reforming initiatives were not simply crowded out by the weight of business required for survival. Because of the international and domestic threats it faced, the Rump sought to present itself as a government of national unity. It attempted to be all things to all men: ideals were sacrificed to expediency, and policies, other than those required for national defence, wavered in the face of a pragmatic concern to achieve broad support and consensus.

The attempt to cobble together a government of national unity, geared to the defence of the regime, took two, interrelated, forms from 1649 to 1651. First, there was an attempt to encourage the involvement of as many MPs as possible in the deliberations of the Rump. Secondly, the policies pursued by this increasingly promiscuous group were designed not to offend the sensibilities of the traditional political nation.

Let us look first at the changing personnel of the Rump. Early in December 1648 the House of Commons, some 470 MPs strong, was whittled by Pride's Purge to a handful of about seventy MPs. The dominant public voice of this group was provided by committed radicals who triumphed in the assertion that power was originally in the people, and who created the new great seal with its confident boast of the restoration of pristine freedom. It was these MPs, men like Marten and Rigby, who contemplated an agenda of legal and social reforms in tandem with their radical ideological conviction. But their ideals were undercut by the attempt to construct at least the impression of national consensus. So those MPs who had fled the House after Pride's Purge were encouraged to return. And only the most minimal affirmation of enthusiasm for the revolutionary acts was required to secure readmission.

In consequence, in February 1649 some seventy-five MPs crept back; fifty more followed in dribs and drabs in the remainder of the year; the Rump swelled from seventy to two hundred MPs, approximately equally balanced between moderates, who sought to distance themselves from the revolutionary actions of January 1649, and radicals who gloried in those events. There was a nice premonition of this phenomenon in the debates concerning the new council of state, the Rump's executive arm, in mid-February 1649. Some radical MPs proposed an oath for the new counsellors in which they declared their full approval of the execution of Charles and the abolition of the Lords: only nineteen of the forty-one counsellors agreed to swear on these terms. Delicate negotiations eventually produced a new oath declaring only a readiness to adhere to the regime as it was currently constituted. Early in 1651, George Bishop, radical sectary and chief of intelligence for the regime, surveyed the Rump's membership and trembled: there were simply 'too few honest hearts', too few who 'honour God by uprightness, believing and activity'. 'A tender heart would weep for the day of visitation that is coming', he concluded bleakly.[15] Incongruously, Bishop's troubled letter was addressed to Oliver Cromwell. Cromwell had been both a major figure in drawing up the compromise concerning the oath for the council of state, and also particularly active in wooing troubled moderate MPs to return to the House after the execution. His general attitude in this period is apparent in his efforts, in this case unsuccessful, to save the House of Lords from legislative abolition: it was madness he argued, to undertake further divisive policies when the Rump 'had more need to study a near union'.[16]

The Rump by the summer of 1649 was a strange hybrid, equally balanced in its make-up between radicals and men who had returned to Westminster to uphold a government – *any* government, generic government – in the face of threatened external assault and internal subversion. The history of legal reform, of schemes that were mooted, then watered down and abandoned, owes much to this admixture. More telling, perhaps, is the legislation that did emerge, which often sought to embody the very divergent policy ideals of variegated groups of MPs or to appeal to a diverse group of constituencies.

The Rump's religious legislation is particularly indicative of the confused and contradictory courses it often pursued as it searched for a broad base of support. In late September 1650 the Rump finally passed a Bill repealing the Elizabethan statutes demanding church attendance, which, though originally directed against Catholics, could be deployed against members of the gathered churches. The Bill had languished for fourteen months since its first introduction, and was probably passed as a sop to Cromwell and the army after Dunbar. But journalists patronised by the Rump downplayed the Bill, preferring to dwell on the Blasphemy Act of the previous month,

> the severity of which votes may stop the slanderous mouths of those that publish abroad such vile reports of this Commonwealth as if [the Rump] intended to countenance impious and licentious practices, under pretence of religion and liberty.[17]

The background to this enactment was the press frenzy in the spring of 1650 about the Ranters, a shadowy group who argued the Calvinist theory of election to an antinomian conclusion. God's elect could not sin, and to 'the pure all things are pure'. This position they cheerfully affirmed with orgies of smoking, drinking and sex. Or so the newspapers and pamphleteers declared, backing their pious denunciation with crude, full-frontal illustrations of Ranter depravities. The Rump decided it could not afford to lose the support of moderate puritans horrified by such immorality, hence the Blasphemy Act. But neither could MPs antagonise sectarians who opposed any challenge to the toleration of religious dissent or threat of state interference in matters of conscience.

The Ranters Ranting

With

The apprehending, examinations, and confession of *Iohn Collins,* *I. Shakespear, Tho. Wiberton,* and five more which are to answer the next Sessions. And severall songs or catches, which were sung at their meetings. Also their severall kinds of mirth, and dancing. Their blasphemous opinions. Their belief concerning heaven and hell. And the reason why one of the same opinion cut off the heads of his own mother and brother. Set forth for the further discovery of this ungodly crew.

LONDON
Printed by *B. Alsop,* 165)

Ranter depravities: title page of *The Ranter Ranting* (1650). The popular press had a field day describing and illustrating the excesses of the Ranters.
(*British Library*)

So the Blasphemy Act was a confused jumble – it enumerates and excoriates in appalled language the horrible theories and practices alleged of Ranter deviants; but the procedures to secure a conviction are of almost impossible complexity, and the punishment for the most shocking assertions and practices was limited to six months' imprisonment.

A similar confusion emerges in the Rump's schemes for the propagation of the Gospel. The projects mooted were designed to ensure that godly ministers, with a strong sense of evangelical mission and committed to preaching, were provided with parochial livings throughout the Commonwealth. Early in 1650 legislation was passed appointing commissioners to secure this end in Wales and the four northern counties. This was a good generic puritan programme, designed to bring evangelical religion to the 'dark corners of the land': the commissioners, chosen from local laymen and divines, were empowered to purge inadequate ministers, and to interrogate the credentials of their prospective replacements. This might have been gratifying to religious radicals, not least because their supporters, particularly in North Wales, dominated the membership of the commissions. But other clauses gave them pause: the Act assumed the old structure of parish, ministerial patronage and tithes. Subsequent demands for further such Acts for other areas of England provoked fierce discussion on the appropriate means of funding the ministry between radical and moderate MPs, and nothing was passed. In North Wales, the zealots deployed the legislation to dismantle the parochial structure, purging ministers in order to use tithe revenues to maintain a series of itinerants, charismatic preachers who often lacked traditional qualifications for the ministry. This creative reading of the legislation troubled conservative MPs, and their nervousness was enhanced by reports of peculation among, and the radical statements attributed to, the commissioners, which were assiduously compiled by their local opponents. Vavasor Powell, it was alleged, 'damned and accursed' lawyers and those who employed them; Walter Cradock preached that university learning was 'an essential ... limb of the kingdom of Antichrist'.[18] In April 1653, when the enabling legislation for Wales expired, the Rump washed its hands of the matter and, with virtually no discussion the Acts were not renewed. The failure to back this radical initiative, and the veiled suggestions of local peculation that the Rump allowed to fester, infuriated the radicals and their powerful supporters in the army. In 1653 Cromwell praised the experiment: 'it being known to many of us that God did kindle a seed there indeed hardly to be paralleled since the primitive times'. He then reflected darkly on the Rump's attitude: 'what discountenance that business of the poor people of God there had ... how signally that business was trodden underfoot in Parliament to the discountenancing of the honest people'.[19]

The Rump was a regime cobbled together in response to crisis and the serious threats of invasion and internal subversion. After Worcester, when those dangers had passed, calls for reform were redoubled. The godly barraged Cromwell and the army with exhortations to consider 'the many burdens and grievances yet unremoved, and the many good things obstructed'.[20] The army pestered, prayed and petitioned: in January 1653 the officers lamented that, 'the work of the Lord hath seemed to stand still, and all the instruments thereof have been men of no might'.[21] But, despite the external pressure, the Rump did little: legislation concerning the church remained ambiguous and ineffectual, law reform made no headway. That was true also of the issue that became key in the aftermath of Worcester, and which led directly to Cromwell's coup in April 1653: the timetable for the Rump's surrender of its authority, and the constitutional arrangement that would succeed it.

The army-backed Agreement of the People of January 1649, with its demand for the termination of the Rump by 30 April of that year, to be followed by new elections designed to secure a properly representative body, gathered dust, despite a few formal pronouncements that the House would rapidly consider 'putting a period to this parliament'.[22] For most of 1649 the House gave intermittent attention to a scheme to expel formally those MPs who refused a loyalty test and to hold by-elections in their constituencies. But the determination of the kind of test – attendance or an oath – and of the detailed list of names of those to be expelled, of course invited time-consuming debate. The Rump also raised the question of whether there should be some prior redistribution of seats before such 'recruiter' elections were held. This proposal answered the old Leveller challenge to the unrepresentative nature of parliament, but it was another issue that simply delayed matters in long, and ultimately abortive, reflection. These discussions dragged on intermittently through 1649 and 1650, punctuated by moments of activity induced by external pressure, such as Cromwell's Dunbar letter.

After Worcester, the question of the constitutional settlement was again revived. On the day Cromwell was triumphantly welcomed in the House, it was voted to take the issue of a new representative under consideration. Pressured by the Lord General, who joined the discussions, it was agreed, first, that the Rump would dissolve (not be recruited) and then that a date would be fixed for that dissolution. But the discussions were protracted and majorities for the line favoured by Cromwell were slim: the motion that a date was to be set was carried only by 49–47 votes. And then the date finally determined upon, on the 18 November 1651, was not until 3 November 1654. With that decision, the Rump, exhausted, again let the matter rest. In the spring it emerged that MPs were still tempted by the recruitment option, though they eventually decided to continue with the new representative legislation.

Army demands for the election of a new representative body in the spring and summer of 1652 achieved only sporadic sparks of activity and then a reversion to lethargy. In January 1653 the army began a period of continuous pressure; the Bill was again revived and pursued, though with a palpable lack of enthusiasm. The clauses of the draft were discussed each Wednesday, but attendance was poor. A date for dissolution was determined, a year earlier than the November 1654 date proposed in 1651; and a property qualification for the franchise was agreed: but discussion was protracted and desultory.

As parliament droned on the hostility of elements of the army boiled over. The council of officers had come close to voting to expel the MPs in March, and such courses were being recommended by some of the radical preachers in London who enjoyed a following in the army. Outlying detachments, inspired by circular letters from the army in London, salivated at the prospect of once again playing a cataclysmic role in the furtherance of reform: temporising and worldly courses must be abandoned, and 'the Saints' would 'become instrumental to raise up the Tabernacle of righteousness, and cause judgement to run down like a stream, and justice like a river'.[23] In response to these threats, Cromwell suggested his compromise first to the council of officers, then to a number of leading MPs. The Rump would dissolve itself immediately, leaving a council of forty or so men – some officers; some MPs – with executive authority; one of their responsibilities would be to inaugurate and police the elections for the new representative body.

In discussions on 19 April with selected MPs, Cromwell believed that he had their agreement that the Bill for the election of a reconstituted parliament would be dropped, and his alternative scheme recommended to the House. When he learned next day that, in an unusually full House, the Bill, far from being abandoned or postponed, was being expedited into law with 'preposterous haste', he was incensed.[24] Rushing to the House, he denounced the men who had betrayed his expectations and dissolved the Rump by military force. Cromwell's personal sense of betrayal is palpable. But what else lies behind his action? In the immediate aftermath of the dissolution, the army asserted positively that the contentious Bill included provision for the recruitment of the House; that existing MPs would have kept their seats, with numbers 'made up by others chosen, and by themselves approved of'.[25] This was a claim that was watered down in later army polemic and Cromwell's statements in justification of his action. Given that the Bill disappeared into Cromwell's pocket, it is impossible to know whether any of its substantive clauses directly tended to recruitment. But it seems very unlikely. More probably, the legislation entailed the continued session of the Rump until the new elections were held in November 1653, and empowered it to exercise a supervisory role over the credentials of those returned. With such authority, Rumpers, adjudicating disputed elections, might well have been sympathetic to the claims of their colleagues or others of their local allies, the 'disaffected, neuters, lawyers, or the like',[26] of whom the army complained. Could that be considered tantamount to recruiting?

What emerges unquestionably from the events in April is the slough of distaste, suspicion and disillusionment that had festered between the army and the Rump. The attempt to bulldoze the oft-delayed legislation through on the 20 April indicates the refusal of many MPs to kow-tow to the army. Confronted with that 'betrayal', the army lashed out with the violence that they had threatened against the civil power intermittently since Worcester.

In this fraught atmosphere of mutual antipathy serious issues were overlooked and essential discussion neglected. The army demanded a new representative assembly. But who would be elected? In November 1651 a religious radical and regicide, Colonel John Jones, diagnosed the problem neatly: the electorate, keenly 'sensible of their present burdens, and not of the reasons and necessity of them',[27] would vote for those who promised immediate tax cuts, not for those seen as responsible for the burdens. More time was needed for people to see the benefits of the new regime. The Rump should be recruited by by-elections, and it should adjourn for some periods, leaving the council to exercise executive authority. But this wise advice came from a commander of the forces in Ireland. His irenic common sense was not shared by his colleagues in the army in England, dealing directly with the Rump on a daily basis and obsessively aware of its flaws.

The army's increasingly jaundiced view of the Rump was a product of the latter's foot-dragging on the key issues of reform. We have already examined part of the explanation for this. The radicals, in their desire to achieve maximum support in the dark days of the winter of 1649, allowed themselves to be swamped by moderates and time-servers, and, particularly, lawyers, who stonewalled and filibustered to obstruct reform proposals from first to last. Radical schemes were anathema to men like Bulstrode Whitelocke, smugly rehearsing their own professional credentials, complacently praising the virtues of the English legal system, and savaging the anarchists who proposed subversive legislation such as that to ensure that proceedings in the courts should be in English.

The army increasingly understood that the members of the Rump were not designed to advance its reformist agenda. But they put a distinctive spin on this. They argued – and it is the stuff of Cromwell's venomous denunciation on 20 April – that the Rump was tainted: its seedy corruption explained both the refusal of MPs to contemplate serious schemes of social or ecclesiastical improvement and their tenacious attempt to cling to power.

Regimes that combine the invocation of high ideals with pomposity and self-interest are peculiarly susceptible to criticism and mockery. In 1654 Milton, who had turned against the Rump, slated the regime of which he had once held such hopes for its combination of a 'parade of insolence' with 'unprincipled peculations'.[28] The growing complacency of MPs is perhaps understandable: by 1651 the successes of the Rump's forces had swiftly changed the tone of international discussion. The Rump moved rapidly from pariah to be cosseted and feted by the great powers. Magnificent receptions, stage-managed by Charles I's old master of ceremonies, were organised for the ambassadors who competed for the favour of the regime. This gave offence to some of the radicals. Colonel John Jones wrote bitterly of the Rumpers and their hangers-on, 'affecting of titular dignities ... empty and scandalous, and serving no end but that of pride and vain glory, which God in our times bears testimony against'.[29] The second accusation, of peculation, had a number of dimensions. Outright bribery was frequently charged against MPs, who were sufficiently sensitive to the issue to expel, imprison and heavily fine one of their number, the unsavoury Lord Howard of Escrick, when charges of pocketing douceurs from royalist delinquents were proved against him. More typical and equally offensive was the Rump's exercise of its authority in the interests of individual members. They enjoyed their control over the pork barrel of patronage, solemnly voting themselves lands, offices and rewards. They furthered each other's interests with protections against creditors and interventions in personal legal disputes. The claims of creditors (a large group, including the public treasury) on the foppish aesthete Sir John Danvers were endlessly postponed; the House frequently interfered on his behalf in his protracted property dispute with his sister. Barely a week before the dissolution of the Rump, the radical MP John Weaver appealed formally to parliament. His father had virtually disinherited him, and he had sought to challenge the will in the court of Chancery; there, he argued, his case had not received a proper hearing and several of his witnesses had been rejected. John Lisle MP, one of the Chancery judges, rose to answer Weaver. He was delighted that the case had come to his colleagues' attention; they would see 'how equally matters are carried in that Court'. And he explained the reasons why Weaver's witnesses had been disqualified. But a stand-off between two MPs was neatly averted. Lisle confessed that, 'in my private judgement', Weaver had been badly treated in the matter of the will; he had not been able to attend his father in his sickness because he was serving the state in Ireland and had been neglected in the will. The Rumpers understood. The petition against Lisle and his colleagues' decision was dropped, while Weaver was granted an estate worth £250 a year out of land forfeited by royalists in Scotland.[30]

MPs also voted one another opportunities for private enrichment. Lord Craven's lands were seized by the Rump on a charge of his negotiating with Charles II, sustained only by the suborned evidence of a couple of destitute royalist officers. The various votes for the seizure of the estate in the House were close: Craven claimed that subsequently there was a gadarene rush of MPs who voted with the slim majority, who 'stepped in with the first to buy the flower of his estate' at significant undervalues.[31]

The Rump also became a by word for jobbery, for what American would call log rolling – the ability of well-organised interest groups to secure the legislation that they required through their connections in the House. The Rump swiftly became a bastion of corporate privilege and vested interest: lobbyists were more welcome than those with projects for the relief of debtors or law reform. Despite much rhetoric about encouraging economic growth through free trade, Acts confirming the monopolies and regulatory powers of London corporations were passed. So too was legislation reviving some of the Caroline fen-drainage projects in eastern England. The expropriated fenmen cited the denunciations of these earlier schemes in the Grand Remonstrance and the Rump's declared concern for property and legal rights in vain. A coterie of MPs with interests in such schemes packed the investigative committees, and then, in a thin House, 'when many of the uninteressed Parliament-men were absent', secured the passage of the Act for the Bedford Level.[32]

The army attributed the ease with which parliament could be manipulated by interest groups not only to the venality and weakness of individual MPs. It was also, they argued, a product of the regime's deficient institutional structure. The Rump combined a heady mix of legislative, executive and judicial power that the Levellers and Ireton had already diagnosed and challenged in the Long Parliament in 1647. Cromwell, in his later criticisms of the Rump, frequently reverted to this theme. The defences of personal liberty and property were 'pitiful' in circumstances when 'the Legislature is perpetually exercised, when the Legislative and Executive powers are always the same'.[33] This weakness is apparent in the Rump's handling of Weaver's case, but, ironically, it was the old Leveller leader, John Lilburne, whose experiences of the failure to separate powers in the Rump were most obviously 'pitiful'. Sir Arthur Hesilrige, the Rump's carpetbagger 'boss' in the north east, sequestered a Durham colliery on the grounds that its owner was a royalist, and then leased the property to the officers of his regiment at a considerable undervalue. Lilburne's family insisted that they had a legal interest in the major part of the property, but Hesilrige and his tame local committee dismissed their claim. John Lilburne, representing his family, sought relief from the Committee of Compounding. Several of its members owed their lucrative appointments to Hesilrige's patronage; Sir Arthur attended the committee hearings, 'sweating, foaming and domineering', successfully browbeating his nominees into allowing him a series of procedural advantages, and then, by a slim four to three majority, into dismissing the Lilburnes' case.[34] Lilburne thereupon published a vitriolic account of the proceedings and petitioned parliament. Upon receipt of the petition, the Rump declared it and the pamphlet scandalous, and, without any formal charge or hearing, fined Lilburne £7000 and banished him from England, with the threat of a death penalty should he dare to return.

This was a spectacular *cause célèbre*, but more generally the Rump's combination of executive and legislative power enhanced delays, confusion and, most damagingly, the erosion of ideals. MPs became enmeshed in the routines of business. The religious visionary Sir Henry Vane immersed himself in the diurnal business of the administration of the navy, and his radical aspirations were eroded; the active regicide Miles Corbett revelled in the trappings and power that he enjoyed as the chairman of the Sequestration Committee. Both men ceased to be assiduous in their attendance at the House.

The Rump for all its populist and Commonwealth rhetoric looked increasingly like a narrow oligarchy, clinging to power for reasons of personal aggrandisement. This was the line advanced by the army in justifying the coup that overthrew it. But MPs might legitimately answer that such an account was hypocritical. It seriously neglected the army's own role as a barrier to reform.

The Rump might recognise that, as a royalist commentator observed, 'what the Army will doe, must be done'.[35] But pragmatic compliance was increasingly delayed and resentful. Men who had been courted assiduously by the smooth ambassadors of the European powers did not take kindly to the cloudy exhortations of the soldiers. The report of every victory before the autumn of 1652 became an opportunity, it seemed, for the commanders to criticise the Rump's foot dragging and tepid commitment to reform, and the pressure became relentless after Worcester. Formal petitions, public prayer meetings, private representations, leaks to the press – all, despite the predilection for the vague and cloudy language of religious zeal, emphasised the army's commitment to the public welfare, and hinted at the Rump's corruption. Even the timid and temporising Whitelocke rebuked Cromwell with some asperity about the Army's 'petitioning ... with their swords in their hands'.[36] The army and its generals were, as Sir Peter Wentworth reminded Cromwell in the bitter exchanges that marked the dissolution of the House on 20 April, the Rump's servants 'who they had so highly trusted and obliged'.[37] The army might intermittently acknowledge this subordinate status. Cromwell, reporting the victory at Inverkeithing, wrote of the Rump as 'you who we serve, as the authority over us', but only as a preface to another pointed injunction that MPs should work with 'uprightness and faithfulness ... that common weal more and more be sought'.[38]

There was more than just wounded *amour propre* in the Rump's growing and ultimately suicidal antipathy to the army. The needs of defence from 1649–51 had, as we have seen, compelled the Rump to establish an efficient military machine. Their efforts were hugely successful, yet there was an obvious downside: the cost was astronomical. To fund its military operations, the Rump could employ the proceeds of the sale of the lands of the church (£1,850,000), the Crown (£2,350,000), and of those royalists whose lands remained under sequestration (£1,230,000), though much of this was assigned to pay off arrears and debts generated before 1649. Taxation was the major source of revenue, and the Rump improved the collection and administration of all the elements in its tax package – customs, excise and the monthly assessment. But increased administrative efficiency did not lead to any reduction in the rates charged on taxpayers. The regressive excise, the target of army as well as Leveller hostility in 1647 and 1648, remained an 'intolerable' burden on the 'shoulders of the poor' in the opinion of radicals.[39] The assessment was set at £90,000 a month in March 1649; the plan was to reduce this to £60,000 at the end of the year, but this scheme was postponed and then wholly abandoned. By the autumn of 1650 the assessment stood at £120,000 a month, and rose to £150,000 during the crisis of the Scots invasion in the summer of 1651; after Worcester, the assessment was cut to £90,000, but this proved premature. In December 1652, with the expenses of the naval war against the Dutch mounting, it reverted to £120,000.

The need to maintain a huge military force, and to maintain it well, had obvious adverse effects on other aspects of the Rump's policies and on its general reputation. The priority given to the interests of the army and navy meant that the regime's civilian creditors were poorly treated. At the end of 1652 the excise was producing £300,000 annually; debts of £378,000 were charged against this sum, but the money was needed for immediate expenditure and those owed money by the government were put off again and again; they were still clamouring for repayment in 1660. In consequence money men were reluctant to invest in government loans. Again, the Rump sought, intermittently, to secure the support of ex-royalists by following a policy of pardon and oblivion for previous political opposition. Yet this policy was undermined as the need for cash encouraged the regime to detect 'royalists', often on technicalities and very dubious evidence, and condemn their estates. This became another source of conflict with the army, who resented the Rump's readiness, in their efforts to widen the net, to renege on the terms of surrender negotiated by its field commanders. But more generally troubling about the Rump's reliance on high and regressive taxation was the damage done to its credentials as a regime committed to anything resembling social reform. Intermittent proposals for the reorganisation of the poor law, or the protection of debtors struck some observers as merely cosmetic, far less beneficial to the public than an end to swingeing taxation. Massive taxation might secure the Rump from its overt enemies, but it was not going to win any battles for the hearts and minds of the populace.

MPs knew this. In the face of army pressure, they might legitimately riposte that, despite its endless, cloudy exhortations, it was the army itself that was the barrier to reform. Social reform, in particular, was chimerical as long as taxes had to be raised to pay a vast and, after September 1651, increasingly unnecessary army. Tax cuts were imperative, and this would require the large-scale disbandment of forces or, perhaps, cuts in pay of 20 to 25 per cent. The Rump contemplated such policies, only to shy away from them. Such discussion was deeply resented in the army, as were the very occasional money-saving schemes that the Rump did inaugurate. In January 1652, following the premature death of Ireton, the Rump appointed Major-General Lambert as lord deputy in Ireland; in May, in a cost-paring exercise, they reorganised the

Irish administration, offering Lambert the less prestigious and less profitable post of commander-in-chief. Lambert refused the post, encouraged in his rejection by his colleagues' expressed concern for 'honest John Lambert' who had been 'so ungratefully treated'.[40]

The army's petition to parliament on 12 August 1652 is a nice illustration of the tension between the soldiers and the Rump over the question of reform. Historians usually consider the petition, published as a tract and widely reported in the press, as moderate in its demands. It is doubtful that MPs thought it so, as its implicit message is absolutely clear: the Rump was a fiscally irresponsible, utterly corrupt regime. The soldiers demanded, as part of a wider package that included law reform and the abolition of tithes, that a series of money-saving exercises should be undertaken. All these latter clauses raised questions on the Rump's stewardship and probity. A more coherent treasury structure, staffed by 'honest and able persons', and able to produce frequent accounts was a necessity. The mismanagement of the excise must be investigated. Loans to parliament, particularly those made by the poor, should be repaid before grants from the revenue were made to reward 'particular persons'. A committee, with no MPs among its members, should be appointed to consider the charge on the public funds occasioned by monopolies, 'plurality of places of profit', sinecures and inflated salary claims.[41] It was a savage indictment. Yet in the course of the discussions leading up to the petition, some in the army may have wished to go further. On 10 August a tract was published that may represent an earlier stage in discussions among the officers, the programme of a more radical faction among them, or merely the enthusiasm of a well-informed radical journalist. It repeated more vigorously both the godly rhetoric and the positive demands of the petition eventually presented, but also demanded – so that 'the poor may no longer be insulted by the rich' – that 'all oppressions and taxes [be] taken off'.[42] Tax cuts! This was either very naïve or exceptionally cynical. But perhaps no more cynical than the milder petition presented, with its suggestion that some marginal exercises in fiscal restructuring were a necessary element of reform. A few well-paid MP sinecurists did not massively inflate the tax bill: where were the taxes going if not to support an army of some 50,000 men? The army itself was the major barrier to the social reform it so incessantly demanded.

7

Why Was Oliver Cromwell
Offered the Crown?

In January 1657, in response to an unsuccessful assassination attempt against Oliver Cromwell, members of the Second Protectorate Parliament, then in session, suggested the Lord Protector be requested to take up 'the government according to the ancient constitution', to preserve liberties by setting them on an 'old and tried foundation'.[1] The request encoded in this language took greater formality in late February, when an MP presented a paper 'tending to the settlement of the nation and of liberty and property'.[2] Its major planks were that Cromwell should become king, and a bicameral legislature be established. On 31 March a new constitution that embodied both these features, was formally offered to Cromwell by the Parliament in the Humble Petition and Advice. After five weeks' discussion Cromwell refused the title of king, though accepting almost all the other provisions of the document.

At one level this spectacular incident is just another of a string of abortive schemes to construct a viable government after the dismissal of the Rump. After the dissolution power devolved upon the council of officers, but they were eager to re-establish civilian government, and, after some argument, it was agreed to invest power in the hands of a 'parliament'. The one hundred and forty-four members of the latter, men 'fearing God, and of approved fidelity and honesty', were handpicked by the army officers after informal consultations with the sectarian congregations in the localities. The Nominated Assembly also known, sardonically, as the Parliament of Saints or, playing on the name of one of its godly members, Praise-God Barbon, as the Barebones Parliament, met in July 1653 and survived until the following 12 December. Its members were split between radical reformers and more cautious moderates who favoured piecemeal and limited change, and little was achieved in increasingly acrimonious debate between the two groups. Eventually, the moderates staged a coup: arriving early at the House they voted their own dissolution, and then went in a body to Whitehall to surrender their authority to Cromwell. His readiness to accept their decision, and very probable involvement in this charade, stemmed in part from disappointment at the infighting within the parliament, in part from the availability of an alternative constitutional settlement. This, the Instrument of Government, had been designed by General John Lambert, who had ostentatiously avoided involvement with the Nominated Assembly, in consultation with other moderates. By its terms, Oliver Cromwell, was appointed head of state with the title Lord Protector; he was formally offered the position on 13 December. As Protector, Cromwell was empowered, with the advice and agreement of a powerful council of state, to legislate and to raise money. These initiatives were to be approved by the votes of a unicameral elected parliament when it first sat.

Parliament, in accordance with the Instrument, met on the 3 September 1654 – the anniversary of Cromwell's victories at Dunbar and at Worcester. Despite the choice of such an auspicious day, the parliament was wholly abortive. None of Cromwell's legislation was approved; no taxes were voted. Fearful that parliament's intransigence was encouraging the plotting of both royalist and radical opponents of the regime, and, worse, was encouraging disaffection in the army, Cromwell dissolved the House at the earliest opportunity. A period of conciliar rule that defied the terms of the Instrument followed. Money was raised and legislation enforced without parliamentary warrant. The sense of arbitrary rule was enhanced when, in the summer of 1655, the administration of the localities was placed under the supervision of military governors, the major-generals. Yet civilian and constitutionalist sentiment was still strong, not least in Cromwell himself and among his intimates, and in the summer of 1656, a parliament, elected in accordance with the Instrument was again summoned. That parliament did little positive for four months until, in the new year, the extraordinary proposal of offering Cromwell the crown was advanced.

There has been much discussion as to why Cromwell refused the proffered crown, but two questions are far less frequently considered. Why was Cromwell offered the title, king, in the first place? And secondly, an issue that turns on the answer to the first question, why did the new settlement, kingship in all but name, fail?

The MPs who offered the crown provided an exceptionally well reasoned justification for the move in their discussions with Cromwell concerning the Humble Petition. They insisted that the law recognised the regal title, and defined the rights and the duties that appertained to the office: 'the whole body of the law is carried upon this wheel, it ... runs through the whole life and veins of the law'. And 'by the law I can say in all generations, this is mine and this is the prince's, and the prince cannot do me wrong, nor the council do me wrong'.[3] Cromwell's current title, Lord Protector, was extra-legal and thus potentially arbitrary. Glynne, the lord chief justice, put it well in an imagined conversation:

> If so be your Highness should do any act, and one should come and say, 'My Lord Protector, why are you sworn to govern by the law, and you do thus and thus?' 'Do I? Why, how am I bound to do?' 'Why, the king could not have done so.' 'Why, but I am not king, I am not bound to do as the king, I am Lord Protector: shew me that the law doth require me to do it as Protector. If I have not acted as Protector, shew me where the law is.'[4]

Kingship was known to the law; the nation wanted the old title so they 'may know your duty to them, and they their duty to you'. This last point is often reiterated by the parliamentary deputation: 'the law knows not a Protector, and requires no obedience from the people to him'.[5] The Second Protectorate Parliament was making a brave attempt to recover, after fifteen years of war and experiment, the formulae that had been invoked by the opponents of the forced loan and ship money, and which had been articulated by the Long Parliament as they demolished the claims and institutional framework of Charles's government in 1641. The ancient constitution and its legal integument were the only conceivable framework for the British polity.

It is hardly surprising that this juridical, legalistic argument was offered primarily by eminent lawyers: Lord Commissioner Whitelocke, Lord Chief Justices Glynne and St John, and Master of the Rolls Lenthall. The legal delegation in the spring of 1657 spoke easily of a popular mandate for the views they were advancing: 'You are called upon ... by the whole people ... by a general and universal consent of the people.'[6] Such statements are hardly convincing, but the attitudes that the lawyers expressed were not unique to their profession. They were supported by a large majority of MPs – 'a sort of lukewarm indifferent country knights, gentlemen and citizens'.[7] We get some sense of the priorities of these men in a series of clever, cutting pen-portraits by one of their opponents: 'Sir John Hubbard, knight baronet of the old stamp, a gentleman of Norfolk, of a considerable estate ... meddled very little, if at all, in throwing down kingship, but hath stickled very much in helping to re-establish and build it up again; and a great Stickler among the late Kinglings, who petitioned the Protector to be King.' Sir Richard Onslow, recognised in 1657 as 'the head of the country party for kingship', was another wealthy knight 'of the old stamp', who had been MP for Surrey in the Long Parliament until imprisoned at Pride's Purge. He was, thought the jaundiced commentator, 'fully for Kingship, and was never otherwise ... And seeing he cannot have young Charles, old Oliver must serve his turn, so he have one.'[8]

We can understand why this group of legal conservatives and traditionalist country gentlemen could conceive of no system of government other than monarchy. But why did they imagine that Oliver Cromwell was an appropriate occupant of this, to them, key office? Why did they think that King Oliver could possibly be a man who would exercise kingship in their interest? The simple answer is that by 1657 many political actors had become keenly aware of the bifurcated Jekyll and Hyde character of Cromwell. From the perspective of the 'kinglings', Cromwell-as-Hyde was a military dictator and the charismatic leader of the radical religious zealots, men who could nerve themselves execute Charles I by claiming a providential mandate for their actions. But he was also Dr Jekyll: a Huntingdonshire squire, who shared the education, cultural assumptions, experience and aspirations of the gentry. In 1654 he evoked 'the ranks and orders of men, whereby England hath been known for hundreds of years: a nobleman, a gentleman, a yeoman ... That is a good interest of the nation and a great one'.[9] This was a man they could recognise, and with whom they believed, by 1656, they could deal.

In the 1650s Cromwell had given plenty of indications of his commitment to radical politics in various guises, and, in that measure, his unfitness for the crown. The millenarian language of the period of the king's execution was still employed: forms of government, he had said in 1647, were ephemeral, 'but dross and dung in comparison with

Christ', established and swept away in the tumultuous progress towards apocalypse. After the dissolution of the Rump, Cromwell, influenced by religious zealots within the army and their civilian supporters, seemed to act on this principle. Power was given to a hand-picked assembly of the godly, the so-called Parliament of Saints, and his speech at their installation was a fervid invocation of millenarian ideals.

> Truly you are called by God ... to rule with him and for him ... I confess I never looked to see such a day as this ... when Jesus Christ should be so owned as He is at this day and in this work. Jesus Christ is owned at this day by your call ... This may be the day to usher in the things which God has promised, which have been prophesied of; which he has set the hearts of His people to wait and expect ... You are at the edge of the promises and the prophecies.[10]

Thus encouraged the assembly undertook a vigorous programme of law reform (approving the abolition of the court of Chancery after a day's debate), challenged the status of the universities, and began to tinker with the system of publicly funded parochial churches, threatening the continuance of tithes and lay patronage.

Cromwell the religious fanatic was a spectre of the 1650s; so too was Cromwell the military dictator. He indicated his commitment to the continued role of the army in English national life on a number of occasions. The Rumpers' discussions of demobilising elements of the army and cutting the pay of those retained in service was, as we have seen, an important element in their dissolution in April 1653. The 'evil intents' of some of the members of the Nominated Parliament to cut army pay was one of the reasons given by the moderates for the surrender of their authority back to Cromwell. The First Protectorate Parliament pursued a similar agenda, proposing the demobilisation of almost half of the army, cutting the taxation earmarked for its maintenance, and reducing the soldiers' pay by 20 per cent. When the parliament was hastily dissolved in February 1655, Cromwell's resentment at the treatment of the soldiers was palpable; he claimed that MPs had deliberately 'starved' the army, 'putting it upon free quarter'.

Cromwell's religious zeal and the privileged place that he accorded the army in his regime came together in a project that horrified the gentry: the rule of the major-generals. In 1655, in response to an abortive royalist rising and the complete failure of the local militias to deal with it, the country was divided into eleven military districts, each headed by a trusted officer, supported by local committees consisting of godly activists. The tasks of this new structure of local government were, first, to prevent royalist insurrections, largely by reorganising and improving the military effectiveness of the local forces. Secondly, to raise a new tax on the royalists, the decimation, which was to pay for this new militia. Finally, to pursue a policy of 'godly reformation': drunkenness, swearing and sabbath-breaking were to be policed and punished; popular recreations, such as bear-baiting and cock-fighting, were to be suppressed, as were ale houses; vagrants and the unemployed were to be ferreted out and forced to work. The major-generals and the local committees publicly enthused at the opportunities presented by the third strand of their commissions. Major-General Boteler reported the eagerness of the Bedfordshire committee to 'make it their business to find out and give me notice of all the prophane and idle gentry and others whose lives are a shame to a Christian Commonwealth'; 'how greedily we shall put down prophaneness', he gloated.[11] Worsley, the most vigorous of the major-generals in the enforcement of the moral agenda, triumphantly reported that in Lancashire 'God hath already put into his people a praying spirit for this great and good work'.[12] The godly mayor of Coventry sent out his militia horsemen each week to round up those travelling on the Sabbath. A servant of Lady Archer was arrested, travelling to buy accoutrements for the speedy funeral of her son, who had died of smallpox and whose rotting body could 'not be kept longer': the mayor consulted three ministers before agreeing that this was a legitimate excuse for travel on a Sunday.[13] It was this third task, with its potential for interference in local government and in the traditional sociability of the gentry, which most appalled the traditional rulers of the counties. 'All sport put down,' wailed Henry Verney, 'the gentry not permitted to meet.'[14]

Godly fanatic; military dictator: Cromwell's credentials as a prospective monarch seemed doubtful. Yet there was another side to the man that gave 'the kinglings' hope that they could woo him to the alternative role. Oliver's continued traditionalism and his powerful desire for a permanent consensual settlement were clearly apparent to observers, in both the tone and the personnel of the regime.

From the inauguration of the Protectorate, official ceremonies and the settings in which these took place were a clear attempt to attach to

The Great Seal of the Protectorate of 1655. It includes a number of traditional monarchical features. The six-barred helmet of a king has the imperial crown upon it; and the crowned lion of England is employed twice in the design.
(*Bodleian Library*)

Cromwell, as the chief magistrate, the symbols and majesty associated with a monarchical regime. The Venetian ambassador reported that 'the obsequious and respectful form observed to the late king' was the model for ceremony after 1654.[15] This aspect of the fashioning of the regime was most apparent in the audiences of foreign dignitaries. Cromwell sat enthroned in the Banqueting House, that temple of Stuart monarchical pretension; the ambassadors approached in a series of choreographed genuflexions, and addressed Cromwell with the most sedulous respect as 'Your Most Serene Highness'.[16] As Protector, Cromwell exercised some of the prerogatives of the crown as the fountain of honour. Foreign ambassadors and supporters of the regime were knighted by him. In June 1655 a new great seal was cut: above the heraldic arms of the Commonwealth, differenced by Cromwell's personal coat of arms, was placed the six-barred helmet of monarchy and an imperial crown. The ambience of royal magnificence surrounding Cromwell, the furniture – paintings, tapestries, rich carpets – and ceremony of a royal court, troubled the godly. Mary Netheway even took exception to the classical statues, 'those monstres', which decorated Cromwell's garden at Hampton Court, reminding him that 'wils the grofes and altars of the idels remaynd untaken away in Jerusalem, the routh of God continued against Israel.'[17]

The traditionalist ambience created by furniture and ceremony was enhanced by the character of those who became the Protector's intimate servants. Moderates were welcomed to his court and increasingly played key roles in it. John Claypole, Oliver's son-in-law and the master of the horse, was a typical country gentleman whose major interests involved hunting, and breeding fighting dogs; the pious Lucy Hutchinson thought him debauched and ungodly. Sir Gilbert Pickering, chamberlain of the household, and Sir Charles Wolseley were godly men, but both were 'knights of the old stamp.' Wolseley was the son of an active royalist and had 'come something late into play on this side'. Pickering had deliberately abandoned sitting at the trial of Charles I and refused the loyalty oath propagated by the Rump. His elaborate dress sense and personal mannerisms also galled the radicals; he was 'so finical, spruce, and so like an old courtier'.[18] Such men at the heart of the Cromwellian court must have looked comfortably familiar to conservatives.

Local government appointments displayed a similar trend and

potential. The JPs appointed by the Nominated Parliament were a group of godly zealots, chosen from outside the charmed circle of traditional authority. It was such men who were again empowered in the summer of 1655 to act as the assistants to the major-generals. But in the interim, with the establishment of the Protectorate, Cromwell invited some of the old rulers of the localities to take up their posts in local government. The early 1654 commission of the peace nominated Presbyterians and country gentry who had been laid aside by, or refused to serve under, the Rump; even some heirs of royalist families were offered the opportunity to serve.

The tone and personnel of the Protectoral regime suggested the traditionalist elements of Cromwell's agenda. What of his policies from 1654? In this, the most important area, there were clear indications that Cromwell shared aspects of both the conservatism of the gentry and of their desire for a settlement on conventional lines. These characteristics could be viewed both in his religious agenda (if in an attenuated form) and in relation to political structure and the constitution.

By 1654 Cromwell had broken with the godly zealots whose aspirations he had encouraged in the calling of the Nominated Parliament. When that body proceeded beyond vague aspirations and began to strike down aspects of the legal and ecclesiastical systems without providing replacements, Cromwell's nerve failed; he reverted to the attitudes of a Huntingdonshire country gentleman, and the assembly was dissolved in mid-December 1653. By April 1657 Cromwell looked back on the whole regrettable incident as 'a story of my weakness and folly ... done in my simplicity'.[19]

The zealots did not view the dissolution in such rueful terms. The events in the spring and summer of 1653 had inspired godly radicals. 'The day of the accomplishment of the Promises ... is dawned', enthused a group of Kentish magistrates, echoing Cromwell's own speech. The hopes of Christopher Feake's congregation in London were expressed in a triumphant hymn written by their minister

> With trembling wee rejoice to see
> Proud Babylon down fall

Ironically, lacking politically correct music, Feake had been obliged to set his messianic words to 'Prelatical Tunes'.[20] So the dissolution of the

Cromwell's identification with the king. In 1655 Pierre Lombart, a French engraver, was paid £20 by the Council for 'several portraits' of Oliver Cromwell. This engraving was clearly inspired by Van Dyck's 1633 equestrian portrait of Charles I attended by his Master of the Horse, one of the great icons of Stuart monarchy. In 1660 Lombart returned to France and, ironically, erased the head of Cromwell from the plate, replacing it by that of Louis XIV. (*Ashmolean Museum, Oxford*)

Nominated Parliament and the establishment of the Protectorate stunned the religious radicals, and drove many of them to outright opposition against the new regime and the apostate who headed it. A week after the dissolution Vavasor Powell, who invited his congregation to pray, 'Lord, wilt Thou have Oliver Cromwell or Jesus Christ to reign over us?', identified Cromwell with Antichrist and Babylon.[21] Similar invective was a continual ground throughout the next five years, enhanced by Cromwell's legislation as Protector that upheld both the basic structure of a national church and tithes as a means of funding it. In the spring of 1655 John Rogers, imprisoned in Windsor Castle, preached that 'the Government was Antichristian, a limb of the Whore and the Beast, that all who are under it are upholders of Babel, Antichrist, Whore, Beast, and shall be destroyed suddenly'.[22] In an interview with 'the Great Man', Rogers told the Protector to his face 'by the word of the Lord, in the majesty, might, strength, power, vigour, life and authority of the Holy Ghost, I can, do, and dare judge you and your actions'.[23] This and similar 'fantastic stuff' tricked out in bloodthirsty biblical rhetoric – 'I will whet my glittering sword ... I will make mine arrows drunk with blood' (Deuteronomy 32: 41, 42) was a favoured text – encouraged a small group of the militant godly to organise a rising, easily crushed in the spring of 1657.[24]

Cromwell's flirtation with the godly radicals was over. He imprisoned their leaders and cashiered army officers who supported them. These developments, and his concern for the maintenance of an effective national church structure and the retention of tithes, were pleasing news to the conservatives. But Cromwell did not move entirely into their camp. As the commission to the major-generals showed, he was still prepared to employ state power to uphold the old puritan programmes of moral reformation. Nor did he abandon his commitment to the centrality of religious toleration for all Christians whose beliefs did not threaten the state. He told Rogers that his role in relation to the zealots of the sects was as a constable. 'I tell you there wants brotherly love, and the several sorts of forms would cut the throats one of another should I not keep the peace.'[25] This position, far more passive than that asserted in the heady rhetorical flights of July 1653, still went too far for moderates, troubled by the proliferation of the sects, and the social subversion which they associated with them.

The sense of a moderate side to Cromwell's convictions with the potential for further development, hinted at in his changing religious agenda, was more apparent in relation to the constitutional system and political structure. In late December, after the self-destruction of the Nominated Parliament, Cromwell was offered the office of Lord Protector with his authority set out in a written constitution, the Instrument of Government. The proposal recalled the vigorous period of discussion between the Levellers and Ireton at the end of 1648, and much of its substance and language was lifted from the version of the Agreement of the People recommended to the Rump by the army officers of January 1649. Legislative power was located in a triennial parliament, its credentials as a representative assembly enhanced by a rationalised constituency structure and a new franchise. The Lord Protector only had the power to delay the passage of legislation – there was to be no absolute veto. Executive authority was shared by the Protector and a council, and the latter was in some measure answerable to the parliament. As in the Agreement, there was a suspicion that even a well-constituted representative assembly could be seduced by power, and transmute, as had the Long Parliament and then the Rump, into an arbitrary oligarchy. So the Instrument included clauses severely limiting parliament's actions as a judicial tribunal, and insisting that parliament could not legislate in matters of religion contrary to the broad tolerationist principles that were embodied in the constitution. More generally, parliament was denied the right to alter the balance of constitutional power as set out in the Instrument.

The Instrument repudiated the charismatic claims to government of the *soi-disant* saints; it also sought to avoid the arbitrary authority of a 'representative' body permanently in session and conjoining legislative, executive and judicial power. It was a settlement rooted firmly in recent experience and conventional assumptions about the nature of political authority. It was as a workable settlement that Cromwell presented it to his first parliament meeting under the Instrument. Emphasising the 'changings and turnings ... all those turnings and tossings' of the previous years, he invited the country gentry arrayed before him to join him in a great cooperative effort: 'the end of your meeting, the great end ... Healing and Settling'.[26]

But parliament would have none of it. Immediately the session began

MPs attacked the Instrument, and in little over a week Cromwell had to insist that those who continued to sit in the House should sign a recognition acknowledging that three aspects of the settlement were non-negotiable. These 'fundamentals' were that government was to be by a single person and parliament; control over the army, in particular, was to be so conjoined. Secondly, that parliament could not legislate to perpetuate itself. Finally, that the liberty of conscience enshrined in the Instrument could not be touched. Some three hundred MPs ultimately took their seats under these terms, but they were still not much disposed to cooperate. Neither legislation nor money Bills were passed while MPs tinkered with the Instrument clause by clause. Much time was spent on fine-tuning extremely peripheral issues – whether the franchise should be extended to copyholders – and on procedural wrangling. Worse, the MPs consistently worried at and sought to erode the fundamental elements that Cromwell had declared off limits, asserting, if not parliamentary sovereignty, a far greater role for the institution than that guaranteed in the Instrument. So parliament claimed control over appointment to the Protectoral council, and insisted that counsellors were answerable to them.

Tempers wore thin as this war of sniping and ambush continued. On 10 November, discussing the issue of Cromwell's power to veto proposed legislation that was clearly contrary to the fundamentals, the House voted that the Protector should have a veto in matters that were to be subsequently enumerated by parliament. Cromwell's supporters, who asserted that such veto powers were intrinsic in the list of fundamentals, were furious. 'We had,' they snarled, 'as much as a vote could do, unmade the Protector.' This intemperate overreaction indicates the 'jealousies' and distrust that divided the House. The debate also provoked a devastating intervention from Major-General Desborough: why, he asked, was Parliament 'reluctant to trust the Lord Protector with the half, that not long since had the whole, and might have kept it without any competitor ... yet he hath given us some part of it?'[27] This was a public relations disaster: it reminded MPs of what they knew only too well: that they sat by kind permission of Cromwell and the army. The Instrument of Government had been produced by John Lambert and his friends as the Nominated Parliament careered into oblivion. Why should a cabal of army officers meeting in some smoke-filled room have the power to impose a constitution on the nation, and deny a right in the representative of the people to discuss its central tenets? Edmund Ludlow thought the Instrument a 'work of darkness', 'in a clandestine manner carried on and huddled up by two or three persons'. Such a view was not the prerogative of unbending republicans: in 1657 a conservative, Downing, scornfully dismissed the Instrument: 'Government is not to be made by six men'.[28]

That the Instrument had no proper constitutional standing, no status, was one major source of the hostility of MPs to it. The other was that it was made by, and in the interests of, the army. The Instrument contained a provision for a standing army of thirty thousand men. This was a major rock of offence, and the First Protectorate Parliament edged around it, aware that outright programmatic attack might be counter-productive. Control of the militia in the Protector and parliament was one of the fundamentals. But what was to happen after Cromwell's death? In a vote of 22 September it was hinted that the arrangement might terminate then and power be vested in parliament alone, and this was made explicit on the 17 November. In January parliament insisted that the local militias, as distinct from the professional forces, should be under parliamentary control. But while the constitutional issue was never directly confronted, parliament did use its financial leverage to shift the balance of effective authority. Again, there was no direct challenge to the Instrument's provision for an army of thirty thousand men, but parliament chose to view the additional troops in service (some twenty-seven thousand) as supernumerary, and anticipated their rapid disbandment. It cut the pay of the army, refused to vote permanent taxation for its maintenance, and reduced the rates of taxation to a level well below that required to fund the surviving troops properly. In 1654–55 the majority of MPs resented both the army and the Instrument as an essentially army document. Their continued hostility led Cromwell to dissolve the parliament as soon as he could within the terms of the Instrument, with neither a tax package nor any public legislation passed.

Parliament had rejected the settlement proffered them by Cromwell, and had unleashed another round of arbitrary government. What followed, the rule of the major-generals, made the intransigence of the MPs seem deeply counter-productive. By rejecting the Instrument, the conservatives had almost compelled Cromwell to act out their worst nightmares, to take up the uncongenial position of a military dictator. Yet some of their leaders may have done it because they recognised how strong the desire for a settlement was in Cromwell: their wholesale rejection of the Instrument might bring him again to the negotiating table, and on more acceptable terms. Certainly the failure of the First Protectorate Parliament made some of Cromwell's inner circle, men who had defended the Instrument in 1654–55, contemplate a more creative approach. And their efforts were to be seconded by MPs who had been at the forefront of the dismantling and revision of that document.

Lawyers, even those in government employ, seem to have deliberately emphasised the dubious status of the regime after parliament's dissolution, and – more than a subtext – the preferability of an alternative settlement. The Instrument had given Cromwell the power to promulgate ordinances and to raise money on his own authority until the sitting of parliament, which was then to formalise these enactments. This the First Protectorate Parliament had notably failed to do, leaving the Cromwellian legislation in a constitutional limbo. This situation created a conundrum for the government lawyers in the aftermath of a royalist insurrection, Penruddock's rising, in the west country in March 1655. The insurgents were easily suppressed, but questions arose over their trial and punishment. What offence had they committed? Cromwell had issued a treason ordinance in the first month of the new regime's existence, but it had not been approved by parliament. Was it still valid? The statute of Edward III, and the common law that had developed around it, defined treason as an offence against the king. The indictments drawn against Penruddock and his accomplices cost Attorney-General Prideaux and his legal team much thought. They relied heavily on detailed narrative and repetitive verbiage, downplaying the vexed question of treason, and focusing on the levying of war as contrary to the 'force of the statute in such case made and provided'. Quite what this referred to was not addressed. Some of the judges remained uneasy, as did the local juries empanelled to hear the cases. Lawyers advised the accused to emphasise the vague and unspecific formulae of the charge in their defence: they should insist 'boldly' that 'the laws of England cannot be changed but by Act of Parliament ... there can be no treason to bear arms against the Lord Protector'.[29] Penruddock and his accomplices were eventually convicted, but the participants in a ludicrously mismanaged and wholly abortive royalist plot in Yorkshire escaped when the judges refused to categorise their actions as treason. A member of the council of state sought to persuade the judges of 'the great concern of the business in hand', but had to admit his failure: 'the difficulty as yet seems incurable ... we cannot agree in principles'.[30] The two recalcitrant judges were dismissed.

A greater public embarrassment swiftly followed. In May 1655 George Cony, a merchant who had refused to pay customs duty and been imprisoned by the council for his temerity, sought habeas corpus. His barristers, an elite group of the leading practitioners, argued that the tax he had refused was illegal, because not approved in parliament, and that his imprisonment was illegal, as contrary to the Act of 1641 which had denied judicial competence to the privy council. Lord Chief Justice Rolle, whose scruples in the Penruddock case had worried the attorney-general, allowed them to air these subversive opinions without interruption and with apparent sympathy. The council acted swiftly; the barristers were imprisoned, and early retirement was arranged for Rolle.

Those who believed that Cromwell's desire for a settlement could survive the bitter collapse of the First Protectorate Parliament, and the move to arbitrary government in reaction to this and to the plots of the royalists and the radicals, could take some comfort in the developments of the next eighteen months. The Cromwellian regime in 1655 and the first half of 1656 was an odd jumble, both in tone and substance. While the major-generals and their zealous local committees rejoiced at the prospect of enforcing godliness and squeezing the royalists financially, they often found themselves frustrated by the Protector's failure to back them up, and his readiness to respond positively to royalist petitions for clemency. General taxation was raised, but by assessment commissioners who were deeply uneasy about the authority under which they acted. The government's law officers proceeded, but in ways that appeared almost to underline the dubious constitutional status of the Protector's authority. Cromwell's half-hearted move into tyranny was ultimately uncongenial to him. Faced with a financial crisis in the summer of 1656, he again summoned parliament. Again his opening speech emphasised cooperation and consensus.

THE QVAKERS DREAM:

O R,
The Devil's Pilgrimage in England :
BEING

An infallible Relation of their severalMeetings,

Shreekings, Shakings, Quakings, Roarings, Yellings, Howlings, Trem·
bligs in the Bodies, and Rimigs in the Bellies : With a Narrative of
their several Arguments, Tenets, Principles, and strange D ctrine : The
strange and wonderful Satanical Apparitions, and the appearing of the
Devil unto them in the likeness of a black Boar, a D g with flaming ey s,
and a black man without a head, causing the Dogs to bark, the Swine
to cry, and the Cattel to run, to the great admiration of all that shall
read the same.

London, Printed for G. Horton, and are to be sold at the Royal
Exchange in Cornhil, 1655.

Anti-Quaker propaganda: title page woodcut from *The Quakers Dream* (1655).
The Quakers were treated to denunciations in the popular press similar to
those accorded to the other radical sects, though they faced far greater official
hostility as their numbers grew rapidly. The faded quality of the four car-
toons that make up this frontispiece is a product of the images (though not
the speech bubbles) having been used twice before. They were first used in an
anti-Ranter tract of December 1651, *The Ranters' Declaration* – in which the
speech bubble in the fourth scene, of nude dancing, delightfully reads, 'Hey
for Christmas'. The block was then reused in a June 1651 tract directed against
a shadowy group of extremists, the Shakers, entitled *The Declaration of John
Robins, the False Prophet.* (*Britsh Library*)

His words were apparently undermined by the refusal to admit over a hundred of the elected MPs to the House – an odd mélange of committed republicans, Presbyterians and the scions of royalist families, selected for exclusion by the major-generals. But despite this shocking start to the session, conservative MPs and members of the council close to Cromwell sought to co-operate in the development of a more creative policy than had their predecessors in 1654–55. The MPs were ostensibly conciliatory: there was no immediate attack on the Instrument, and parliament passed new treason legislation and gave formal approval to the war against Spain. What they did not do was to vote money to fund that war. Despite the absence of a taxation package, the glacial slowness of their proceedings, and the time accorded private rather than public business, Cromwell chose to encourage them. The stasis in the House was, however, deceptive. It is clear from the correspondence of foreign ambassadors and of some of the Irish representatives, that a good deal of negotiation was occurring behind the scenes in relation to a major alteration in the constitutional status of the regime.

Early in December the silence concerning the status of the Instrument was finally broken, but in a highly oblique manner, when the case of James Nayler was brought to the attention of the House. Nayler, a leader of the Quaker movement, had, on 24 October, ridden into Bristol in a theatrical parody of Christ's entry into Jerusalem; he was. attended by a crowd of his adoring female disciples chanting 'Holy, Holy, Holy, Lord God of Sabaoth'. The Bristol magistrates arrested him and then forwarded the matter to parliament; a committee of MPs interrogated Nayler during November. Upon their report, the House was obliged to consider what should be done with him.

No doubt many MPs who insisted that Nayler's blasphemous charade would draw down the wrath of an offended deity firmly believed that only penalties of Mosaic rigour were appropriate to his case. No doubt many of the gentry were delighted with the prospect of savagely punishing the leader of a sect that was growing apace, and whose symbolic actions and ferocious rhetoric they viewed as subversive of social order and hierarchy. But the Nayler case had important political ramifications, which many leading MPs must have seen.

First, the elaborate pieces of street theatre favoured by the Quakers, their messianic language, and their furious denunciation of all other religious groups, offended some of the leaders of the army as much as they did conservative gentlemen and lawyers. The first to speak after the reading of the investigating committee's report was Major-General Philip Skippon, the 'Christian Centurion', a man of enormous moral authority, still suffering from the wounds he had received at Naseby. 'It has always been my opinion that the growth of these things is more dangerous than the most intestine or foreign enemies ... their principals strike at both magistracy and ministry ... Should we not be as jealous of God's honour as our own?' Death was the appropriate sentence. William Boteler, one of the most active and most hated among the major-generals, immediately seconded Skippon: the Quakers 'are despisers of your government, contemn your magistracy and ministry, and trample it under their feet'.[31] He specified stoning as the appropriate form of execution. But some of their colleagues in the army did not agree with their prescription. Desborough sought time for further consideration while Lambert insisted on the need for proper procedures. The country gentry and lawyer alliance must have rejoiced inwardly to see the military bloc, the men who encouraged Cromwell's radical and pro-military posture, so fractured.

Secondly, the Nayler case entailed, by implication, an attack on the Instrument. 'These Quakers, Ranters, Levellers, Socinians, and all sorts', complained Skippon, 'bolster themselves under thirty-seven and thirty-eight of Government.'[32] The fact that the clauses of the Instrument concerning liberty of conscience did not clearly condemn Nayler led MPs, determined on savage punishment, to ride roughshod over the entire constitution. A number of possible mechanisms to secure Nayler's condemnation were mooted, but ultimately the House agreed that it had inherited the judicial power of the House of Lords, and so could act as a high court, with almost limitless authority to define offences and determine punishments. This assertion that the power of parliament was a matter of precedent and was not circumscribed by the Instrument, resurrected the prospect of the worst excesses of the Rump. The decision to take this line, bypassing the restrictions of the Instrument, was encouraged by government lawyers – Glynne, Lenthall, Whitelocke – the men who had already hinted at the legal nakedness of the Protectorate in 1655. Parliament, despite the efforts of a vocal minority, spared Nayler's life. But he was branded, his tongue was bored through, and he was savagely whipped through the streets of London on the intrinsic authority of parliament asserted without reference to the constitutional scheme by which the MPs had been summoned.

Parliament's decision in the Nayler case represented both a covert blow against Lambert's constitutional settlement, and splintered the military bloc. The next incident entailed the humiliation of the army as a political force. On Christmas Day 1656, Desborough introduced a 'short Bill' to continue the decimation tax upon the royalists, and with it the new militia forces, and the role of major-generals and godly commissioners in local government. Desborough was seeking to take advantage of the thinness of the House, many of the country gentry having returned to their homes to celebrate the festivities of the season. The ploy worked; by a vote of 88 to 63 the House agreed that the Bill should be brought in next day. Mysteriously it was not. The Bill did not emerge until 7 January, immediately after Twelfth Night, when the revellers were returning from their Christmas celebrations, and it was in a different form from that originally proposed by Desborough. It ordered the levy of the decimation, but also implied, by granting legal indemnity to those who had acted in 1655–56, that the project had previously been illegal.

The debate, 'mettled and serious', begun on 7 January and continued intermittently, as a consequence of the Speaker's illnesses, concluded on the 29th with the Bill's rejection by 128 to 88 votes. Occasional explosions of bitter anti-army resentment from country gentlemen punctuated the debate, but the arguments of the major speakers against decimation were judicious and temperate. They argued that the project was contrary to the Rump's Act of Oblivion, granting amnesty to ex-royalists who had recognised the regime; that it punished both royalist plotters and those who lived quietly under the government; that it would create a group permanently disaffected to the government. These were themes close to Cromwell's stated intentions of 'healing and settling'. So too was their emphasis on the tendency of the major-generals to 'cantonise' the nation, to establish arbitrary military authorities that were destructive of England's tradition of a centralised state acting under a common law. The angry frustration of the army officers seethed throughout the debates. The suave offer of indemnity for their illegal activities roused them to particular fury: 'For the indemnity, we are much beholden to those gentlemen that would give it us', said Desborough sardonically, 'It is our swords must indemnify us. It is that must procure our safety.'[33] Their attempt to argue that their opponents were simply disaffected wreckers was undercut when, the day after striking down the Bill, the House voted a further £400,000 for the government.

These were the incidents – and the silences – in Cromwell's second Parliament that provide a context for the offer of the crown. Which political actors were responsible for this convoluted but creative development? It is not surprising to find the leaders of the country gentry hounding Nayler or denouncing the decimation tax. But men like the later 'kinglings' Hobart and Onslow, who had been at the forefront of the attack on the Instrument in 1654–55, did not play a similar aggressive role in 1656. Direct assault on the Instrument was eschewed by the gentry; rather they subtly emphasised the uncertainties and anomalies of the constitutional situation. A number of Cromwell's counsellors and officials began a cooperation with the country gentry that continued through the offer of the crown. It was their 'singular industry' and 'prudence' that was praised by an MP enthusiastically reporting the proposed settlement – 'there is much of English freedom in this constitution'.[34] The legal bloc, the men who were to present the constitutional argument for kingship to Cromwell, distanced themselves from military rule in the decimation debates and from the Instrument in their discussions of the legality of punishing Nayler. Among the civilian counsellors, Sir Charles Wolseley and Roger Boyle, Lord Broghill, president of the Cromwellian council governing Scotland, who had joined in defending the Instrument in 1654 often in confrontations with Onslow, stood out as men seeking to alter the constitutional basis of the regime in 1656 and 1657. Broghill was the chief of a group of Irish MPs who spoke and voted solidly against the military element, and his London residence was the centre for his organisation. In November, as rumours of the possibility of Cromwell taking the crown proliferated, it was noted that 'the Nights are very long at Cork house'.[35]

The most interesting figure in this period of indirect manoeuvre is Cromwell himself. In October and November he was aware of the behind the scenes suggestions of the need for a change in the constitutional structure, and sought to persuade the proponents of the

Instrument among his 'faithful servants' of his commitment to it.[36] But his tolerance of parliament's procrastination must have troubled those of his counsellors who sought to sustain the political influence of the army, and who were wedded to an inclusive interpretation of religious toleration. There is a strong sense of his attempt to be all things to all men in the autumn. His shift away from the military men and the Instrument became clearer at the turn of the year. All commentators found it significant that it was the Protector's squire son-in-law, John Claypole, who spoke first on the 7 January on the Bill for Decimation – and spoke against it. Perhaps more revealing was Cromwell's Christmas Day letter to the House, pretending ignorance of the fate of James Nayler (whose savage punishment had already begun) and asking by what authority they had acted in this case. This threw the cat among the constitutional pigeons, but the puzzled tone was *faux naïf*, and a measure of collusion must be suspected. Certainly several speakers, mostly lawyers, who had cheerfully condemned Nayler and subsequently favoured the offer of the crown, appear to have relished the opportunity to point out the inadequacy of the structure of authority established under the Instrument.

Throughout the first five months of parliament's sitting the civilians – lawyers; country gentry; the Irish squadron – sought to detach Cromwell from the military men who acted as a brake on his conservative sentiments. By 23 February they felt confident enough to offer their draft of an alternative settlement, a civilian constitution, rooted in tradition, custom and law, and authorised by parliament. Their success in wooing Cromwell, in nurturing the conservative side of his nature, appeared to be confirmed powerfully four days later. Cromwell met with a group of junior officers, presenting a petition against the title of king, who were joined by a team of army heavyweights, general officers led by Lambert. The latter's attempt to organise a unified army front was shattered by Cromwell, who used the occasion to excoriate the major-generals in front of a no doubt flabbergasted audience of their subordinates. He rehearsed the various policies that the army grandees had obliged him to undertake, and the dismal series of failures that had resulted. He defended the projected second House as a 'balancing power' against a sovereign unicameral chamber, reminding them 'the case of James Nayler might happen to be your own case'. He asked why

The apotheosis of Oliver Cromwell: 'The Embleme of England's Distractions as also her Attained and Further Expected Freedom and Happiness'. Probably by William Fairthorne (1658). Oliver Cromwell tramples the whore of Babylon and the serpents of Error and Faction, surrounded by symbols of the conspiracies he has overthrown and the peace he has brought. The three kingdoms, crowned and robed, offer him the victor's laurels. Cromwell's death limited the sales of the icon, but the plate, with a few minor alterations, was reused in 1689. Cromwell's head was erased and replaced with a portrait of William III.
(*Ashmolean Museum, Oxford*)

the title 'king' was now so offensive to the generals, when they had offered it to him in a early version of the Instrument (*that* information must have surprised many of the audience). He concluded with a powerful affirmation of the civilian position: the Instrument was demonstrably 'an imperfect thing'. 'It is time to come to a settlement and lay aside arbitrary proceedings, so unacceptable to the nation.'[37]

Cromwell had distanced himself from his army adherents, and shattered the united front they had sought to present against the civilians. Those who reported the meeting of 27 February were triumphant and confident. Too soon. The House debated the Humble Petition, passing the first clause (postponed to the end of the discussions) establishing the royal title by 123 to 62 votes after two days debate on 25 March. Cromwell was presented with the finished document on 31st; three days later, the Protector declared that he was unable to accept the scheme with the royal title. The surprised and dispirited 'kinglings' rallied sufficient support to vote to repeat their offer, and to discuss with Cromwell his objections to the document as a whole. In series of meetings with the Protector the lawyers emphasised the essential place of the king as the integument of the English constitution, while the House busied itself with refining other aspects of the project which Cromwell had challenged. On 30 April the revised document was forwarded to Cromwell. On 8 May Cromwell made the response that 'amazed his most real servants': 'I cannot undertake this government with the title of King.'[38]

The army leaders were triumphant; the 'kinglings' angry and disheartened. After this great climacteric, the commitment of many MPs waned. On 19 May it was agreed that the title Lord Protector should replace that of king, and the amended draft of the Humble Petition was passed by 54 to 50 on the 22nd; Cromwell accepted the revised document on the 25th. Parliament was then prorogued in June after passing some legislation and an Assessment Act; the MPs promised a 'richer vintage' to follow these 'few grapes' when they reconvened in the new year.

In the negotiations from February 1657 Cromwell had apparently achieved much: the anomalies and illegalities of rule under the Instrument were resolved. Parliament had voted a civilian constitution, backed by the authority of the representatives of the people; taxes could be raised and rebels punished without the corrosive questions of legal propriety. He had rejected the royal title, but many of the ancillary trappings of kingship were deployed to boost the new regime. On 26 June 1657 Cromwell was formally inaugurated as the head of state, seated on the throne of Edward I and wearing a robe of purple velvet lined with ermine, 'the habit anciently used at the solemn investiture of princes'. Next month one of Cromwell's supporters was given a hereditary peerage. The writ declared, 'Amongst other of the prerogatives which adorn the imperial crown of these nations none is of greater excellency or doth more amplify our favour than to be the fountain of honour.'[39] Unbending republicans were disgusted: Cromwell's court was 'more chargeable to the Commonwealth' than that of Charles I, snorted Colonel Alured.[40]

But Cromwell was *not* king, and the subsequent failure of the new constitution is in large part attributable to his rejection of the title. The country gentry, 'under great discouragement and discontent', left Westminster in droves after Cromwell's speech on 8 May. In consequence, a last-ditch attempt by the constitutionalists to define the powers and duties of the Lord Protector in terms of those previously appertaining to the king failed in a thin House. The proponents of this compromise argued that without it Oliver as Protector 'would be looked upon only as a military officer, and without all bounds and limits'.[41] This was indeed the common perception, but less, one senses, because of the legalistic argument than because the gentry recognised why Cromwell had rejected their offer and the degree to which they had failed to nurture the traditionalist, conservative side of his personality. Cromwell ultimately could not desert his old military and godly allies. They had responded to the offer of the crown with a torrent of sermons, petitions and letters against this 'fearful apostasy'. They appealed to Cromwell's common experience with them of God's power in the past, reminding him that the opponents of kingship were 'those who have been accounted the horsemen and the chariots of Israel ... to whom usually God reveals his mind'. They stressed that the men who promoted the constitutional change, 'your new pretending friends', were turncoats and timeservers, 'men who have hanged upon the outside of the cause of Christ'. They complained that those who rejoiced at the projected change in the localities were enemies of the saints, who 'openly boast of laying level the Lord's blessed work amongst his poor people'. And, uniformly, they insisted that God had 'signally born testimony' against kingship, and had destroyed it.[42] These appeals, couched in rhetoric that resonated with his own earlier charismatic experiences, Cromwell found irresistible. He would not 'seek to set up that that providence hath destroyed and laid in the dust, and I would not build Jericho again'.[43] Cromwell would not, *could not* break his connections with the army and the sects. The conservative alliance of lawyers and country gentry had failed to wean him from his old friends.

Their frustration emerged in the second session of the parliament that reconvened on 20 January 1658. The membership of the House was somewhat changed. Some thirty MPs had been promoted to the new 'Upper House' bolted on by the Humble Petition and Advice; there were also some newcomers, men from among the group of radical republicans and conservatives who had been denied admission at its first sitting. Two weeks later an enraged Cromwell dissolved them. Nothing had been done, and the sniping at the new settlement, particularly the second chamber, by some MPs, had encouraged radicals outside parliament to commence a petitioning campaign and to seek support from within the army.

Historians seeking to explain this disaster have emphasised two elements. First, the role played by the republicans newly admitted to the House, men like Sir Arthur Hesilrige, skilled in the filibuster and the destructive manipulation of procedure to ensure stalemate. Secondly, the fact that many of the most committed Cromwellians had been promoted to the Upper House, where they watched helplessly as the Commons refused to recognise their existence. But Cromwell posed the real question that needs to be answered, and which these explanations do not answer, in his ferocious speech at the dissolution: 'And what is like to come upon this but even present blood and confusion? And if it be so, I do assign it to this cause: Your not assenting to what you did invite me to by the Petition and Advice, as that which might be the settlement of the nation.'[44] Why did a substantial majority in parliament vote for the Humble Petition and Advice, in the spring of 1657, and then stand by stolidly, watching the pantomime antics of Hesilrige and his friends which rendered the settlement unworkable in the following January?

The answer is because Cromwell was not king. His refusal to accept the title indicated that he was not wedded to the policies of the gentry and the lawyers, of the civilian conservatives. He was still not fully theirs. Cromwell could not entirely close with the 'kinglings' because he could not reject the language and sentiments of his old comrades. In the face of his painful tergiversation and final rejection of the crown, the traditionalists lost faith in the whole project in which they had invested so much. The country gentry who trickled away from parliament in May and June 1657, and who passively watched the destructive posturing of the republicans in the following January, were responding to Cromwell's refusal to play the role designed for him. Similar frustration and disappointment led to the temporary retirement of Broghill, sulking on his Irish estates in the summer of 1657, and to the refusal of the old peers led by Lord Saye to sit in the new upper chamber. Healing and settling, however attractive to Cromwell, could not be promoted on terms that obliged him to abandon his old allies in the army and among the godly congregations; he was still determined to 'endear and engage the hearts of the saints'.[45]

Seven months after the dissolution of the parliament Oliver Cromwell was dead. The precipitate dissolution had enabled Cromwell to halt the campaign of petitioning by the sects and within the army, though it obliged him to purge a number of army officers, notably Lambert and, significantly, all the captains of his own regiment of horse. The government staggered on, enjoying considerable international success, but desperately underfunded. 'We are at that pass for money, that we are forced to go a begging to particular aldermen of London ... and I fear we shall be denied', wrote Thurloe in July.[46] The divisions within the council that had exploded during the kingship debate continued to rack that body, and to torture Cromwell. Disputes over membership and minor exercises of patronage festered. Moderates thought their army opponents, like Desborough, 'ignorant of law and right', too quick to dismiss issues of legality and due process, too ready to 'fly to that law, the sword, which is in their own hands'.[47] In June the military element on the council were once again vigorously promoting the establishment of a local militia funded by a tax on the royalists. The moderate counsellors hoped to encourage the Protector to undertake further purges of the radical elements in the army, to call another parliament, and to entertain new propositions for a settlement; even to reconsider taking the royal title.

The regime muddled on, held together only by Cromwell's determination and energy, which was flagging under the weight of personal illness and family crisis. The Protector's younger son, Henry, as lord deputy in Ireland set out his understanding of the bleak situation powerfully in a June letter to Thurloe. There was simply no constitutional settlement. The regime's survival depended entirely on his father 'and upon his peculiar skill and faculty and personal interest in the army as now modelled and commanded ... I say beneath the immediate hand of God (if I know anything of the affairs in England) there is no other reason why we are not in blood this day.'[48] His words were prescient.

On 3 September 1658, the anniversary of his great victories at Dunbar and Worcester, Cromwell died, his passing accompanied by a great tempest of wind and rain. His successor, ostensibly nominated by Oliver according to the terms of the Humble Petition and Advice, was his son Richard, a man of no military and negligible governmental experience. The febrile displays of loyal enthusiasm from the localities do little to disguise the essential fragility of the regime. Weak leadership, conciliar division, financial breakdown, and army ambition were a recipe for disaster. By the spring of 1659 the patience of the generals for a regime that could not pay the soldiers and which seemed increasingly sympathetic to civilian interests was eroding fast.

8

Was There an English Revolution?

Richard Cromwell, Oliver's elder son, was nominated, so the council insisted, by his father on his deathbed in accordance with the terms of the Humble Petition and Advice, and succeeded to the office of Lord Protector. It was a surprising choice. Richard had little experience of soldiering, administration or high politics. He had lived as a country gentleman, sharing the traditional recreations of his class. His lack of any hint of zealous religious conviction (which certainly troubled his father), of any army connection, and, more particularly, of any involvement in the complex turns of events in the previous five years may have made him an attractive prospect to moderates. But the rejoicing – bells, bonfires, peals of ordnance, fountains running claret – that greeted his accession, and the waves of petitions declaring unswerving loyalty to his regime, are indicative less of active enthusiasm for Richard among local conservatives than of a belief that the survival of the Protectorate in *any* hands was the only bulwark against a reversion to military rule, to sectarian extremism, even to chaos. Petitioners stressed that the Humble Petition guaranteed the Protector's position, but also that it was the touchstone of 'just and good Government according to the Law'.[1] Moderates at the centre, those who had backed the kingship project and knew the weaknesses of the attenuated constitutional settlement that had resulted from Oliver Cromwell's refusal of the crown, were far less sanguine about the regime's chance's of survival than were their local cohorts.

The new Protector and his defeatist entourage, fearful of the resentment of the army, fearful of the influence of the radicals, did virtually nothing for three months. The summoning of parliament was delayed until February, while the regime spiralled further into bankruptcy. When parliament finally sat, the government's programme, little more than a desperate bid to secure essential taxation, was delayed by the verbal stamina and sophisticated mastery of parliamentary procedure of a cadre of radical MPs, 'the lesser party, but ... all speakers, zealous, diligent'.[2] Filibusters and procedural quirks were supplemented with telling arguments which elicited considerable sympathy from the majority of moderate MPs. These men, while temperamentally disposed to prefer the Protectorate to a republican utopia or the return of the Rump, were troubled by the ramshackle structure of the regime. They echoed the radicals' charges that the Cromwellian 'upper house' was stuffed with 'mean people'; they shared the radicals' suspicions of the Scots and Irish MPs, military men 'chosen from hence that never saw Scotland but in a map'.[3] In consequence little constructive was done, and the English army, seeing no financial provision forthcoming and infuriated by the anti-militarist rhetoric employed by MPs of all persuasions, obliged Richard Cromwell to dissolve his parliament on 22 April. In the next month they dismissed Richard, ended the Protectorate, and restored the Rump MPs to authority.

The new regime proved fragile. It survived a rebellion by a coalition of royalists and Presbyterians, smashed by General John Lambert's professionals at Winnington Bridge in Cheshire on 19 August, but the victory was merely the prelude to another military coup. Inspired by their providential victory – having 'been again saved by the Lord, and ... had a late view of his appearances as of old' – and antagonised by the Rump's attempts to assert full civilian control over the military, on 13 October the English army, led by Lambert and Desborough, again expelled the Rump.[4] Ten weeks later, the generals, humiliated by their inability to rule in the absence of a functioning central government, invited the Rump MPs to return to Westminster. This latter volte-face was a product of divisions among the leaders of the English army, of the uneasy dissatisfaction of their men, and of the insistence of George Monck, general of the forces in Scotland, on military obedience to the civil power. In defence of this ideal Monck marched his forces south, occupying London early in February. On 21 February 1660 he approved the return of the seventy-three surviving victims of Pride's Purge to Westminster Hall; they outnumbered the remaining Rumpers, and on 16 March the Long Parliament finally dissolved itself. A new parliament, which was to agree the restoration of Charles II, met on 25 April.

'Gyant Disborough', an illustration from Thomas Flatman's post-Restoration satire, *Don Juan Lamberto: or A Comical History of the Late Times* (2nd edn, 1661). It catches nicely both the hopelessness of Richard Cromwell (the 'Meek Knight') in the face of army hostility, and the character of John Desborough, the least sympathetic of Oliver Cromwell's military associates to the sensitivities of civilians and conservatives.

(*Ashmolean Museum, Oxford*)

In reviewing the tumultuous events over the twenty years leading up to Restoration, an obvious question to ask is whether there was an English Revolution. A royalist panegyrist, writing in 1661, had no doubt. 'Revolution! Revolution! Our King proclaimed! Restored!'[5] The writer, of course, was using the term in its contemporary senses. A revolution was, first, a completed circular movement, a return to a starting point: the Restoration of Charles II was certainly that. But, in the course of the previous decades of war and experiment, 'revolution' has developed a second meaning: of a rapid, surprising, perhaps violent political change. The word had begun to acquire this sense in the aftermath of the regicide, and the term was frequently used in relation to the political instability of 1653. It was also apposite to describe the fevered course of events, of coups and revolts – 'the late revolutions' – in the twenty months following the death of Oliver Cromwell.[6] So our enthusiastic royalist was playing with this usage also, the usage which shades into the modern sense of 'revolution' – a fundamental alteration of in the structure and culture of politics and society. So was there an English Revolution? The monarchy was restored in 1660, after a series of regime changes in the period 1640–60, but had any seismic changes occurred in the deeper structures of social and political relations that were akin to those in France after 1789 or Russia after 1917?

In 1649 it had seemed very obvious that there had been. The execution of the king was a moment at once both traumatic and cathartic. It shattered conventional expectations, plunging men into despair as they contemplated the breakdown of all social relations within the traditional hierarchy of which Charles had been the apex and guarantor. It aroused a fierce apocalyptic delight among radicals and encouraged their most visionary aspirations. 'In this day of the Lord's wrath', Joseph Salmon exhorted his colleagues in the army shortly after the execution, 'you strike through King, Gentry and Nobility, they all fall before you: You have a Commission from the Lord to scourge England's Oppressors.'[7] The Rump government, in its public pronouncements, encouraged such hopes for significant change with its 1649 Great Seal, with its proud inscription, 'in the first year of freedom ... restored' and May proclamation of England as 'a Commonwealth and Free State', ruled 'for the good of the people' by their representatives.[8]

But such expectations were doomed to disappointment. The Rump turned its attention from any kind of potentially divisive social reform as it sought to defend the republic against foreign enemies and domestic insurgents, and, in that endeavour, to create a government of national unity. Cromwell's letter after Dunbar, and the final defeat of the Scots at Worcester a year later, kept radical hopes alive. It was after this decisive battle that Gerrard Winstanley powerfully reminded Cromwell of the actual and implicit promises made at the trial and execution of the Charles I. That event had encouraged Winstanley to establish a commune of 'Diggers' in Surrey, working the common land together and practising community of goods; but their crops and equipment had been vandalised and destroyed by local landlords, ministers and farmers, with the connivance of the army, and their experiment had been abandoned. In November 1651 Winstanley sought Cromwell's backing for another attempt to create a society without private property. 'Kingly power', paradoxically, had survived the execution of the king: it was still embodied in the practices of a hegemonic establishment of reactionary landlords, lawyers and clergymen. To 'remove the Conqueror's power out of the King's hands unto other men's, maintaining the old laws still', would, Winstanley insisted, 'lay the foundation of greater slavery to posterity than ever you knew'.[9]

Cromwell did not accept Winstanley's utopian scheme, but, with the dissolution of the Rump and the summoning of the Parliament of Saints, he again energised those who sought to develop the implications of 'those mighty works and wonders' that God 'hath wrought in these lands'. 'Greater and more high things ... in way of removing wickedness and oppression' were anticipated by the godly MPs gathering in Westminster.[10] The dissolution of the parliament and establishment of the Protectorate blasted such hopes. Radicals were reduced to publishing Cromwell's euphoric speech of 4 July 1653, encouraging the members to undertake their providentially mandated task of 'bearing good fruits to the nation', in an effort to embarrass the new Lord Protector who had publicly dismissed the 1653 experiment.[11]

The death of Cromwell and the fall of the Protectorate, despite the intervening record of disappointment and betrayal, resurrected some of the euphoric hopes for structural change sparked by the execution and declarations of 1649. And yet the political landscape had changed dramatically by 1659: the decade had seen the *strengthening* of the social order that seemed so desperately fragile after the execution of the king.

Reflecting on events since the beginning of 1658, with the offer of the Humble Petition and Advice, a radical critic complained that 'the old spirit of gentry' had been 'brought in play again'.[12] A decade earlier that had seemed a very unlikely eventuality. The day before the regicide, a moderate Norfolk parliamentarian, Sir Valentine Pell, trembled as he considered 'the perils and eminent dangers hanging over our heads, that little else can be expected but a general sudden confusion. Oh, my bowels do yearn within me to think that I should live to hear and see the miseries and calamities like to ensue ... The honest heart must break.'[13] But the 'sudden confusion' that he anticipated did not follow. The radical MPs who connived in the purge the Commons, abolished the House of Lords, executed the king and proclaimed the Commonwealth invited conservatives, initially horrified by these events, to rejoin them in parliament. Similar invitations were offered to many leading gentlemen, otherwise conservative, to act for the regime in the localities: a few – Sir Thomas Bowes and Sir William Rowe in Essex; the earl of Denbigh and Sir Simon Archer in Warwickshire – accepted the opportunity to undertake their traditional roles as magistrates.

The establishment of the Protectorate enhanced the involvement of traditional power-brokers in the regime. In his speech to his first parliament Oliver Cromwell played to his gentry audience. He denounced those radicals who haunted their nightmares – 'men of Levelling principles'; millenarian zealots. He insisted that a favourite text for radical exegesis, Ezekiel 21.27, had been 'very much abused'.[14] He asserted his own devotion to the traditional social hierarchy – 'A nobleman, a gentleman, a yeoman ... that is a good interest of the nation, and a great one'. And he invited his auditors, 'the natural magistracy of the nation', to assist him in his government as legislators and as JPs.[15] Despite the troubling anomaly of the rule of the major-generals, Cromwell returned to his conservative theme when he first met his second parliament: 'we would keep up the nobility and gentry'.[16] Those who offered the crown to the Protector were anticipating both that more gentlemen 'of the old stamp' like Sir John Hobart and Sir Richard Onslow would support the initiative, and that such men had sufficient social authority to balance the hold of the army over the government. This was the view of George Monck, writing a letter of advice to Richard Cromwell at his accession. Monck was more robust in his assessment of Richard's chances than most of the new Protector's counsellors. Richard could, unlike his father, disassociate himself from the generals. He should invite moderates into his council; he should immediately seek to work with parliament, encouraging the old peers to attend the 'Other House' and increase the numbers of 'the leading gentry of the ... counties' in that body – Monck specifically mentioned Sir George Booth for Cheshire and Sir John Hobart for Norfolk. He should court the leading Presbyterian ministers. Two policy initiatives must immediately be undertaken. First, Richard Cromwell should affirm the need for a national church bound together by a common statement of faith, and with power to prosecute the 'blasphemy and prophaneness' that currently flourished, to the horror of the social elites, in the absence of such mechanisms. Secondly, the rocketing costs of the army and the navy must be cut. Ships must be laid up and under-strength regiments consolidated; more fundamentally, local militias, officered by the gentry, should take over many of the responsibilities which now fell to expensive professional detachments. The regime, Monck argued firmly, would flourish if it identified itself with 'those of power and interest among the people'.[17]

The reconstruction of elite hegemony upon which Monck relied in his advice had been achieved largely because the gentry had already rebuilt their economic position and with it their social power. At the end of the Civil War, Sir John Oglander, bewailing 'the tyrannical misery that the gentlemen of England did endure', reported that 'there were in Yorkshire a hundred families extinct or undone, so that none of them could appear again as gentlemen. Death, plunder, sales and sequestration sent them to another world or beggar's bush, and so in all – or most – shires'.[18] This was an overstatement by a particularly jaundiced commentator, of course, but the war had certainly damaged the prosperity of the landowning classes. High taxation and free quarter were universal; wanton destruction and plunder had drained regions over which the war had been fought; and the income of royalist estates had been seized, and would only be returned upon the payment of a significant composition fine. For a few gentry families, already in difficulties, the multiple demands of war were the last straw and they sold up. But the bulk of the gentry weathered the crisis. This is most apparent if we consider the group deepest hit by multiple financial demands occasioned by the war, the royalists. Over three thousand of them recovered their sequestered estates upon payment of a fine, usually in the range of double the annual value of the estate. Seven hundred or so, either because they refused to swear the oaths demanded as a prerequisite to negotiating a fine, or because they were particularly tainted by their Civil War actions, had their estates sold by the government. But in some three-quarters of these cases the lands were bought back by trustees acting on behalf of the old owner, upon payment of something like six years' annual value of the estate. Raising these sums required careful and time-consuming management of both income and expenditure – in the mid-1650s a Kentish royalist complained that all his time was taken up 'with the business of farming'.[19] But by that period many of his colleagues were enjoying a modest prosperity, and some were extending their holdings, or, like Sir George Sondes at Lees Court, building magnificent houses.

The gentry were able to stage this economic retrenchment because the governments of the Interregnum gave them every opportunity to do so. We can best understand this if we consider the alternative policies demanded by the radicals. Many of the latter challenged the role of the gentry in English society. Zealots hoped that the Nominated Parliament would 'lay aside' titles, such as knight and esquire, 'as a vain glorious thing'. Quakers also denounced 'honours and titles' and backed their objections by refusing hat-honour and deferential forms of address – 'hollow, deceitful, unwarrantable ... the inventions of the beast'.[20] More practically, they attacked the social inequalities that resulted from the gentry's privileged positions as landowners.

While the gentry complained bitterly of the weight of taxation that fell upon them, radicals argued that the burden was still distributed inequitably, and that the gentry were the beneficiaries of a regressive system of taxation. They demanded a higher land or income tax; the government should 'lean principally upon the richest' and end the 'intolerable' excise duty on consumption.[21] Nothing was done in this respect, and under the Protectorate Cromwell and his parliaments sought to cut or abandon the assessment, throwing the entire burden onto indirect forms of taxation. Radicals also argued that a discriminatory taxation policy should be pursued. The fiscal burden on active supporters of the parliamentary cause should be lightened; deficits should be funded by confiscation and sale; and mulcts should fall more heavily on the royalists, 'those who were the causers of them'.[22] The 1655–56 decimation tax was the one gesture in this direction, but it ran counter to most governmental policy and was swiftly abandoned.

Landlord–tenant relations were also challenged, particularly in 1649 and again a decade later. Radical critics emphasised the anomaly whereby parliament had abolished the court of wards, and with it the quasi-feudal dependence of landlords upon the crown, but had failed to provide any comparable protection to those manorial tenants with copyhold tenure. They still owed homage to their lords, 'a badge and bruit of the Norman slavery', and, more practically, were subject to arbitrary rents and fines, and liable for humiliating 'bond-services'.[23] 'Lords have enough', argued the Quaker leader, George Fox, in 1659, without the windfall profits that could be screwed from the relics of servile tenure.[24]

That was not Sir Ralph Verney's view. Sir Ralph, fighting the consequences of plunder, sequestration and debt on an estate in no man's land for the bulk of the war, tripled his rental income by aggressive management – buying out smallholdings, consolidating farms and enclosure. In 1650 he justified himself against the charge that he was a harsh landlord: 'no man', he wrote, 'is bound to suffer his tenants to reap the benefit of his land because they are poor; that were a ready way indeed to make them rich, and him poor'.[25] In the absence of the legislative interference demanded by the radicals, the gentry were able to continue the reorganisation of their estates to exploit market opportunities with minimal regard for the interest of their tenants. The failure of another favoured radical project, the abolition of the court of Chancery, also advantaged the gentry. The law concerning settlements and mortgages, which the gentry increasingly used to organise and protect their estates and to raise cash on the security of their lands, was developed under Chancery's jurisdiction. The Nominated Parliament voted the abolition of the court, but, with a fierce rear-guard action from the conservatives, failed to agree the enacting legislation before the assembly was dissolved. As Protector, Oliver Cromwell sought to restructure the court in the interests of cheapening litigation, but did not challenge its jurisdictional competence. Equally typically, after their October 1659 coup against the Rump, the officers sought to bolster their radical credentials by again discussing the abolition of Chancery.

The economic position of the gentry was steadily rebuilt after 1649 in part because the Rump was not prepared to consider any of the radical schemes that would have entailed some measure of economic or social restructuring. The energies of the government focused on the defence of the regime, and once this was secured in 1651 the conservative social tendencies of the majority of the MPs guaranteed that there would be no fundamental change. Under Cromwell, after the abortive experiment of the Nominated Parliament and despite the aberration of the major-generals, this trend was enhanced. The assessment was reduced and the jurisdiction of Chancery affirmed. Cromwell also began to reintegrate the gentry into his administration of the localities.

The war and the regicide had posed a more immediate and practical threat to another plank of gentry authority, besides the radicals' challenge to their social and economic hegemony: they lost their control of the agencies of local government. From 1649 (earlier in areas which had supported the king) until 1654, the localities had been governed, very efficiently, largely by outsiders to the traditional establishment: taxes were raised, felons hanged, the poor relieved, bridges and roads maintained by men who could not have aspired to a place on the bench before 1642. Under both Oliver and Richard Cromwell moderates who had refused to serve the Rump and even the heirs of royalist fathers were offered the chance to reclaim their traditional role in local government. In the 1650s the gentry steadily gained in confidence. Their economic base had not been fundamentally assailed, and positions in parliament and local government were again available to many of them. The divisions of the Civil War were patched up, as ties of family and locality were reaffirmed in hospitality and traditional forms of conviviality, such as horse-racing and hunting.

After the return and enthronement of Charles II the gentry warmly congratulated themselves on their central role in that welcome outcome; typical is an MP's comment in 1670, 'the gentlemen were the instrumental cause of the King's Restoration'.[26] The self-serving hyperbole, however, carries a measure of truth. The majority of MPs in Richard Cromwell's parliament, as in that of 1656, consisted of conservative gentlemen. They were reluctant to see the wrecking policies of the republicans triumph, and they intermittently cooperated with the government clique in an unavailing effort to ensure the survival of the regime, as established by the Humble Petition. But their enthusiasm for the Protectorate was distinctly qualified. Negatively, they distrusted the continued role of the army as a 'fourth estate', a recognised political actor, with 'colonels, swordsmen and commanders of armies' heavily represented in the upper House. But they approved of the re-establishment of a two-tiered legislature, and argued that 'the ancient nobility' should not have been 'neglected and set aside' in the new structure.[27] The smug praise that the radicals lavished on the Rump's achievements roused their fury, and they insisted on the huge burden of taxes and the neglect of religion between 1649 and 1653. Overall, they sought a return to the 'ancient constitution' and they favoured the Humble Petition only in so far as it guaranteed the key values of the traditional political structure and culture. The 'foundation of your rights' was *not* the Humble Petition, insisted men like Sir George Booth and Richard Knightley, rather they were enshrined in Magna Carta, in Edward I's *De Tallagio Non Concedo*, and in the Petition of Right. The radicals jeered at this mode of thinking: 'no thought is to be taken now of what was done by John of Gaunt and such fellows'. But traditionalists were unperturbed. Nor did they immediately reject the consequence of their traditionalist perspective, as it was stated by Vane: 'if you be minded to resort to the old Government, you are not many steps from the old family'.[28]

The dissolution of Richard's parliament, and the end of the Protectorate, forced this moderate group, terrified by the direction of events at the centre, into new courses of action. A good number contemplated rebellion. The only rising that eventually occurred, led by Sir George Booth, was easily suppressed, but this was the tip of an iceberg of local discontent and conspiracy. Throughout England active supporters of the Protectorate, Presbyterian gentry and ministers, men too young to have involved themselves in the earlier wars and old royalists plotted together against the Rump. Booth's manifestos indicate the concerns and the self-fashioning of the Rump's opponents. In three documents, Booth sought to justify his stand and to encourage others to join him in an effort to establish a properly representative parliament either by new elections, or by the restoration of the members of the Long Parliament ousted by Pride in December 1648. He argued that the policies of the restored Rump were unprecedented and illegal. Huge sums were demanded in taxation backed by threats of the employment of military force and imprisonment against those who refused. In consequence liberty and property, guaranteed as the sacred 'Birthright' of Englishmen by Magna Carta and the Petition of Right, risked 'total extinguishment'; religion, too, had no settled foundation. The government's policies offended not just against abstract legal rights. The Rump, in its choice of local agents to enforce its monstrous agenda, was seeking to 'depress the nobility and understanding commons'. As 'considerable members of our country' in whom 'English blood abideth', Booth and his supporters took up arms against 'slavery'.[29]

The defeat of Booth's rising represented only a temporary intermission in the propaganda and pressure of the traditionalists. General Monck's intervention, and the gnomic pronouncements that accompanied his advance into England, encouraged the moderates, despite his declared support for the Rump, to deluge him with petitions. These had the same goal for which Booth had risen – a free parliament, in this case backed not by military force but by the threat of a tax strike. And the petitioners used essentially the same language that Booth had employed: the burden of 'unheard of taxes'; and the need to uphold the 'undoubted Birthright and Liberty', and the 'Fundamental Laws', of 'all the free born people of England'.[30] The subscribers portrayed themselves in similar terms to those employed by Booth and his supporters; they were 'the most considerable of the gentry' of Devon; the 'most of the chief gentlemen and freeholders' of Berkshire. Such claims were not unwarranted. The organisation of the petitions, which can be examined in some detail in several counties, involved much the same groups who emerge in a more shadowy guise as involved in the summer rebellion. Throughout England the petitions were organised by conjunctions of members of the elite, though of very different backgrounds: the sons of active royalists; quietists who had lain low throughout the Civil War, and 'murmured not but made a soft complaint';[31] those who had been ousted or had retired from local office in 1648; and vigorous proponents of the offer of the crown to Cromwell. The reconstituted local elite based in the traditional social hierarchy backed the conservative rhetoric of the petitions.

Ultimately Monck followed the policy suggested in this wave of petitions from the localities and from the City of London. The general's antipathy to 'the intolerable slavery of a sword government' was always asserted in relation to a sense of public opinion: 'I know England cannot, nay, will not endure it.' The sense of local communities united behind their traditional leaders, calling for a return to a civilian regime firmly located in the values of the ancient constitution, and the sense of the Rump's negligible support in the localities, except for 'a mean and schismatical party',[32] certainly weighed in Monck's evaluation of the optimal route to re-establish a viable government.

A two-year period of extraordinary political volatility, of the 'greatest turnings and revolutions',[33] culminated in a climactic revolution – now using the word in its best established contemporary sense – the Restoration of the Stuarts. The gentry congratulated themselves, with some cause, on their role in this: 'it was the loyal gentry that brought him home'.[34] But the major player in the Restoration was a general, George Monck, and an army, the English force occupying Scotland. The role of the army, convoluted and paradoxical, is the next element in the evaluation of the attenuated revolution that England experienced in the period following the execution of the king.

The army had been at the cutting edge of radical action between 1647 and 1653. It had proposed constitutional schemes, purged parliament and played the major role in the execution of the king. After the security of the Commonwealth was assured in September 1651, it had lobbied and bullied the Rump to make good its promises of reform, dissolved that body when it failed to act, and set up the theocratic experiment of the Parliament of Saints. After the death of Oliver Cromwell, the army reverted to the themes of this earlier period of reformist political engagement and to the language of godly reform. In September they reminded Richard Cromwell that the 'work of reformation tending to good life and manners' should be promoted 'vigorously', insisting on the need for good magistrates and a purged and reformed ministry.[35] The reform of 'law and manners' and a similar emphasis on the purging of local officers, 'plucking the wicked out of their places', occurred in the army's April petition to the Protector, and the same themes were repeated in the 12 May petition to the restored Rump, with a few more specifics, including law reform and the reform of the universities.[36] The restored Rump's abject failure to make any progress on the matters raised in May, was emphasised in the September petition from the northern brigade, flush with victory against Booth. After the expulsion of the Rump in October, it was reported that the general council of the army was considering the abolition of tithes and of the court of Chancery.

This reformist rhetoric was an attempt by the generals to take the moral high ground and to embarrass the various civilian regimes. But it was also an attempt to persuade their subalterns of their continued commitment to the high ideals of 1649 and 1653. Certainly the unease of the junior officers in the face of policies pursued by their generals that could easily be portrayed as self-interested was a feature of the febrile politics of the army in this period. Petitions and pamphlets from civilian radicals continually pressed the junior officers and soldiers to 'do our first works and remember the loves of our virginity', to recall 'those virgin days', 'the days of innocency and simplicity'.[37] The army must repent its apostasy in furthering the ambition of Oliver Cromwell. It must 'remember from whence you are fallen and do your first works; return and stand to or fall with the GOOD OLD CAUSE'.[38] The latter was a splendidly vague concept, 'set out', as the Presbyterian William Prynne noted caustically, 'with glorious general words and painted varnishes, without acquainting [us] particularly, really and ingenuously what it is'.[39] But, however nebulous, the catchphrase carried enormous emotive power. The restoration of the Rump in May by the generals, who would have preferred the continuance of the Protectorate with Richard Cromwell as a cipher, owed much to pressure from the junior officers. The concern of the soldiers for an ill-defined Good Old Cause involving the resurrection of the most radical aspirations of the period before 1654, and their suspicions of unspecified backslidings among the generals, also underpinned the turmoil in the army when Lambert and his allies suppressed the restored Rump in October 1659.

But it would be wrong to characterise the army as simply a hothouse of radical ideas. Despite its insistence in 1647 that it was 'no mere mercenary army', even in those days of 'innocency and simplicity' recalled with such nostalgia a decade later there was an important dimension of corporate self-interest to its actions. This aspect of its behaviour became predominant as the most vigorous of the radicals among its ranks died or were purged, and were replaced by men at all levels of the command structure who saw soldiering as a career. The army's professional agenda of privileged status and regular pay necessitated a large-scale centralised administrative structure. And to guarantee that this agenda would be prosecuted by a sympathetic government the army violently interfered in politics in 1648, 1653 and twice in 1659. Its favoured constitutional schemes sought increasingly to construct a formal political role for itself as an independent estate of the realm. From the perspective of the Levellers the kind of regime required by the army could never have reformist aspirations, because it was too remote from the people it ostensibly represented. But, as was also noted by the Levellers and again by those who found army agitation for reform after Worcester hypocritical, the army's devouring need for money was the major block to reform. Improvement in social conditions could not be expected under the burden of taxation, particularly the regressive taxation, upon which the army was reliant. The army might exhort parliament to alter the legal penalties governing the treatment of debtors: but how far was the structural problem of debt a product of the demands of the soldiers for money? Reducing the size of the army and cutting its pay, then, were prerequisite to reform. But that was simply not viable, as the Rumpers painfully discovered in March 1653.

The army's privileged role in the political process, and its upkeep, were the key issues, increasingly well defined and emphasised, in the period after the death of Oliver Cromwell. In October 1659 the army made its fullest pitch for a quasi–independent political status. They demanded that Charles Fleetwood should be given life tenure of the post of commander-in-chief; that no officer should be dismissed except by the verdict of a court-martial; that appointments to posts should not be subject to direct parliamentary interference; and that the rights of the army to petition should be affirmed. The 'design' of this petition, wrote an officer who was troubled by it, was 'to create an interest in the army, distinct to that of the parliament and nation'.[40] Most of the issues that suggested the army's ambition to be an independent 'corporation' had come up in the preceding year. At Richard Cromwell's accession, some of his advisers had been troubled by the readiness of the 'cabal' of ambitious officers to challenge his position, 'not a general of the army, as his father was'.[41] Next month the army had begun to foment a series of demands in secret meetings – that Fleetwood should be commander-in-chief, with power to issue commissions; and that no officer should be deprived of his command without a hearing before a military tribunal. In November meetings ostensibly for prayer and religious instruction had developed a political edge, with demands that officers cashiered by Oliver Cromwell – most notably John Lambert – should be reinstated. In March the generals persuaded Richard to sanction the formal convention of a general council of the army, and the petition that was subsequently presented by that body hinted at the officers' serious distrust of the parliament then in session. In their wish-list, presented to the restored Rump of May 1659, the army urged the need for a select senate, its members appointed for life, to be established, equal in authority with the representatives elected to the Commons. This looked suspiciously like an attempt to guarantee the generals, who had just lost their positions in the Protectoral Upper House, a similar veto power in the new republican constitution.

The second issue that exercised the army leaders in the period 1658–60 concerned the pay of their forces. In the army's May and October petitions, which led respectively to the demise of both the Protectorate and the recalled Rump, 'the necessitous condition of the poor soldiers', 'in great extremity for want of pay', was emphasised.[42] Officers had exhausted their cash and their credit to supply their men, and the latter had been obliged to buy food and lodging by borrowing at extortionate rates of interest on the security of their eventual payment of arrears. Lambert made a similar point in a letter to the Rump after the defeat of Booth's rising, and several petitions from groups of soldiers were published complaining that, 'destitute of food and drink', they had 'sold and pawned all they had'.[43] The problem was easy to diagnose; impossible to resolve. Oliver Cromwell, hoping to secure civilian support, had cut the assessment and the books simply did not balance. In April 1658, parliament learned that the debt stood at £2,500,000 (£890,000 of which was owed to the army in England), and that the annual shortfall was a third of a million.

Richard Cromwell's parliament did little more than wring its hands over the prospect of bankruptcy, talking vaguely of retrenchment and of the collection of monies stuck in the administrative pipeline. The restored Rump was more aware of the need to placate the army, and made a series of series of gestures to deal with 'the extreme wants of the Soldiery'.[44] The rates of pay of the troops around London were raised. Attempts were made to negotiate short-term loans. Monies raised by the sale of Cromwell's palaces were to be used to secure the pensions of army widows and orphans, and of those disabled in the service. The annual sum due for the monthly assessment was to be collected in the first three months of the financial year, and two months' pay was to be issued as soon as the money came in. But it is clear from the repetition of parliament's orders, particularly after the defeat of Booth's rising when army grievances were more loudly expressed, that, despite lavish promises, little money actually trickled down to the soldiers or to their dependants. In September the Rump voted to triple the monthly assessment, but the slow progress of the resolution through the House suggested that there were serious doubts about the political viability of this proposal. The threat of a taxpayers' strike hung over all the discussions in this period. It was enhanced when the Rump, fearing army intervention in October, voted that anyone attempting to raise taxes without parliamentary warrant was a traitor. The refusal to pay taxes until a body with better representative credentials than the Rump approved them was the theme of many of the county petitions that deluged Monck as he moved south to London in the new year.

Army petitions incessantly demanded regular pay, and the payment of arrears and of pensions. These very real employment-related grievances in part explain the generals' suspicion of the civil authorities and the attempt to secure a quasi–independent political status for the army that also inform these documents. But a key military figure in 1658–59 increasingly dissented from the diagnosis and schemes of his colleagues. While the leaders of the English army sought to establish themselves as an independent estate of the realm, George Monck pursued a very different agenda. At Richard Cromwell's accession Monck had advised the new Protector to make a virtue of his civilian background, and to challenge the warlords. First, he must undertake military retrenchment. Such a cost-cutting exercise would have another advantage. It could be a cover to purge 'insolent spirits' from among the army officers. Monck dismissed the possibility that this provocative course of action could have repercussions: 'here is not an officer in the army upon any discontent, that has interest enough to draw two men after him, if he be out of place'.[45] After the fall of the Protectorate Monck was prepared to accept the first political experiment attempted by his English colleagues, the reconvening of the Rump. When that body tactlessly meddled in his administration of his army, Monck questioned the quality of the information that had led them to interfere, but agreed on their right to do so. 'Obedience is my great principle', he wrote, and referred to his early service in the Dutch forces, 'where soldiers received and obeyed commands, but gave none'.[46] He refused to accede to the second army intervention, the October putsch against the Rump, and prepared to resist his colleagues. To that end he followed his earlier advice to Richard Cromwell, purging his regiments of officers and men whose loyalty he doubted, particularly religious extremists. In his manifestos he insisted on the need to uphold the civil power, as a key aspect of the rights of Englishmen, lecturing the zealous Fleetwood that God had witnessed 'against power of raising money without the people's consent first had'.[47] The concomitant of this argument he used to win the support of his troops. He guaranteed that a grateful parliament would pay their arrears. Money was still at the heart of the soldiers' concerns.

The army played a highly ambivalent role in this period. It could articulate the most radical sentiments in the series of representations that punctuated the various coups, justifying its interventions in terms of them. Yet it was suspicious of any schemes for military demobilisation, insisted on lavish provision for itself, and sought to guarantee its continuing influence in the government. The army's bifurcated agenda left it ultimately divided and utterly demoralised: in November 1659 civilians gleefully reported that the soldiers 'say they will not fight, but will make a ring for their officers to fight in'.[48] The army's self-interested involvement in the political process was one of the reasons for the failure to pursue a more radical initiative, to institute any fundamental change in the structure of a centralised polity and a traditionally ordered society. The other was the divisions that split those who did think in terms of a more radical, even revolutionary, restructuring of state and society.

In the spring of 1659 civilian radicals were united in hostility to the regime of Richard Cromwell. Republicans elected to parliament worked to challenge the constitution of the Protectorate and delay the passage of legislation. 'If Pope Alexander ... Caesar Borgia and Machiavel should all consent together, they could not lay a foundation for a more absolute tyranny' than the Humble Petition, said John Hobart.[49] Experienced ex-Rumpers, skilled in the partial manipulation of procedure and the filibuster led the group – on 7 February Sir Arthur Heselrige spent three hours on a speech lauding the Rump and its achievements. They could not outvote the combination of government officials and conservative country gentry to overthrow the key constitutional provision of the Protectorate, but their substantive points and their mastery of procedure created and spun out delays. And they also encouraged the conservatives to voice their anti-military suspicions, assiduously reporting these tirades in the press to enhance the army's paranoia about its prospects for pay and its very survival. At the same time radical pamphlets and sermons created further ferment in the army, cleverly exploiting the uncertainties of the junior officers about recent political developments and their susceptibility to the potent mantra of the Good Old Cause.

The tactics of the radicals succeeded brilliantly. A military coup compelled Richard Cromwell to dissolve his parliament, and the nostalgia of the subaltern officers for the imagined pristine purity of the pre-Protectorate period obliged the generals to recall the Rump. This was another triumph for radical propaganda, working on the heated sensibilities of the junior officers: the association of the Good Old Cause with the 'Good Old Parliament'.[50]

But at this point fissures began to appear among those who had combined to overthrow the Protectorate. Most obviously, delays in the development of a new form of government revealed serious divisions within the restored Rump itself. In Richard Cromwell's parliament the republican opposition had been fertile in their suggestion of properly based constitutional schemes, and fluent in their presentation, as they mocked the ramshackle structure established by the Humble Petition and Advice. But developing a new structure of government proved more contentious. By October, when the army intervened, the committee appointed to draft the new constitution had made some progress. But nothing had been done on the extent of the franchise, whether open or restrictive, nor on the issue of whether there should be a senate with power to check the legislative supremacy of the elected house. And discussion had been punctuated by some major arguments, not least between two of the most experienced and influential Rumpers, Sir Arthur Haselrig and Sir Henry Vane.

Heselrige, in Vane's opinion, was too wedded to the form of the Rump in its first, 1649–53, manifestation. His plan for recruiter elections was largely designed, as the army had suggested in 1653, to perpetuate the authority of the current clique, to settle 'the government as Sir Arthur would have it'.[51] Beyond that, Vane felt the Heselrige was prepared to place too much unchecked power in the hands of the representative. Vane had little affection for democracy; the better part, he believed should not be subordinated to a majority. In consequence, he successfully insisted on the inclusion of some 'Fundamentals' in the constitutional draft, notably a ban of kingship and wide-ranging religious toleration that could not be altered by the MPs. But his plan to check their power further by the introduction of a senate was anathema to Heselrige, not least because it was one of the planks of the army's agenda. Heselrige's angry suspicion that Vane was in cahoots with the generals, a charge that gained some credibility when Vane cooperated with them after the October coup, was a major dimension of the tension between the two men.

Such divisions among the leaders of the restored Rump were symptomatic of wider splits among the radical coalition in 1658–59, splits that had eroded the potential for revolutionary action throughout the period after the execution of the king. The most obvious fault line divided the secular republicans and the godly zealots. The unprecedented volatility of the period invited imaginative reflection. Thinkers like Walwyn, Milton and Harrington sought to encode the chaotic course of events into alternative theoretical frameworks, based on the principles of classical republicanism. But such thinkers received only minority support and could never dominate the political process. Secular schemes had limited appeal for the majority of radicals, whose concerns focused on their charismatic religious convictions. Indeed, such schemes, lacking any serious attempt to locate their authority in a biblical hermeneutic, were suspect. So charges of scepticism, even atheism, against Walwyn had been used effectively to blacken the Levellers and their inventive constitutional schemes by their erstwhile

Baptist and sectarian allies in 1649. But the dissolution of that alliance owed more to the judgement of the Baptist leaders that the Rump would protect religious freedom, and that Leveller hostility to the regime might prove totally destructive of all that had been achieved. Ultimately most of the godly radicals were unconcerned with forms of government, provided that they then were guaranteed toleration. Beyond that priority, the godly were troubled by the continued existence of a state church, supported by tithes and involving the traditional forms of patronage. They might also express a general interest in the reform of the law or the condition of the poor, but their affirmation of these goals was intermittent. More of their diurnal energy was channelled into the construction of alternative communities based on the affirmation of individual charismatic insight. And in this process they exhausted themselves in debilitating internecine disputes between the various sects and within them. Baptist churches tore themselves apart over such issues as the right of women to preach, on whether a meal should precede the communion service, and whether the communion should also involve the washing of feet. By 1654 it was reported of the Lothbury church that 'God hath sent a dividing spirit'; in the same year Morgan Llwyd's poetry, once triumphalist, expressed his sadness at the bickering and disarray in his Wrexham church: 'the churches brawl, their members fall'.[52]

The fall of the Protectorate in 1659 was greeted with euphoria by the godly. But the restored Rump was not guaranteed their uncritical support. Many were suspicious of a regime that included too many men who had prostituted themselves during the Protectorate – Lenthall, St John and Whitelocke, fresh from defending the offer of the crown to Cromwell, were not the obvious embodiments of the Good Old Cause. And the godly could still remember the broken promises, peculation and self-interest that had led to the dissolution of the Rump in April 1653, and, enthusiastically, the reformist schemes of the Nominated Parliament. It was then that the Good Old Cause, defined as 'NO KING BUT JESUS', had been upheld and promoted, as it had certainly not been by the Rump.[53] Some saw the restoration of the Rump as, at best, an interim solution, a *pis aller*, and agreed to suspend judgement until its policies were clearer. By September increasingly negative evaluations were emerging. From the perspective of the godly, very little had been achieved. A chorus of civilian tracts assailed the regime's lethargy, being joined by petitions from men 'who desire to fear the Lord' in the army.[54]

The criticism of the Rump's torpid performance focused on two issues where radical expectations had not been met, one of tactics, one of substance. First, the radicals demanded a thorough purge of those MPs, officials, army commanders and local magistrates who had temporised with the Protectorate. Arguing that only those who had exhibited 'a sincere, single, thorough spirit for Christ his Cause and Interest in these latter days' deserved preferment, the author of *A True Catalogue* insisted that all who had promoted the Cromwellian regime should be ousted. Nothing had been done, of course, because many apostate timeservers sat in parliament. But the author's animus extended beyond that obvious target group; his catalogue of self-interested 'salary men' included the leading republican spokesman Sir Arthur Heselrige.[55] The Rump made some gestures to these concerns, seeking advice from local radicals on the temper of the magistrates and militia officers, but did little to act upon their recommendations. In November 1659 the Rumpers replaced the religious radical, John Canne, as the editor of the chief government newspapers, with the supple timeserver Marchamont Nedham. Nedham had been the most brilliant propagandist of the Rump government from 1649–53, but then had employed his formidable skills in the service of the Protectorate. The godly were appalled. For them, Nedham was 'that blasphemous Rabshakah': in reply he jeered at their favoured mode of discourse, 'bringing in a whole catalogue of dreaming Rabbis to jostle out' proper constitutional thinking.[56]

The second substantive issue, the financial provision for a national church, had a similar history. The restored Rump welcomed petitions from the sects against tithes but proceeded to vote the continuance of the contentious maintenance. Tithes were to be paid 'until' – a word subsequently changed to the yet more vague 'unless' – parliament devised an alternative. This declaration was to be published and promulgated at the assizes by the judges. In these two aspects of policy the Rumpers appeared ready to surrender the interests of their sectarian allies, and risk the divisive consequences, in their effort to make bridges to parochial ministers and the traditional ruling elite in the localities.

'The old nature is still standing', wrote a disappointed Quaker after negotiating with one of the Rump's committees.[57]

In 1658–60 the radicals were divided on a series of issues. They feuded, as they had since 1649, over the optimal constitutional structure, and over the continued existence of a national church and the degree of toleration to be permitted within it. Both these issues intersected with a third matter of contention: the degree to which a radical government should seek to enlist the support, active or passive, of the army and of the traditional social and governmental elite. Maintaining the delicate balance between the godly, the soldiers and the country gentry, which Oliver Cromwell had been barely able to sustain, was beyond any of the regimes that succeeded on his death. But it was still part of the agenda of them all. The attempt to do so explains the tortuous course of politics after September 1658.

The decade following the execution of the king did not witness the overarching transformation of the structure of society and of political culture so vividly imagined by some radical thinkers. Those who most desired changes were divided on key issues of the organisation of church and state. The army, despite its powerfully expressed commitments to reform, was also dedicated to the contradictory agenda of maintaining its comfortable status within the regimes. With the tacit consent of military and civilian radicals, and with the active encouragement of some of them, notably Oliver Cromwell, the traditional political elite survived the crisis and regained their strength. In the immediate aftermath of the establishment of the republic the gentry had been shattered and demoralised. The radical aspirations of the Nominated Parliament, the interventionist and divisive rule of the major-generals, and the chaotic 'revolutions' following Oliver Cromwell's death, all resurrected the spectres that had haunted men like Sir Valentine Pell in 1649. But they could now confront them with a united front, and with an ideological position that commanded a very general agreement. The wide dispersal and social density of the conceptual framework of the ancient constitution, the ideals of government and law embodied in defining documents, had driven the resistance to Charles's government in 1639. In the flux of events of 1659 and 1660, the 'revolutions', it represented the key unifying element. It was this unanimity that persuaded

Monck that the best way to secure the professional agenda of the army – or least of his army – was to identify with the language and the policy prescription of the gentry.

The 'ancient constitution' was as much an incantation and a chimera as was 'the Good Old Cause'. The outbreak of war in 1642 and the subsequent political turmoil had demonstrated that there was negligible consensus about the detailed content of the constitutional package it implied. In February 1659 Sir Anthony Ashley Cooper remarked that if Richard Cromwell's power was to be defined solely in relation to 'the ancient laws', 'Shall we not leave him to those ancient doubts and disputes which have cost us so much blood?'[58] As the euphoria of the Restoration passed, Ashley Cooper's words proved prescient. And they were an appropriate text for his personal role in the constitutional disputes between Whigs and Tories that fed into the Exclusion Crisis and that led, ultimately, to the overthrow of James II in 1688.

Consideration of events later in the century provokes further reflection on the overarching significance of the period between 1640 and 1660 within the development of the English polity, and to a final consideration of the appropriateness of the label of 'revolution'. Elements of the distinctive political culture of late seventeenth-century England, involving a broad-based political nation, well informed and actively engaged, were certainly reinforced powerfully in the Civil War period. These aspects were not wholly novel; their earlier existence was in part responsible for the king's isolation in 1640. But the deepening of characteristics that were already part of the English experience represented a qualitative structural change, which, if not revolutionary, was hugely significant. We can best approach these issues through two statistical series.

The first of these concerns the output of the publishing industry. In the decade 1630–39 an average of 624 titles were published each year. In 1641, if we include the individual numbers of the weekly newsbook, the number of published titles leapt to 2042, and that number almost doubled in the next year. The 1642 Everest of 4038 titles was unsurpassed for the remainder of the century, but only in the Plague and Great Fire years of 1665 and 1666 did the number of publications dip below the one thousand mark, despite attempts to police press output by the

Cromwellian and then the Restoration governments. Over three thousand titles were published in each of the years of political melt-down – in 1648, 1659–1660, 1682 and 1688. The raw numbers conceal fundamental changes in the form taken by publications and their content. From 1640, the majority of published works were pamphlets and newsbooks, cheap to buy and easily distributed.

The second sequence of statistical information focuses on taxation. In the reign of Charles I prior to 1640 the government extracted an average of £632,000 annually in taxation. During the war years, with many areas subject to the demands of both belligerents and with the burden enhanced by the unsanctioned requisitions of local commanders, and by free quarter and plunder, comparable figures cannot be calculated. But from 1649 until the Restoration the sum raised by the central governments more than doubled, to about one and a half million pounds per annum. The next great quantum leap occurred after the overthrow of James II in 1688. With Britain involved in a draining continental war until 1714, the sum which was raised by taxation rose to almost four and a half million pounds a year. Significantly, while the crushing weight of taxation during the Interregnum had been the subject of endless complaint, taxes fell scarcely at all after the Restoration. There was, however, a shift in the balance between direct and indirect taxation; a greater proportion of the money was raised through duties on trade and on consumption.

Of these series, the former, indicating the explosion of publication in the Civil War period is the better known and has been the more discussed by historians. In his great defence of unlicensed printing, *Areopagetica*, published in November 1644 John Milton set out a marvellous vision of the constructive role of print in advancing abstract truth and individual self-awareness. Groups of readers, thoughtful and serious, instructed by civic virtue and godly zeal, would read and would discuss their reading critically and creatively. Such strenuous reading and discussion would reinforce and refine their political and religious convictions, create ever wider communities of readers as ideas were exchanged, and bring new and hitherto unimagined truths to light. Books that advanced erroneous opinions should not be suppressed; that would only drive such opinions underground. Error should be engaged with openly in the creative acts of reading and discussion, and in that way it would both be refuted and play a role in the advancement of truth. Reading would destroy intellectual torpor and the false consciousness that it supported. A new, dynamic citizen body would be created: 'Methinks I see in my mind a noble and puissant nation rousing herself like a strong man after sleep and shaking her invincible locks.'[59]

Historians like Christopher Hill have argued by this utopian vision was in some measure actualised in the Civil War and Interregnum. Radical ideas were honed and disseminated in groups of readers and discussants, and then informed political action. Accounts of the Levellers in their meetings in pubs in the London suburbs in 1647 and 1648, or of the Rota Club, debating republican solutions in 1659 at a Westminster coffee house, emphasise that books were interactive: reading provoked debate; and debate produced new published statements. The argument that print played a vital role in the creation of radical sentiment in this period is often backed by denunciations from conservatives of its dangerous consequences. In 1647 the Presbyterian preacher Richard Vines, in a nice comment on distribution networks, complained that heretical opinion 'is carried up and down in books and cried at men's doors every day'.[60] Earlier, in the summer of 1642, the king bewailed the unprecedented situation in which 'all presses are open to vent whatsoever [the parliamentarians] think fit to say to the people'.[61]

Yet this kind of evidence is double-edged. Vines's sermon was, of course, printed, and Charles was answering a charge that his supporters were employing a press at York: his tone was apologetic – the papers printed by the York press 'have been extorted from us by such provocations, have not been before offered to a king'– but he insisted that parliament's employment of the press obliged him to follow suit.[62] Printing was not uniquely available for the dispersal of the radical critiques of the state or the social structure emphasised by Hill. Conservatives, too, could deploy the press to focus opinion and to construct political parties; they did so with notable success in 1659 and 1660. The unconsidered, conventional beliefs that Milton imagined would be swept away by open reading and debate could as easily be reinforced by those processes. Conservatives proved as skilled as their radical opponents in employing the new demotic forms and voices, presenting their own cases, and contesting the views of their opponents in a variety of literary genres – logical demonstration, denunciation, parody and mockery. The complexity of the situation is nicely caught in the attack on heresy launched by the Presbyterian Thomas Edwards in 1645 and 1646. Edwards wrote of the evils perpetrated by 'audacious men and their daring books'; such books should be burned, such men disciplined.[63] Yet his attack was through the press and his writing mirrored the crude *ad hominem* denunciation for which he chastised his opponents. And he gloated over the swift sale achieved by his works and the letters of support that poured in from avid readers in the provinces. The radical propagandist William Walwyn was appalled by Edwards's relentless vituperation: the authorities should take action against 'this unparalleled use of the press which you have taken, to name in public so many of their faithful adherents in so reproachful a manner'.[64]

The swift circulation of news and opinion through the press did not wholly conform to the utopian vision hymned by Milton, but it did powerfully reinforce and enhance the construction of a political nation that was broadly based both geographically and socially. Printing eroded blinkered localism and extended political understanding, already well developed, into classes below the gentry and the municipal elites. It is in this context that we must understand the second statistical series, concerning taxation. The experience of the Civil War showed, most obviously, that England could bear a far greater weight of taxation without risking the destruction of its economy than had previously been imagined. And it showed that taxation, if it was to be successful, had to entail the consent and involvement of the political nation. The representatives of the taxpayers in parliament voted the taxation; with direct taxation, the taxpayers played the major role in laying and levying the sums. These practices, too, had pre-war precedents, not only in relation to revenue but to the enforcement of the criminal law and the administration of social policies. But the construction of a well-informed body of citizens, and their vital involvement in the business of government, characteristics which differentiated England from its continental counterparts and rivals in the eighteenth century, owed much to the experience of the Civil War and Interregnum. The dynamic reinforcement and realisation of these aspects in the period 1640 to 1660 represented, if not a revolution, a significant acceleration in the process of the development of a distinctive English polity and political culture.

Notes

Notes to Introduction

1. Conrad Russell, *The Fall of the British Monarchies, 1637–1642* (Oxford, 1991), pp. 144–45.
2. So Ruth E. Mayers, chastising historians who had written on the failure of the restored Rump in 1659: *1659: The Crisis of the Commonwealth* (Woodbridge, 2004), p. 6.
3. Alan Everitt, *The Local Community and the Great Rebellion* (London, 1969), pp. 5, 8; Alan Everitt, *Change in the Provinces* (Leicester, 1969), pp. 47, 48.
4. Glenn Burgess, *Absolute Monarchy and the Stuart Constitution* (New Haven, 1996), p. 2.
5. Sean Kelsey, 'The Death of Charles I', *Historical Journal*, 45 (2002), p. 727.

Notes to Chapter 1: Why Did Charles I Call the Long Parliament?

1. Royal declaration of 10 March 1629, S. R. Gardiner, *The Constitutional Documents of the Puritan Revolution, 1625–1660* (3rd edn, Oxford, 1906), pp. 84, 97.
2. Royal Proclamation of 27 March, S. R. Gardiner, *The History of England from the Accession of James I to the Outbreak of the Civil War*, 10 vols (1896), vii, pp. 81–82.
3. Contemporary account of events in St Giles on 23 July 1637, Gardiner, *History of England*, viii, p. 315.
4. Charles I to the duke of Hamilton, 25 August 1637, Kevin Sharpe, *The Personal Rule of Charles I* (1992), p. 789.
5. Peyton to Henry Oxinden, 26 November 1638, Sharpe, *Personal Rule*, p. 797.
6. Contemporary account of the discussion between the king and Sir Thomas Wilsford, M. C. Fissel, *The Bishops' Wars: Charles I's Campaigns against Scotland* (Cambridge, 1994), p. 22.

7. Conrad Russell, *The Fall of the British Monarchies, 1637–1642* (Oxford, 1991), p. 93.

8. Windebank, a privy counsellor, to the English ambassador in Madrid, Russell, *Fall of the British Monarchies*, pp. 92–93.

9. Contemporary accounts: for Lincolnshire, Clive Holmes, *Seventeenth Century Lincolnshire* (Lincoln, 1980), p. 138; for Northamptonshire, Bedfordshire Record Office, J. 1369.

10. Earl of Northumberland to earl of Leicester, Sharpe, *Personal Rule*, pp. 857–58.

11. Russell, *Fall of the British Monarchies*, p. 126.

12. Earl of Northumberland to earl of Leicester, Russell, *Fall of the British Monarchies*, p. 123.

13. The lawyer, William Lambarde, in his 1582 handbook for magistrates, Felicity Heal and Clive Holmes, *The Gentry in England and Wales, 1500–1700* (Basingstoke, 1994), p. 167.

14. Heal and Holmes, *The Gentry*, p. 175.

15. Register of the privy council, M. C. Fissel, *The Bishops' Wars: Charles I's Campaigns against Scotland, 1638–1640* (Cambridge, 1994), p. 208.

16. Edward, Viscount Conway's 'Relation': Bodleian Library, MS Clarendon 19, fol. 165.

17. Reports from the sheriffs to the privy council, from *CSPD, 1640*, pp. 1, 230, 317, 579, 599.

18. Reports from sheriffs to the privy council: *CSPD, 1640*, pp. 266, 300, 599, 657; National Archives, SP 16/464/24.

19. Wandesforde's 'Book of Instructions', Heal and Holmes, *The Gentry*, p. 199.

20. Jury charges quoted are *HMC Verulam*, pp. 186–87 (Hertfordshire); Warwickshire RO, CR 136 B711 (Warwickshire); Conyers Read (ed.), *William Lambarde and Local Government* (Ithaca, New York, 1962), pp. 161–65 (Kent).

21. Clive Holmes, 'Liberty, Taxation and Property', in J. H. Hexter (ed.), *Parliament and Liberty from the Reign of Elizabeth to the English Civil War* (Stanford, California, 1992), p. 136.

22. Report of the Bedford meeting by Richard Taylor JP, Richard Cust, *The Forced Loan and English Politics* (Oxford, 1987), p. 161.

23. Report on the meeting at Lincoln from the commissioners, Cust, *The Forced Loan*, p. 175.

24. Narrative, probably by the sheriff, Sir Peter Wentworth, National Archives, SP16/327/126.

25. The sheriff, Sir Humphrey Mildmay, to the council, John Walter, *Under-*

standing Popular Violence in the English Revolution (Cambridge, 1999), p. 141.

26. Report of the Venetian ambassador, William Hunt, *The Puritan Moment* (Cambridge, Massachusetts, 1983) p. 270.

27. Alison Gill, 'Ship Money during the Personal Rule of Charles I: Politics, Ideology and the Law, 1634 to 1640' (unpublished Ph.D. thesis, Sheffield University, 1990), p. 416.

28. S. P. Salt, 'Sir Simonds D'Ewes and the Levying of Ship-Money, 1635–1640', *Historical Journal*, 37 (1994), p. 257.

29. Thomas Pychard to the Council, *CSPD, 1640*, p. 315.

30. The sheriff, Sir Walter Norton, to the council, Clive Holmes, 'The County Community in Stuart Historiography', *Journal of British Studies*, 19 (1980), p. 66.

31. Coventry's Star Chamber charge, John Rushworth, *Historical Collections*, 8 vols (London, 1680–1701), ii, pp. 297–98.

32. *Articles of Accusation, Exhibited by the Commons . . . against Sir John Bramston* (1641), p. 33.

33. Sheriffs of Nottinghamshire and Cheshire to the council, *CSPD, 1637–38*, pp. 443, 451.

34. Holmes, *Seventeenth-Century Lincolnshire* , p. 133.

35. Sharpe, *Personal Rule*, p. 865.

36. *CSPD, 1640*, p. 7.

37. Nicholas Tyacke, *Anti-Calvinists: The Rise of English Arminianism, c. 1590–1640* (Oxford, 1987) p. 236.

38. Petition to Laud, Tyacke, *Anti-Calvinists*, p. 189.

39. Documents relating to the case in the court of Ecclesiastical High Commission against Vicars, Holmes, *Seventeenth-Century Lincolnshire*, pp. 42–43, 62–63.

40. Visitation articles, Tyacke, *Anti-Calvinists*, pp. 206, 207.

41. Curll to the president of Magdalen College, Oxford, 1636, Kenneth Fincham, 'Episcopal Government, 1603–1640', in K. Fincham (ed.), *The Early Stuart Church* (Basingstoke, 1993), p. 83.

42. The Northampton lawyer, Robert Woodford, in his diary, Tyacke, *Anti-Calvinsts*, p. 209.

43. [William Prynne], *Newes from Ipswich* (Ipswich, 1636), sig. 2, 2v; Henry Burton, *For God and the King* (1636), pp. 15, 159.

44. Woodford, in his diary: see John Fielding, 'Opposition to the Personal Rule of Charles I: The Diary of Robert Woodford', *Historical Journal*, 31 (1988), p. 778.

45. 'A Satire to the Chief Rulers', C. J. Sissons, *Lost Plays of Shakespeare's Age* (Cambridge, 1936), p. 193.
46. John Ley to Bishop Bridgeman, Tyacke, *Anti-Calvinists*, p. 223.
47. Julian Davies, *The Caroline Captivity of the Church* (Oxford, 1992), p. 284.
48. Laud's diary, Andrew Foster, 'The Clerical Estate Revitalised', in Fincham (ed.), *Early Stuart Church*, p. 141.
49. For Titley, Holmes, *Lincolnshire*, pp. 114–16; for Drake, Harold Smith, *The Ecclesiastical History of Essex* (Colchester, 1932), pp. 76–81, 180.
50. D. Parsons (ed.), *The Diary and Correspondence of Sir Henry Slingsby* (1836), pp. 19–21.
51. Preamble to the canons, Russell, *The Fall of the British Monarchies*, p. 137.
52. The pamphlet, *Information from the Scottish Nation*, in John Bruce (ed.), *Notes of the Treaty Carried on at Ripon*, Camden Society, old series, 100 (1869), p. 71.
53. Information of the Rev. John Michaelson, K. W. Shipps, 'Lay Patronage of East Anglian Puritan Clerics in Pre-Revolutionary England' (unpublished Ph.D. thesis, Yale University, 1971), p. 407.
54. Sir Edward Osborne to Lord Conway, D. Scott, 'Hannibal at Our Gates: Loyalists and Fifth-Columnists during the Bishops' Wars: The Case of Yorkshire', *Historical Research*, 70 (1997), p. 282.
55. Russell, *The Fall of the British Monarchies*, p. 153.

Notes to Chapter 2: How Did the King Gain Support in Parliament?

1. Contemporary accounts, C. V. Wedgwood, *Thomas Wentworth, First Earl of Strafford, 1593–1641: A Revaluation* (1961), pp. 386, 389.
2. Wedgwood, *Strafford*, p. 372.
3. The king's speech on the scaffold, 30 January 1649, C. V. Wedgwood, *The Trial of Charles I* (1964), p. 190.
4. Quotations are from the Remonstrance and the petition presented to the king with the Remonstrance, S. R. Gardiner (ed.), *The Constitutional Documents of the Puritan Revolution* (3rd edn, Oxford, 1906), pp. 202–32; quotations from pp. 203, 206, 225.
5. Memoir of Sir Philip Warwick, S. R. Gardiner, *History of England from the Accession of James I to the Outbreak of the Civil War, 1603–1642*, 10 vols (1896), x, p. 77.
6. Anthony Fletcher, *The Outbreak of the English Civil War* (1981), p. 74.
7. Contemporary pamphlet, Gardiner, *History of England, 1603–42*, ix, p. 327.
8. Hyde's recollection of a conversation with Essex, Gardiner, *History of England, 1603–42*, ix, p. 341.

9. Herne, pleading for Laud, C. V. Wedgwood, *The King's War* (London, 1958), p. 361.
10. Contemporary account of Strafford's trial, Gardiner, *History of England, 1603–42*, ix, pp. 331–32.
11. Speech by Sir John Culpepper MP, Conrad Russell, *The Fall of the British Monarchies, 1637–1642* (Oxford, 1991), p. 288.
12. Newsletter of April 1641, to Sir John Lambe, Russell, *The Fall of the British Monarchies*, p. 291. Sir John Temple to earl of Leicester, Fletcher, *The Outbreak of the English Civil War*, p. 34.
13. Sir John Temple to earl of Leicester, Fletcher, *The Outbreak of the English Civil War*, p. 34.
14. For the Ten Propositions, see Gardiner, *Constitutional Documents*, p. 164.
15. Gardiner, *History of England, 1603–42*, ix, pp. 56–57
16. Hyde's speech in the Commons, Brian Wormald, *Clarendon: Politics, Historiography and Religion, 1640–1660* (Cambridge, 1951), p. 20.
17. Scottish Commissioners in London, to their colleagues in Newcastle, Russell, *The Fall of the British Monarchies*, p. 198.
18. Speech of Sir Simonds D'Ewes, Harold Shaw, *A History of the English Church during the Civil Wars and Commonwealth*, 2 vols, (1900), i, p. 22.
19. Letter from the Scots commissioner, Robert Baillie, Shaw *A History of the English Church*, i, p. 18.
20. The petition is in Gardiner, *Constitutional Documents*, pp. 137–44.
21. Scottish Commissioners in London to their colleagues in Newcastle, Gardiner, *History of England, 1603–42*, ix, p. 247.
22. John Pyne to Thomas Smythe, Fletcher, *The Outbreak of the English Civil War*, p. 97.
23. D'Ewes's Diary, Russell, *The Fall of the British Monarchies*, p. 426.
24. D'Ewes's speech, Fletcher, *The Outbreak of the English Civil War*, p. 100; Wray's speeches on religion, Clive Holmes, *Seventeenth-Century Lincolnshire* (Lincoln, 1980), p. 144.
25. Gardiner, *History of England, 1603–42*, ix, p. 285.
26. Speeches by Strode and Pym, Fletcher, *The Outbreak of the English Civil War*, p. 155 and Gardiner, *History of England, 1603–42*, x, p. 76.
27. Fletcher, *The Outbreak of the English Civil War*, p. 150.
28. Dering's account, W. M. Lamont, *Godly Rule, 1603–1660* (1969), p. 81.
29. Letters to Sir Edward Dering from two Kentish ministers, Thomas Wilson and Richard Culmer, in L. B. Larkin (ed.), *Proceedings Principally in the County of Kent*, Camden Society, old series, 80 (1862), pp. 40, 120.
30. Digby's speech, Gardiner, *History of England, 1603–42*, ix, p. 277; Waller's speech, Fletcher, *The Outbreak of the English Civil War*, p. 123.

31. Clive Holmes, *The Suffolk Committees for Scandalous Ministers, 1644–1646* (Ipswich, 1970), p. 9

32. Sir John Danvers to Sir Edward Dering, Fletcher, *The Outbreak of the English Civil War*, p. 111.

33. Thomas Knyvett to John Buxton: Cambridge University Library, Buxton MSS, box 97, c. 108.

34. *A Discoverie of Six Women Preachers* (1641).

35. Robert Abbott's letters to Sir Edward Dering, Derek Hirst, 'The Defection of Sir Edward Dering, 1640–1641', *Historical Journal*, 15 (1972), p. 206; Alan Everitt, *The Community of Kent and the Great Rebellion* (Leicester, 1966), p. 87.

36. Royalist newspaper account, Brian Manning, *The English People and the English Revolution* (1976), p. 36.

37. Richard Baxter's autobiography, Manning, *The English People and the English Revolution*, p. 35.

38. Holmes, *Seventeenth-Century Lincolnshire*, p. 154.

39. Fletcher, *The Outbreak of the English Civil War*, p. 123.

40. Robert Greville, Lord Brooke, *A Discourse Opening the Nature of that Episcopacie which is Exercised in England* (1641), p. 122.

Notes to Chapter 3: How Did the King Get an Army?

1. Newsbook account, Joyce Lee Malcolm, *Caesar's Due: Loyalty and King Charles* (1983), p. 32.

2. Pamphlet version of the petition, John Walter, *Understanding Popular Violence in the English Revolution* (Cambridge, 1999), p. 322.

3. The petition signed at Dunmow, Clive Holmes, *The Eastern Association in the English Civil War* (Cambridge, 1974), pp. 34–35.

4. Charles I's answer to the Nineteen Propositions, Conrad Russell, *The Fall of the British Monarchies, 1637–1642* (Oxford, 1991), p. 515.

5. Edward Symmons's account of his treatment, Holmes, *The Eastern Association*, p. 35.

6. Kentish petition, and the commentary in the journal of Sir Roger Twysden, Alan Everitt, *The Community of Kent and the Great Rebellion, 1640–1660* (Leicester, 1966), pp. 97, 100.

7. Everitt, *The Community of Kent*, p. 92.

8. John Morrill, *Cheshire, 1630–1660: County Government and Society during the English Revolution* (Oxford, 1974), p. 50.

9. Walter, *Understanding Popular Violence*, p. 127.

10. Letters from Herefordshire JPs to Sir Robert Harley, and Lady Brilliana

Harley to her son, Edward, Jacqueline Eales, *Puritans and Roundheads: The Harleys of Brampton Bryan and the Outbreak of the English Civil War* (Cambridge, 1990), pp. 134, 136.

11. Nottinghamshire gentry to Sir Thomas Hutchinson MP, Anthony Fletcher, *The Outbreak of the English Civil War* (1981), p. 307.

12. *Answer to the Nineteen Propositions*, and instructions to the assize judges, Walter, *Understanding Popular Violence*, pp. 19–20, 129.

13. Affidavit of John Peacock, Holmes, *The Eastern Association*, p. 44.

14. Letter to the earl of Middlesex from his steward, Dan Beaver, 'The Great Deer Massacre: Animals, Honor and Communication in Early Modern England', *Journal of British Studies*, 38 (1999), p. 187.

15. Reports of Sheriff Heron and the JPs, Holmes, *Lincolnshire*, pp. 154–55.

16. Walter, *Understanding Popular Violence*, p. 325.

17. Walter, *Understanding Popular Violence*, p. 154.

18. Holmes, *Eastern Association*, p. 33.

19. Fletcher, *The Outbreak of the English Civil War*, pp. 270–71.

20. John Morrill, *Revolt in the Provinces* (2nd edn, 1999), p. 63.

21. Tract explaining the actions of the Lincolnshire men, Holmes, *Lincolnshire*, pp. 147–50, 156–57.

22. Parliamentary commissioners to the Speaker, R. N. Worth (ed.), *The Buller Papers* (privately printed, 1895), p. 55.

23. Edward Hyde, earl of Clarendon, *The History of the Rebellion*, ed. W. Dunn Macray, 6 vols (Oxford, 1888), ii, p. 449.

24. Correspondence of Sir John Holland, Sir John Potts and Sir John Spelman, Holmes, *Eastern Association*, pp. 57, 61.

25. A contemporary account and criticism of the Yorkshire treaty, *Reasons Why Sir John Hotham Cannot in Honour Agree to the Treaty of Pacification* (1642), p. 3.

26. Jeremiah Burroughs, *The Glorious Name of God, the Lord of Hosts* (1643), pp. 5, 73.

27. Account of Edward Symmons, Eales, *Puritans and Roundheads*, p. 176.

28. John Hampden to Sir Thomas Barrington; newsbook account: Holmes, *Eastern Association*, pp. 34, 38.

29. Thomas Jenyson JP, P. I. King and Joan Wake, 'The Matter of Isham Cross', *Northamptonshire Past and Present*, 1 part 3 (1950), p. 24.

30. William Beamont (ed.), *A Discourse of the Warr in Lancashire, Written by Major Edward Robinson, after 1651*, Chetham Society, 62 (1864), p. 10.

31. A. J. Hopper, '*The Readiness of the People*': The Formation and Emergence of the Army of the Fairfaxes, 1642–3 (York, 1997), p. 7.

32. Burroughs, *The Glorious Name of God*, p. 5.

33. Wharton's letters in Stuart Peachey, *The Edgehill Campaign and the Letters of Nehemiah Wharton* (Leigh-on-Sea, 1989), pp. 5, 22.
34. Margaret, duchess of Newcastle, *The Life of William Cavendish, Duke of Newcastle*, ed. C. H. Firth (London, 1886) p. 19; P. R. Newman, 'The King's Servants: Conscience, Principle and Sacrifice in Armed Royalism', in John Morrill, Paul Slack, Daniel Woolf (eds), *Public Duty and Private Conscience in Seventeenth-Century England* (Oxford, 1993), pp 226, 230.
35. Salusbury to his sister, Lady Lloyd, National Library of Wales, MS 5390D.
36. Courtenay to Sir Richard Buller, Mark Stoyle, *Loyalty and Locality: Popular Allegiance in Devon during the English Civil War* (Exeter, 1994), p. 205.
37. Clarendon, *History*, ii, pp. 367, 372.
38. *The Stanley Papers, Part III*, ed. F. R Raines, Chetham Society, 70 (1867), 'The History and Antiquities of the Isle of Man', by the earl of Derby, pp. 1, 8; Sir Bevill Greville to his wife, Eliot Warburton (ed.), *Memoirs of Prince Rupert and the Cavaliers*, 3 vols (1849), i, pp. 420–21.
39. Published letter from 'an eminent Cavalier', Malcolm, *Caesar's Due*, p. 45.
40. Davenport's account, J. S. Morrill, 'William Davenport and the 'Silent Majority' of Early Stuart England', *Journal of the Chester Archaeological Society*, 58 (1975), p. 128.
41. Coningsby's defence of his proceedings, Bodleian Library, MS Tanner 303, fol. 114.
42. Parliamentary newsbooks, J. R. Phillips, *The Civil War in Wales and the Marches*, 2 vols (1874), ii, pp. 16, 19, 24; Ann Hughes, *Politics, Society and Civil War in Warwickshire, 1620–1660* (Cambridge, 1987), p. 149.
43. Richard Baxter, *Reliquiae Baxterianae*, ed. Matthew Sylvester, (1696), pp. 42, 44.
44. Contemporary newsbooks, Brian Manning, *The English People and the English Revolution* (1976), p. 246.
45. Contemporary narrative of the siege, G. Ormerod (ed.), *Tracts Relating to Military Proceedings in Lancashire*, Chetham Society, 2 (1844), p. 179.
46. Wharton's letters, Peachey (ed.), *The Edgehill Campaign and the Letters of Nehemiah Wharton*, p. 22.
47. Everitt, *The Community of Kent*, p. 97.

Notes to Chapter 4: Why Did Parliament Win the Civil War?

1. Thomas Carlyle, *The Letters and Speeches of Oliver Cromwell*, 3 vols, ed. S. C. Lomas (London, 1904), iii, 65.
2. Letter of May 1644 from Digby to the earl of Ormond, in Thomas Carte,

Life of James, Duke of Ormonde 3 vols (1735–36), iii, *A Collection of Letters*, p. 298.

3. Letter of 27 May 1644 from Ormond to Archbishop Williams, in Mark Stoyle, *Soldiers and Strangers: An Ethnic History of the English Civil War* (New Haven and London, 2005), p. 60.

4. Edward Drake's diary of the siege, A. R. Bayley, *The Great Civil War in Dorset* (Taunton, 1910), pp. 149, 164.

5. City petition, Maurice Ashley, *Financial and Commercial Policy under the Cromwellian Protectorate* (Oxford, 1934), p. 98.

6. Lord Byron to the earl of Ormond, S. R. Gardiner, *The History of the Great Civil War, 1642–1649*, 4 vols (1894), i, p. 295–96; Hopton's autobiographical history of the war, Stoyle, *Soldiers and Strangers*, p. 62.

7. The bitter sarcasm is that of Robert Baillie, a Presbyterian divine and Scottish Commissioner in London, Clive Holmes, *The Eastern Association in the English Civil War* (Cambridge, 1974), p. 208

8. Rupert's Diary, Eliot Warburton (ed.), *Memoirs of Prince Rupert and the Cavaliers*, 3 vols (1849) ii, p. 468.

9. Derby's book of private devotions, Ernest Broxap, *The Great Civil War in Lancashire* (Manchester, 1910), p. 147.

10. Fitzwilliam Coningsby's defence, Bodleian Library, Tanner MS 303, fol. 125v; Scudamore's published *Defence*, Ian Atherton (ed.), *Sir Barnabas Scudamore's Defence* (Akron, Ohio, 1992), p. 55.

11. Contemporary accounts of the siege of Manchester, G. Ormerod (ed.), *Tracts Relating to Military Proceedings in Lancashire*, Chetham Society, 2 (1844), pp. 56, 107, 122; Broxap, *Great Civil War in Lancashire*, p. 49; Brian Manning, *The English People and the English Revolution* (1976), p. 209.

12. Contemporary tract, and subsequent recollections by the parliamentarians John Hodgson and Joseph Lister, A. J. Hopper, '*The Readiness of the People': The Formation and Emergence of the Army of the Fairfaxes, 1642–3* (York, 1997), p. 10.

13. Contemporary account, Manning, *English People*, p. 217.

14. Sir Thomas Fairfax to his father, Lord Fairfax, Hopper, *Readiness of the People*, p. 11.

15. The information of William Child, 1644 23 February, William Phillips (ed.), 'The Ottley Papers Relating to the Civil War', *Transactions of the Shropshire Archaeological and Natural History Society*, 8 (1896), pp. 228–29.

16. London newspaper account of the exchanges between Blake and Wyndham, Emanuel Green, 'The Siege and Defence of Taunton', *Proceedings*

of the Somersetshire Archaeological and Natural History Society, 25 (1879), part 2, pp. 37–38.

17. Cromwell's deposition against Manchester, Holmes, *Eastern Association*, pp. 197–98.

18. Letter from Willoughby to Denbigh, June 1644, Clive Holmes, *Seventeenth-Century Lincolnshire* (Lincoln, 1980), p. 184.

19. Cromwell to the Committee of the Eastern Association, Holmes, *Eastern Association*, p. 92.

20. Christopher Hill, *God's Englishman: Oliver Cromwell and the English Revolution* (1970), p. 67.

21. Biography of Springate by his wife, Margaret, Alan Everitt, *The Community of Kent and the Great Rebellion* (Leicester, 1966), p. 148.

22. Protest of the Hertfordshire MPs to the Commons, Holmes, *Eastern Association*, p. 192.

23. Warwickshire petition to the House of Lords, Ann Hughes, *Politics, Society and Civil War in Warwickshire, 1620–1660* (Cambridge, 1987), p. 179; Rev. George Carter to Sir Simonds D'Ewes, Clive Holmes (ed.), *The Suffolk Committees of Scandalous Ministers*, Suffolk Record Society, 13 (1970), pp. 108, 111, 112.

24. Post-Civil War account by Worcester of his service to the king's cause, *HMC 12th Report*, appendix 9 (1891), p. 60.

25. Sir John Mennes to Prince Rupert, February 1644; Lord Byron to Lord Digby, April 1645, J. R. Phillips, *The Civil War in Wales and the Marches*, 2 vols (1874), ii, pp. 136, 246.

26. *HMC 12th Report*, appendix. 9 (1891), p. 42.

27. Letter from Wyndham to Prince Rupert, January 1645, Warburton (ed.), *Prince Rupert*, iii, pp. 47–48.

28. William Waring to Sir Francis Otley, January 1644, Ronald Hutton, *The Royalist War Effort, 1642–1646* (1982), p. 127; Archbishop Williams to Lord Digby, April 1645, Phillips, *Civil War in Wales and the Marches*, ii, p. 244.

29. Kent committee to corporation of Sandwich, Everitt, *Community of Kent*, pp. 136–37.

30. Sir John Holland's speech to the Commons, Holmes, *Eastern Association*, p. 191.

31. Norfolk committee to the Commons, October 1644; Luke Voyce to the central committee of sequestration, 1645: Holmes, *Eastern Association*, p. 192.

32. Petition to the king from the Marcher Association, January 1645, Atherton, *Scudamore's Defence*, p. 11.

33. Letters to Prince Rupert from Dudley Wyatt (16 January 1645), Prince Maurice (29 January) and Barnaby Scudamore (20 February), British Library, Additional MS 18982, fos 16, 27, 33.

34. Lord Byron to Lord Digby, April 1645, in Phillips, *Civil War in Wales and the Marches*, ii, p. 246.

35. David Underdown, *Somerset in the Civil War and Interregnum* (Newton Abbot, 1973), p. 92.

36. *The Desires and Resolutions of the Clubmen of ... Dorset and Wiltshire* (July 1645), p. 1; Worcester declaration in the newsbook, *The Kingdomes Weekly Intelligencer*, no. 91 (March 1645), p. 728.

37. Edward Hyde, earl of Clarendon, *The History of the Rebellion* ed. W. Dunn Macray, 6 vols (Oxford, 1888), ii, p. 472.

38. An anonymous account of the siege of Colchester, *HMC 12th Report*, appendix 9, pp. 21, 26, 28–29.

39. Colonel Slingsby's account of the battle of Roundway Down, C. E. H. Chadwyck Healey (ed.), *Bellum Civile: Hopton's Narrative of his Campaign in the West*, Somerset Record Society, 18 (1902), p. 95.

Notes to Chapter 5: Why Was the King Executed?

1. The king's speech on the scaffold, C. V. Wedgwood, *The Trial of Charles I* (2001), pp. 190, 191

2. The king in debate with the president of the court, 22 January 1649, ibid., p. 140.

3. From the charge against the king, read on 20 January by the prosecutor, John Cook, ibid., p. 130.

4. Charles I to Lord Digby, 26 March 1646, Thomas Carte, *History of the Life of James, Duke of Ormonde*, 3 vols (London, 1735–36), iii, p. 452.

5. Sir John Berkeley's account of the negotiations, *A Narrative of John Ashburnham*, 2 vols (London, 1830), ii, appendix, p. cliv.

6. Charles I to William Hopkins, 9 October 1648, C. W. Firebrace, *Honest Harry* (London, 1932), p. 344.

7. John Crewe to John Swynfen, David Underdown, *Pride's Purge* (Oxford, 1971), p. 111.

8. Robert Baillie to Mr Dickson, March 1646, S. R. Gardiner, *History of the Great Civil War*, 4 vols (London, 1894), iii, p. 84.

9. Keith Lindley and David Scott (eds), *The Journal of Thomas Juxon, 1644–1647*, Camden Society, fifth series, 13 (1999), pp. 87, 148.

10. Accusation in the army's impeachment of the eleven Members: *A Particular Charge or Impeachment* (1647), p. 28.

11. Thomas Newsham to the Committee of Duchy House, Anne Hughes, *Politics, Society and Civil War in Warwickshire, 1620–1660* (Cambridge, 1987), p. 248.

12. Newsbook, *Scottish Dove*, 119 (21–29 January 1646), p. 945.

13. Message from the House of Lords to the Commons, 9 April 1647, *Lords' Journal*, ix, p. 131.

14. Quotations are from Colonel King's public speech, Clive Holmes, 'Colonel King and Lincolnshire Politics, 1642–1646' *Historical Journal*, 16 (1973), pp. 478, 483.

15. T. J., *A Brief Representation and Discovery of the Notorious Falsehood and Dissimulation Contained in a Book Styled The Gospel Way Confirmed by Miracles* (1649).

16. Tract (1647) by Humphrey Willis, an opponent of the Somerset committee, David Underdown, *Somerset in the Civil War and Interregnum* (Newton Abbot, 1973), p. 134.

17. Thomas Edwards, *The Second Part of Gangraena* (1646), p. 122, claiming to be quoting a sermon by the Baptist Samuel Oates.

18. Edwards, *The Third Part of Gangraena* (1646), pp. 17–18, 251.

19. Published version of an army petition of March 1647, *An Appologie of the Soldiers to All Their Commission Officers*, p. 2.

20. Quotations from the *Solemn Engagement* and the *Representation of the Army*, in A. S. P. Woodhouse (ed.), *Puritanism and Liberty* (London, 1938), pp. 402, 404, 407.

21. *A Copie of a Letter Sent from the Agitators ... to All the Honest Seamen*, dated 21 June 1647.

22. A letter of 28 September, 1647 to Sir Thomas Fairfax published by John Lilburne in *The Juglers Discovered* (1647), p. 3.

23. Account of the General Council meeting and the subsequent fast on 21/22 December, John Rushworth, *Historical Collections*, 8 vols (London, 1680–1701), vii, p. 943.

24. Extracts from Lilburne's tract, *Legal Fundamental Liberties*, are reproduced in Woodhouse (ed.), *Puritanism and Liberty*, pp. 342–55.

25. *The Remonstrance of the Army*, in *The Old Parliamentary History*, iii, columns 1073–1127; quotation from col. 1125.

26. Woodhouse (ed.), *Puritanism and Liberty*, p. 477.

27. Bishop in discussion at Putney, 1 November 1647, C. H. Firth (ed.), *The Clarke Papers*, i, Camden Society, new series, 49 (1891), p. 383.

28. From later accounts of the meeting in *The None-Such Charles his Character* (1651), pp. 173–75; William Allen, *A Faithful Memorial of that Remarkable Meeting of Many of the Officers ... at Windsor* (1659), in

NOTES TO PAGES 119–131

Walter Scott (ed.), *A Collection of Tracts [from the Library] of Lord Somers*, 13 vols (2nd edn, London, 1809–15), vi, pp. 498–501.

29. Petition of Colonel Saunders's regiment in *The Declaration and Humble Representation of the Officers and Soldiers* (1648), pp. 1–2; of Colonel Harrison's regiment in *Severall Petitions Presented to his Excellency* (1648), pp. 4–5.

30. Cromwell in discussion at Putney, 1 November 1647, Firth (ed.), *Clarke Papers*, i, p. 379.

31. Letter from Cromwell to Hammond, 25 November 1648, Thomas Carlyle, *The Letters and Speeches of Oliver Cromwell*, 3 vols, ed. S. C. Lomas (London, 1904), i, pp. 393, 400.

32. Sir Thomas Wroth, in a debate in the Commons in January 1648, David Underdown (ed.), 'The Parliamentary Diary of John Boys', *Bulletin of the Institute of Historical Research*, 39 (1966), p. 155.

Notes to Chapter 6: Why Was the Rump Dissolved?

1. Ludlow's account of the dissolution, S. R. Gardiner, *History of the Commonwealth and Protectorate*, 4 vols (1903), ii, p. 263.

2. Captain John Streater, recalling Cromwell's speech in a pamphlet of 1659, Ian Gentles, *The New Model Army in England, Ireland and Scotland, 1645–1653* (Oxford, 1992), p. 432.

3. Petitions to Cromwell and the Army from Herefordshire (7 May); Bedfordshire (13 May); Chester (15 May), John Nickolls (ed.), *Original Letters and Papers of State Addressed to Oliver Cromwell* (1743), pp. 92–93.

4. S. R. Gardiner (ed.), *Constitutional Documents of the Puritan Revolution, 1625–1660* (3rd edn, Oxford, 1906), p. 339.

5. John Moyle to Robert Bennet, November 1650, Folger Shakespeare Library, MS X d 483 (71).

6. Pamphlet, A. L. Morton, *The World of the Ranters* (1970), p. 177.

7. From Richard Overton's pamphlet, *The Hunting of the Foxes* (published 21 March 1649), D. M. Wolfe (ed.), *Leveller Manifestos of the Puritan Revolution* (New York, 1944), p. 370.

8. Ibid., p. 368.

9. Cromwell's letter to Speaker Lenthall, 4 September 1650, Thomas Carlyle, *The Letters and Speeches of Oliver Cromwell*, 3 vols, ed. S. C. Lomas (London, 1904), ii, p. 106.

10. Commons Journal, Blair Worden, *The Rump Parliament* (Cambridge, 1974), p. 204.

11. From notes on the committee's meeting of 11 June 1652, British Library, Additional MS 35863 fol. 83.

12. *The Faithful Scout*, February 1652, Worden, *Rump Parliament*, p. 280.

13. Ludlow's Memoirs, Worden, *Rump Parliament*, p. 114; Cromwell's speech of 21 April 1657, Nancy L. Matthews, *William Sheppard: Cromwell's Law Reformer* (Cambridge, 1984), p. 190 n. 110.

14. *The Prisoners Remonstrance* (1649), p. 4.

15. Nickolls (ed.), *Original Letters*, p. 50.

16. Report in a royalist newsletter, David Underdown, *Pride's Purge* (Oxford, 1971), p. 202.

17. *Mercurius Politicus*, Worden, *Rump Parliament*, p. 239.

18. [Alexander Griffiths], *Mercurius Cambro-Britannicus* (1652), pp. 6, 7.

19. *Letters and Speeches of Oliver Cromwell*, ii, pp. 282–83.

20. Letter to Cromwell of February 1652 from several churches in the west midlands, Nickolls (ed.), *Original Letters*, pp. 80–81.

21. Army council to detached units of the army, Austin Woolrych, *Commonwealth to Protectorate* (Oxford, 1986), p. 51.

22. Newsbook account, Worden, *Rump Parliament*, p. 194.

23. Artillery officers at Edinburgh to the council of officers, 9 March 1653, in the newsbook, *A Perfect Diurnall of Some Passages and Proceedings of and in Relation to the Armies*, no. 174, p. 2607.

24. Cromwell in his speech to the Barebones Parliament, *Letters and Speeches*, ii, p. 280.

25. Newsbook, published on 21 April, Worden, *Rump Parliament*, p. 350.

26. Army newsletter of 23 April, Worden, *Rump Parliament*, p. 351.

27. John Jones to Dr William Stane, 19 November 1651, Worden, *Rump Parliament*, p. 288.

28. In his 1654 *Second Defence* against continental attacks on events in England since 1648, Sarah Barber, *Regicide and Republicanism* (Edinburgh, 1998), p. 206.

29. John Jones to his kinsman, Scout Master General Henry Jones, Sean Kelsey, *Inventing a Republic* (Manchester, 1997), p. 141.

30. Spencer Research Library, Kansas University, MS D 87, notebook of John Lisle, fos. 152–152v; *Journal of the House of Commons*, vii, pp. 277–78.

31. *A True and Perfect Narrative of the Several Proceedings in the Case concerning the Lord Craven* (1653), p. 24.

32. From a hostile account of the Rump's legislation, *The Anti-Projector: or The History of the Fen Project* (n.d. but 1653), p. (4).

33. Cromwell's speech to the Kingship Committee, 21 April 1657, *Letters and Speeches*, iii, p. 95.

34. John Lilburne, *A Just Reproofe to Haberdashers-Hall* (1651), p. 15.

35. Daniel O'Neale's political analysis for Hyde, C. H. Firth, 'Cromwell and the Expulsion of the Long Parliament in 1653', *English Historical Review*, 8 (1893), p. 530.

36. Whitelocke's complaint to Cromwell, Gentles, *The New Model Army*, p. 420.

37. C. H. Firth (ed.), *Ludlow's Memoirs*, 2 vols (Oxford, 1894), i, p. 353.

38. *Letters and Speeches*, ii, p. 204.

39. Mr Chidley to Cromwell, February 1651, Nickolls (ed.), *Original Letters*, p. 59.

40. A later account (1659) from Colonel Bamfylde to Secretary Thurloe, Firth (ed.), *Ludlow's Memoirs*, i, p. 353.

41. *To the Supreame Authoritie the Parliament of the Commonwealth of England* (1652), clauses 4, 5, 8, 9.

42. *A Declaration of the Armie to his Excellency the Lord General Cromwell* (1652), p. 6.

Notes to Chapter 7: Why Was Oliver Cromwell Offered the Crown?

1. The MPs Ashe and Downing, speaking on 19 January, J. T. Rutt (ed.), *The Diary of Thomas Burton* 4 vols (London, 1828), i, pp. 362, 365.

2. Journal of the House of Commons, C. H. Firth, *The Last Years of the Protectorate*, 2 vols (London, 1909), i, p. 130.

3. Lenthall, speaking in the conference with Cromwell on 11 April, *Monarchy Asserted* (1660), in Walter Scott (ed.), *A Collection of Tracts [from the Library] of Lord Somers*, 13 vols (2nd edn, London, 1809–15), vi, pp. 356–57.

4. Glynne, on 11 April, ibid., p. 359.

5. Wolseley, on 11 April, ibid., p. 360.

6. Glynne, on 11 April, ibid., p. 359.

7. From a radical tract of 1658, *A Second Narrative of the Late Parliament (So Called)*, in W. Oldys and T. Park (eds), *The Harleian Miscellany* 10 vols (London, 1808–13), iii, p. 467.

8. Ibid., p. 464.

9. Speech to the first Protectorate Parliament, 4 September 1654, Thomas Carlyle, *The Letters and Speeches of Oliver Cromwell*, ed. S. C. Lomas, 3 vols (London, 1904), ii, p. 342.

10. Speech to the Nominated Parliament, *Letters and Speeches*, ii, pp. 291, 295, 298, 299.

11. Thomas Birch (ed.), *Thurloe State Papers*, 7 vols (London, 1742), iv, pp. 208, 218.

12. Worsley to Thurloe, November 1655, Christopher Durston, *Cromwell's Major-Generals* (Manchester, 2001), p. 155.

13. Levi Fox (ed.), 'The Diary of Robert Beake', *Miscellany*, Dugdale Society, 31 (1977), pp. 117–18.

14. Henry Verney to Sir Ralph Verney, December 1655, David Underdown, 'Settlement in the Counties, 1653–1658', in G. E. Aylmer (ed.), *The Interregnum* (London, 1972), p. 176.

15. Report of the Venetian ambassador, Roy Sherwood, *Oliver Cromwell: King in All But Name, 1653–1658* (Stroud, 1997), p. 9.

16. Newsbook account of the reception of the French ambassador, Sherwood, *Oliver Cromwell*, p. 23.

17. John Nickolls (ed.), *Original Letters and Papers of State* (London, 1743), p. 115.

18. *Second Narrative*, in *Harleian Miscellany*, iii, pp. 445, 446.

19. *Letters and Speeches*, iii, p. 99.

20. Petition in August edition of the newspaper, *Mercurius Politicus*; tract by an opponent of Feake's: Bernard Capp, *The Fifth Monarchy Men* (London, 1972), pp. 67, 68.

21. Report of Powell's sermon to the Council, Capp, *Fifth Monarchy Men*, p. 101.

22. Report by Governor of Windsor Castle, Bodleian Library, MS Rawlinson A 26, fol. 243.

23. An account of the interview by Rogers's supporters, Edward Rogers, *Life and Opinions of a Fifth-Monarchy-Man* (London, 1867), pp. 189, 197.

24. Reports to the government, *Thurloe State Papers*, iii, pp. 136–37; v, pp. 60–61.

25. Report of Cromwell's interview with John Rogers, Rogers, *Life and Opinions*, p. 215.

26. *Letters and Speeches*, ii, pp. 340, 341.

27. Report of 10 November debate in Goddard's diary, *Burton's Diary*, i, pp. lxiv, lxvi-lxvii.

28. Ludlow, *Memoirs*, Barry Coward, *The Cromwellian Protectorate* (Manchester, 2002), p. 25; Downing speaking in parliament, 19 January 1657, *Burton's Diary*, i, pp. 364–65.

29. The indictment, and a brief for the accused, April 1655, *Thurloe State Papers*, iii, pp. 370–71, 391–93.

30. Strickland to Thurloe, 17 April 1655, *Thurloe State Papers*, iii, 385.

31. *Burton's Diary*, i, pp. 24–25, 26.

32. *Burton's Diary*, i, pp. 49–50

33. *Burton's Diary*, i, pp. 316–17.

34. Robert Beake to Leonard Piddock, 28 March 1657, Coventry Archives, BA/H/Q/A79/302.

35. John Bridge to Henry Cromwell, November 1656, C. H. Firth, 'Cromwell and the Crown', 2 parts, *English Historical Review*, 17 (1902), 18 (1903), quote is ibid., 17, p. 439.

36. Sir Gilbert Pickering to General Montagu, November 1656, Bodleian Library, MS Carte 73, fol. 47.

37. *Burton's Diary*, i, p. 384, anonymous letter of 7 March; Anthony Morgan to Henry Cromwell, 3 March, Firth, 'Cromwell and the Crown', ii, p. 60.

38. Firth, 'Cromwell and the Crown', ii, pp. 75, 76.

39. Newspaper account of the inauguration, Roy Sherwood, *The Court of Oliver Cromwell* (London, 1977), p. 160; writ cited ibid., p. 164.

40. Matthew Alured, *The Case of Colonel Matthew Alured* (1659), p. 6.

41. Letters of 12 and 19 May, Thurloe to Henry Cromwell, *Thurloe State Papers*, v, pp. 281, 291.

42. Representations from the churches in Gloucestershire (n.d.); from Captain Bradford (4 March 1657); from the Anabaptist ministers of London (3 April): Nickolls (ed.), *State Papers*, pp. 140–43.

43. Cromwell's speeches during the kingship discussion, Blair Worden, 'Oliver Cromwell and the Sin of Achan', in David L. Smith (ed.), *Cromwell and the Interregnum* (Oxford, 2003), pp. 58, 59.

44. *Letters and Speeches*, iii, p. 192.

45. Petition from the churches in Gloucestershire (n.d.), Nickolls (ed.), *State Papers*, pp. 140–43.

46. Thurloe to Henry Cromwell, Firth, *The Last Years of the Protectorate*, ii, p. 258.

47. Henry Cromwell to Thurloe, February 1657, *Thurloe State Papers*, vi, p. 790.

48. Henry Cromwell to Thurloe, June 1657, Firth, *Last Years of the Protectorate*, ii, 276–77.

Notes to Chapter 8: Was There an English Revolution?

1. Norwich petition, in *A True Catalogue ... of the Several Places ... where ... Richard Cromwell was Proclaimed Lord Protector* (1659), p. 29.

2. Barwick to Hyde, April 1659, Thomas Birch (ed.), *Thurloe State Papers*, 7 vols (London, 1742), vii, p. 647.

3. Speeches of Archer, Northcote and Skipwith in parliament, 4 and 11 March, J. T. Rutt (ed.), *The Diary of Thomas Burton*, 4 vols (London, 1828), iv, pp 10, 33, 129.

4. Army pamphlet, David Farr, *John Lambert: Parliamentary Soldier and Cromwellian Major-General, 1619–1684* (Woodbridge, 2003), p. 194.

5. Christopher Hill, 'The Word "Revolution"', in his *A Nation of Change and Novelty* (London, 1990), p. 112.

6. George Bishop, *Mene Tekel: or The Council of the Officers of the Army* (1659, published in September), p. 5.

7. Joseph Salmon, *A Rout, A Rout* (1649 – published 10 February), sig. (A2v).

8. S. R. Gardiner, *The Constitutional Documents of the Puritan Revolution, 1625–1660* (3rd edn, Oxford, 1906), p. 388.

9. George H. Sabine (ed.), *The Works of Gerrard Winstanley* (New York, 1965), p. 502.

10. L.D., *An Exact Relation of the Proceedings and Transactions of the Late Parliament* (1654), sig. (A2v): L.D. is almost certainly the MP, Samuel Highland, a radical Baptist.

11. Thomas Carlyle, *The Letters and Speeches of Oliver Cromwell*, ed. S. C. Lomas, 3 vols (London, 1904), ii, p. 292. The speech was first published in October 1654.

12. *The Cause of God and These Nations* (March 1659), p. 4.

13. Cambridge University Library, Cholmondely (Houghton) MSS; Pell Papers, Correspondence, no. 112.

14. 'I will overturn, overturn, overturn': for the radical Abiezer Coppe's employment of this passage, see David Loewenstein, *Representing Revolution in Milton and his Contemporaries: Religion, Politics, and Polemics in Radical Puritanism* (Cambridge, 2001), pp. 100, 103, 104.

15. Speech of 4 September 1654, *Letters and Speeches*, pp. 342, 346, 350.

16. Speech of 17 September 1656, *Letters and Speeches*, p. 540.

17. The letter is undated: *Thurloe State Papers*, vii, pp. 387–88.

18. C. F. Aspinall-Oglander (ed.), *A Royalist's Notebook:The Commonplace Book of Sir John Oglander* (London, 1936), p. 109.

19. Alan Everitt, *The Community of Kent and the Great Rebellion, 1640–1660* (Leicester, 1966) p. 277.

20. Samuel Hering (1653), J. T. Cliffe, *Puritans in Conflict* (London, 1988), p. 182; Martin Mason (1655), Clive Holmes, *Seventeenth-Century Lincolnshire* (Lincoln, 1980), pp. 205–6.

21. J. W., *A Mite to the Treasury* (April, 1653), p. 15; Mr Chidley to Cromwell, February 1651, John Nickolls (ed.), *Original Letters and Papers of State Addressed to Oliver Cromwell* (London, 1743), p. 59.

22. Petition of from Norfolk, Bernard Capp, *The Fifth Monarchy Men* (London, 1972), p. 56.

23. Petition from Buckinghamshire, February 1649, in the radical newspaper, *The Moderate*, 32, p. 313.

24. Samuel Duncon, *Several Proposals Offered by a Friend to Peace and Truth* (1659), article 14; George Fox, *To the Parliament of the Commonwealth of England* (1659), article 32.

25. John Broad, *Transforming English Rural Society* (Cambridge, 2004), p. 275.

26. Felicity Heal and Clive Holmes, *The Gentry in England and Wales, 1500–1700* (Basingstoke, 1994), p. 227.

27. Speech by Edgar, 8 February, *Burton's Diary*, iv, p. 124.

28. Speeches of 9 and 17 February, by Vane and Neville, *Burton's Diary*, iii, pp. 180, 331.

29. Booth's manifestos, from which the quotations in this paragraph are taken, are *The Declaration of the Lords, Gentlemen, Citizens, Freeholders and Yeomen* and *A Letter from Sir George Booth to a Friend of His*, both 2 August 1659; on 9 August Booth issued *An Express from the Knights and Gentlemen now Engaged with Sir George Booth*.

30. Quotations from *A Letter from Divers of the Gentry of the County of Lincolne*; *The Remonstrance of the Knights, Gentlemen and Freeholders of the County of Gloucester*; *The Humble Address and Hearty Desires of the Gentlemen ... of Northampton*; *Wee the Knights, Gentlemen, Minister and Freeholders of ... Warwick*. All the addresses echo this language.

31. William Somner of Kent, Everitt, *Community of Kent*, p. 307.

32. The phrase is from *A Letter from Sir George Booth*.

33. *Some Reasons Humbly Proposed to the Officers of the Army* (April 1659), p. 4.

34. Sir John Bramston, in his autobiography, Heal and Holmes, *The Gentry in England and Wales, 1500–1700* (Basingstoke, 1994), p. 227.

35. *True Catalogue*, p. 21.

36. Davies, *Restoration*, p. 77.

37. Pamphlets from the spring of 1659, A. H. Woolrych, 'The Good Old Cause and the Fall of the Protectorate', *Cambridge Historical Journal*, 13 (1957), pp. 139–40.

38. *Twelve Plain Proposals Offered to the Honest and Faithful Officers*, published on 28 April 1659

39. Woolrych, 'Good Old Cause', p. 159.

40. Captain Needham to Charles Fleetwood, *Thurloe State Papers*, vii, p. 754.

41. Thurloe (7 September) and Fauconberg (28 September) to Henry Cromwell, *Thurloe State Papers*, vii, pp. 374, 413.

42. May petition, Godfrey Davies, *The Restoration of Charles II, 1658–1660* (Oxford, 1955), p. 77; October petition, *A True Narrative*, p. 11.

43. *To the Right Honourable the ... Parliament: The Humble Petition of the Sentinels in the Regiment Formerly Belonging to Major General Goffe* (1659).

44. The Commons Journal, Ruth E. Mayers, *The Crisis of the Commonwealth* (Woodbridge, 2004), p. 59.

45. *Thurloe State Papers*, vii, pp. 387–88.

46. Letter to the Speaker, 18 June 1659, C. H. Firth (ed.), *The Clarke Papers*, iv, Camden Society, new series, 62 (1901), p. 22.

47. Letter of 20 October, *A True Narrative of the Proceedings in Parliament, the Council of State, General Council of the Army and Committee of Safety* (1659), p. 30.

48. Josiah Berners to John Hobart, 29 November 1659, *Clarke Papers*, iv, p. 300.

49. Speech in parliament 28 February 1659, *Burton's Diary*, iii, p. 543.

50. *The Humble Remonstrance of the Commission Officers and Private Soldiers of Major General Goff's Regiment* (26 April 1659)

51. James D. Ogilvie (ed.), *Diary of Archibald Johnston of Wariston, 1655–1660*, Publications of the Scottish History Society, third series, 34 (1940), p. 139.

52. Champlain Burrage (ed.), 'A True and Short Declaration', *Transactions of the Baptist Historical Society*, 2 (1910–11), p. 149; T. E. Ellis and J. H. Davies (eds), *Gweithiau Morgan Llwyd o Wynedd*, 2 vols (Bangor, 1899–1908), i, pp. 96–98.

53. John Canne, *A Seasonable Word* (10 May 1659), p. 5.

54. Edward Phillips, *Continuation of Baker's Chronicle* (1674), p. 673.

55. *True Catalogue*, pp. 15, 59.

56. Capp, *Fifth Monarchy Men*, p. 162

57. Alexander Parker to Fox, June 1659, A. R. Barclay (ed.), *Letters ... of Early Friends* (London, 1841), p. 70.

58. *Burton's Diary*, iii, p. 228.

59. Joad Raymond, *Pamphlets and Pamphleteering in Early Modern Britain* (Cambridge, 2003), p. 274.

60. Ann Hughes, *Gangraena and the Struggle for the English Revolution* (Oxford, 2004), p. 381 n. 157.

61. Royal declaration, in Raymond, *Pamphlets and Pamphleteering*, p. 208.

62. *His Majesties Answer, to a Book Intituled the Declaration* (Cambridge, 1642), pp. 5–6.

63. Hughes, *Gangraena*, p. 361.

64. Walwyn's tract against Edwards, in Hughes, *Gangraena*, p. 413.

Bibliographic Essay

Overview

The best overview of the period from the Personal Rule of Charles to the Restoration of his son is Austin Woolrych's *Britain in Revolution, 1625–1660* (Oxford, 2002). It provides a thorough and reliable narrative. It suffers from the classic problem of general works on this complex period: Woolrych's analysis, often acute, can get buried beneath the weight of detail. Jonathan Scott's *England's Troubles: Seventeenth-Century English Political Instability in European Context* (Cambridge, 2000) is a fascinating attempt to locate the period between 1640 and 1660 in a longer history of political instability and rebuilding. Its arguments are consistently engaging, but its discussion of detail is necessarily selective. Ronald Hutton, in chapters 1–4 of his *Debates in Stuart History* (Basingstoke, 2004), reflects – often with interestingly different conclusions – on the historiographical developments discussed in the introduction to this book.

Biographies

Biographies are also a good way of approaching the period as a whole. The recently published *Oxford Dictionary of National Biography* (Oxford, 2004) provides a series of short biographies of many of the major actors in the Civil War and Interregnum. These vary in quality, but John Morrill's study of Oliver Cromwell (in volume 14) must be singled out as a superb example of the biographer's craft. Cromwell has been generally fortunate in his biographers. The best of the recent studies is J. C. Davis, *Oliver Cromwell* (London, 2001), but Christopher Hill's older *God's Englishman: Oliver Cromwell and the English Revolution* (London, 1970) is still engaging and provocative.

Local Studies

Much research on early modern England in the last forty years has taken the form of local studies. Such work can be very narrow in focus, but several books that concentrate upon the Civil War and Interregnum, or that contain extensive discussion of the period, display an awareness of the broader issues and provide lively discussion. Alan Everitt, *The Community of Kent and the Great Rebellion, 1640–1660* (Leicester, 1966) was the trailblazing work in this field; its sensitivity and elegant presentation ensure that it is still an essential work. I also recommend John Morrill, *Cheshire, 1630–1660: County Government and Society during the English Revolution* (Oxford, 1977); A. R. Warmington, *Civil War, Interregnum and Restoration in Gloucestershire, 1640–1672* (Woodbridge, 1997); Clive Holmes, *Seventeenth-Century Lincolnshire* (Lincoln, 1980); David Underdown, *Somerset in the Civil War and Interregnum* (Newton Abbot, 1973); Anthony Fletcher, *A County Community in Peace and War: Sussex, 1600–1660* (London, 1975); and Ann Hughes, *Politics, Society and Civil War in Warwickshire, 1620–1660* (Cambridge, 1987).

Collections of Essays

Much work on the period has taken the form of articles in various scholarly journals. Some collections of particularly important work from such journals have been published, and four of these will be referred to below in the chapter sections of this bibliography.

Richard Cust and Ann Hughes (eds), *The English Civil War* (London, 1997).

Peter Gaunt (ed.), *The English Civil War: The Essential Readings* (Oxford, 2000).

John Morrill (ed.), *The Nature of the English Revolution* (London, 1993).

David L. Smith (ed.), *Cromwell and the Interregnum* (Oxford, 2003).

CHAPTER BIBLIOGRAPHIES

Chapter 1: Why Did Charles I Call the Long Parliament?

I disagree profoundly with the emphases and conclusions of Kevin Sharpe's *The Personal Rule of Charles I* (London, 1992), but its revisionist account, stressing the success of the king's policies and the support that they received from his English subjects, is thorough, challenging and beautifully presented. Mark Kishlansky has developed an aspect of Sharpe's argument, in *Past and Present.* I find Richard Cust's emphasis, in his *Charles I: A Political Biography* (Harlow, 2005), on Charles's failure to comprehend the structures of English government and the limitations of royal authority that these imposed altogether more convincing.

Nicholas Tyacke's article, 'Puritanism, Arminianism and Counter-Revolution', in Cust and Hughes (eds), *The English Civil War* (chap. 5), is still the best account of the challenge of Arminiansm to Calvinist orthodoxy, though it underestimates, to my mind, the threat posed by the Puritans to a uniform national church.

My account of the pressures of Charles's policies in the provinces owes much to the local studies listed above, to T. G. Barnes's *Somerset 1625: A County's Government during the 'Personal Rule'* (1961), and to the work of my graduate student, Henrik Langelueddecke; his forthcoming article, in the *Journal of British Studies*, ' "I finde all men & my officers all soe unwilling": The Collection of Ship Money, 1635–1640' is particularly important. John Morrill's *Revolt in the Provinces: The People of England and the Tragedies of War, 1630–1648* (London, 1998), de-emphasises (with Sharpe) the constitutional hostility to ship-money; I find this analysis less convincing than Morrill's discussion of the local response to the Civil War which form the second and third parts of this influential book.

On the failure of Charles's resort to arms against his rebellious Scottish subjects, the best studies are Conrad Russell, *The Fall of the British Monarchies* (Oxford, 1991), and M. C. Fissel, *The Bishops' Wars: Charles I's Campaigns against Scotland, 1638–1640* (Cambridge, 1994).

Three books with the same title, *The Causes of the English Civil War*, are also relevant to the arguments developed in this chapter. While the works by Ann Hughes (2nd edn, Basingstoke, 1998) and Norah Carlin (London, 1999) are excellent and perceptive works of synthesis, Conrad Russell's work (Oxford, 1990) is simply brilliant; a provocative and original masterpiece. Russell's Ford lectures at Oxford, from which the book developed, were a major inspiration for this book.

Chapter 2: How Did the King Gain Support in Parliament?

Conrad Russell's *The Fall of the British Monarchies* is not an easy book. Russell revelled in detail in this work, and, as part of his revisionist agenda, in the contingent. The trees are far more apparent than the wood. But it is an essential basis for further study.

David Smith's *Constitutional Royalism and the Search for a Settlement, c. 1640–1649* (Cambridge, 1994) provides a subtle examination of the convictions of developing royalist group at Westminster. B. H. G. Wormald's work, *Clarendon: Politics, History and Religion* (Cambridge, 1951), is idiosyncratic but perceptive on nascent royalist support.

The religious debates are well discussed by John Morrill, in 'The Attack on the Church of England in the Long Parliament', in Morrill (ed.), *The Nature of the English Revolution*, (chap. 4). Derek Hirst's article, 'The Defection of Sir Edward Dering', in Gaunt (ed.), *The English Civil War: The Essential Readings* (chap. 9), is a telling study of the growing disquiet of an influential MP.

Anthony Fletcher's *The Outbreak of the English Civil War* (London, 1981) is an excellent account of the response of the localities to events at Westminster.

That is also the focus of David Cressy's new work, *England on Edge: Crisis and Revolution, 1640–1642* (Oxford, 2005); this is particularly strong on the importance of the eruption of printed works in 1641, and on disputes over religion at the level of the parish.

Chapter 3: How Did the King Get an Army?

This discussion is highly dependent on the local studies listed above (p. 224), and on Morrill's *Revolt in the Provinces*. East Anglia's response is examined in Clive Holmes, *The Eastern Association in the English Civil War* (Cambridge, 1974).

Recent work on the development of parties in the localities, and of the respective armies has taken a number of directions. John Adamson has argued the dependence of both sides on traditional ties of dependence and deference to raise forces in his 'The Baronial Context of the English Civil War', in Cust and Hughes (eds), *The English Civil War* (chap. 3). Joyce Lee Malcolm, in *Caesar's Due: Loyalty and King Charles, 1642–1646* (London, 1983), has stressed that the royalists attempted to raise men by such mechanisms, but that they failed. John Walter's detailed study of Essex, *Understanding Popular Violence in the English Revolution: The Colchester Plunderers* (Cambridge, 1999), though narrow in its specific focus, is very convincing in its account of the power of parliamentary propaganda to mobilise sections of the populace. A. J. Hopper, 'The Readiness of the People': The Formation and Emergence of the Army of the Fairfaxes, 1642–3* (York, 1997), is good on the religious motivations of the Yorkshire parliamentarians.

David Underdown, in *Revel, Riot and Rebellion: Popular Politics and Popular Culture in England* (Oxford, 1985), attempted to locate popular commitment, royalist or parliamentarian, in particular local ecological patterns and the social structures and cultures dependent on these; his arguments have been questioned and modified by John Morill, 'The Ecology of Allegiance in the English Civil War', in Morrill (ed.), *The Nature of the English Revolution* (chap. 11); and, in a detailed case study, by Mark Stoyle, *Loyalty and Locality: Popular Allegiance in Devon during the English Civil War* (Exeter, 1994).

Chapter 4:. Why Did Parliament Win the Civil War?

Macolm Wanklyn and Frank Jones, *A Military History of the English Civil War* (Harlow, 2005), which, with dark denunciations of hindsight and determinism, insists on parity of resource and thus on 'operational factors' as key to parliament's victory, is the most recent example of the kind of discussion I find so unconvincing. Ann Hughes, in her article 'The King, the Parliament and the Localities during the English Civil War', in Cust and Hughes (eds),

The English Civil War (chap. 10), first stated some of the issues discussed in this chapter.

On the royalist forces, Ronald Hutton's *The Royalist War Effort, 1642–1646* (London, 1982) is by far the best overview. Some of its emphases are controversial, but P. R. Newman's challenge, 'The Royalist Party in Arms: The Peerage and Army Command', in Colin Jones, Malyn Newit, Stephen Roberts (eds), *Politics and People in Revolutionary England* (Oxford 1986), is not convincing. Underdown's *Revel, Riot and Rebellion* is excellent on the challenge to the royal administration from the Clubmen.

Mark Stoyle, in *Soldiers and Strangers: An Ethnic History of the English Civil War* (New Haven & London, 2005), has argued the dependence of Charles's military effort upon foreigners – Cornish, Welsh and Irish, as well as mercenaries – and that parliament, in reaction, effectively asserted its English credentials. On the parliamentary side, David Scott, *Politics and War in the Three Stuart Kingdoms, 1637–1649* (Basingstoke, 2004), provides a useful synopsis of a number of detailed studies of events at Wesminster during the war years. Clive Holmes's *Eastern Association* examines the rise and ultimate supersession of one of the pre-New Model Armies. On the New Model itself, Mark Kishlansky's *The Rise of the New Model Army* (Cambridge, 1979) develops an exciting, but overstated argument. Safer is the more pedestrian work of Ian Gentles, *The New Model Army in England, Ireland and Scotland, 1645–1653* (Oxford, 1992).

The local studies listed above (p. 224) contain much information on the impact of the war in terms of taxation, conscription and local government in the counties. That is the theme of Martyn Bennett's rich *The Civil Wars Experienced: Britain and Ireland, 1638–1661* (London, 2000), which is at its best on the period of the First Civil War. Philip Tennant's *Edgehill and Beyond: The People's War in the South Midlands, 1642–1645* (Stroud, 1992) is an exceptional micro-study of the organisation of the war and its costs on a much-disputed area.

Chapter 5: Why Was the King Executed?

On the dominance of Holles's party at Westminster, Mark Kishlansky's article, 'The Emergence of Adversary Politics in the Long Parliament', in Cust and Hughes (eds), *The English Civil War* (chap. 5), provides a slimmed down version of the argument developed at length in his *The Rise of the New Model Army*. That argument, though overstated, catches the venom that marked debate at Westminster in 1646 and 1647. On the Presbyterian attack on the sects, see the new work by Ann Hughes, *Gangraena and the Struggle for the English Revolution* (Oxford, 2005).

The grievances of the Army are analysed well in Kishlansky, *The Rise of the New Model Army*; in Ian Gentles, *The New Model Army*, and in John Morrill's essay. 'Mutiny and Discontent in English Provincial Armies, 1645–1647' in Morrill (ed.), *The Nature of the English Revolution* (chap. 17).

There are no good recent books on the Levellers, but several helpful articles. Three are very acute. David Wooton's 'From Rebellion to Revolution: The Crisis of the Winter of 1642/3 and the Origins of Civil War Radicalism', in Cust and Hughes (eds), *The English Civil War* (chap. 13), and J. C. Davis, 'The Levellers and Christianity', in Gaunt (ed.), *The English Civil War: The Essential Readings* (chap. 12), analyse the development of the Levellers' agenda. John Morrill's 'The Army Revolt of 1647' in Morrill (ed.), *The Nature of the English Revolution* (chap 16), examines the tension between army demands and the Levellers' civilian programme of decentralisation. Murray Tolmie's *The Triumph of the Saints: The Separate Churches of London, 1616–1649* (Cambridge, 1977), chaps 6–8, is an excellent account of the fraught relationship between the Levellers and the Baptist churches.

Subsequent manoeuvres between the parliament, the army and the civilian levellers prior to the Second Civil War are brilliantly analysed in Austin Woolrych, *Soldiers and Statesmen: The General Council of the Army and its Debates, 1647–1648* (Oxford, 1987). A number of the articles in Michael Mendle (ed.), *The Putney Debates of 1647: The Army, the Levellers and the English State* (Cambridge, 2001) are very helpful on events in the autumn of 1647, particularly on the role of the Levellers. So too is chapter 6 of James Holstun's *Ehud's Dagger: Class Struggle and the English Revolution* (London, 2000), which catches the distrust and anger below the surface politeness of the debates.

On the Second Civil War Robert Ashton's *Counter-Revolution: The Second Civil War and its Origins* (New Haven, 1994), is rich in detail, though its discursive argument is often hard to follow.

The army's irruption into the political process in November and December 1648, and the execution of the king, is subtly discussed in David Underdown, *Pride's Purge: Politics in the Puritan Revolution* (Oxford, 1971). Jason Peachey (ed.), *The Regicides and the Execution of Charles I* (Basingstoke, 2001) contains a number of interesting essays; that by John Adamson, 'The Frightened Junto: Perceptions of Ireland, and the Last Attempts at a Settlement with Charles I' (chap. 2), is particularly challenging. Some of Adamson's ideas are developed by Sean Kelsey in a number of articles: the most important are 'The Trial of Charles I', *English Historical Review*, 118 (2003), pp. 583–616 and 'The Death of Charles I', *Historical Journal* 45 (2002), pp. 727–54. Both Adamson and Kelsey have illuminated the intentions of some of the participants in the trial; both, to my mind, understate the powerful demand for the expiation of the king's blood-guilt. On this see Patricia Crawford, 'Charles Stuart, That Man of Blood', in Gaunt (ed.), *The English Civil War: The Essential Readings* (chap. 13).

Chapter 6: Why Was the Rump Dissolved?

Blair Worden's *The Rump Parliament* (Cambridge, 1974) is essential reading for a fuller understanding of the themes developed in this chapter; on topics such as taxation, law reform, or the church settlement his work requires little supplementation. On the dissolution of the Rump, Austin Woolrych, *Commonwealth to Protectorate** (Oxford, 1982), challenges some of Worden's arguments, though both subscribe to a similar overall evaluation of the Rump and its demise. Sean Kelsey, *Inventing a Republic: The Political Culture of the English Commonwealth* (Manchester, 1997), and Sarah Barber, *Regicide and Republicanism: Politics and Ethics in the English Revolution* (Edinburgh, 1998), provide insights into the Rump's self-fashioning; both authors are more charitable to the Commonwealth regime than are Worden or myself.

On the relationship between parliament and the army, see Gentles, *The New Model Army*.

The religious policies of the Rump, and the perceived threat posed by radical extremists, are nicely handled in J. C. Davis, *Fear, Myth and History: The Ranters and the Historians* (Cambridge, 1986).

Chapter 7: Why Was Cromwell Offered the Crown?

Blair Worden's brilliant article, contextualising Cromwell's refusal of the crown, 'Oliver Cromwell and the Sin of Achan', in Smith (ed.), *Cromwell and the Interregnum* (chap. 2), has been most influential in the formation of my views. Austin Woolrych's assessment of the Protectorate is also interesting, 'The Cromwellian Protectorate: A Military Dictatorship?', in Smith (ed.), *Cromwell and the Interregnum* (chap. 3).

Woolrych, *Commonwealth to Protectorate* is excellent on Cromwell's flirtation with the radicals in 1653, and the resurrection of his conservative temperament in the face of their legislative proposals.

The period from Cromwell's acceptance of the *Instrument of Government* to his dissolution of his first parliament has not been the subject of a sustained modern study. S. R. Gardiner's *History of the Commonwealth and the Protectorate*, 4 vols (London, 1903), iii, chaps 35–37, is still the best discussion Additional analysis is provided by articles by Peter Gaunt, ' "The Single Person's Confidants and Dependents"? Oliver Cromwell and his Protectorial Councillors', and David Smith, 'Oliver Cromwell, the First Protectorate Parliament and Religious Reform', both in Smith (ed.), *Cromwell and the Interregnum* (chaps 4 and 7); also by Gaunt, 'Oliver Cromwell and his Protectorate Parliaments', in Ivan Roots (ed.) *'Into Another Mould': Aspects of the Interregnum* (2nd edn, Exeter, 1998).

On local government, and the introduction of the major-generals, see Anthony Fletcher, 'Oliver Cromwell and the Localities: The Problem of Consent', in Smith (ed.) *Cromwell and the Interregnum* (chap. 5), Stephen Roberts, 'Local Government Reform in England and Wales', in Roots (ed.) *'Into Another Mould'*, and Christopher Durston, *Cromwell's Major-Generals: Godly Government during the English Revolution* (Manchester, 2001).

On the Quakers, and on the response they elicited, see the sensitive study of Nayler by Leo Damrosch, *The Sorrows of the Quaker Jesus* (Cambridge, Massachusetts, 1996). There is no good published study of the 1656 parliament. The best work on this crucial meeting is in chapter 5 of Patrick Little, *Lord Broghill and the Cromwellian Union with Ireland and Scotland* (Woodbridge, 2004), and in the 1990 Yale University Ph.D. thesis by Carol Egloff; her two-part article 'The Search for a Cromwellian Settlement: Exclusion from the Second Protectorate Parliament', *Parliamentary History*, 17 (1998), pp. 178–97, 301–11, gives some taste of the power of her analysis.

Chapter 8: Was There an English Revolution?

On the contemporary understanding of the term 'revolution', Ilan Rachum's 'The Meaning of "Revolution" in the English Revolution (1648–1660)', *Journal of the History of Ideas*, 56 (1995), pp. 195–215, is a very thorough analysis. More readable is Christopher Hill's 'The Word "Revolution"', in his *A Nation of Change and Novelty* (London, 1990).

The best study of the period from the death of Oliver to the Restoration is still Austin Woolrych's introduction (pp. 1–228) to the revised edition of vol. 7 of *The Complete Prose Works of John Milton* (New Haven, 1980). Ronald Hutton's *The Restoration: A Political and Religious History of England and Wales, 1658–1667* (Oxford, 1985), parts 1 and 2, is a lively, occasionally erratic, survey. Ruth E. Mayers, in *1659: The Crisis of the Commonwealth* (London, 2004) provides a wealth of interesting detail, but in service of an argument – that the Rump was a competent regime that could well have survived but for chance and misunderstanding – that I find wholly untenable. Barry Reay, *The Quakers and the English Revolution* (London, 1985), chap. 5, demonstrates both active Quaker involvement in the politics of this period, and the hostility of conservatives to the Friends.

Derek Massarella has analysed the continuities of army policy throughout the Interregnum: 'The Politics of the Army and the Quest for a Settlement', in Roots (ed.) *'Into Another Mould'*.

The division among the radicals, and the energy spent in internecine disputes, was a theme of Christopher Hill's exciting and readable, *The World Turned Upside Down: Radical Ideas during the English Revolution* (London, 1972).

John Broad has written an excellent study of the responses of a single gentry family to the pressures of wartime finance, and of their recovery in the late 1650s: *Transforming English Rural Society: The Verneys and the Claydons, 1600–1820* (Cambridge 2004), chaps 3 and 4. More generally see Felicity Heal and Clive Holmes, *The Gentry in England and Wales, 1500–1700* (Basingstoke, 1994), chaps 4, 5, and 6.

Joad Raymond, *Pamphlets and Pamphleteering in Early Modern Britiain* (Cambridge, 2003), provides information on the output of the presses, and a brilliant interpretative reading of its significance. Hughes, *Gangraena and the Struggle for the English Revolution* is an excellent case study of the role of print in the creation of the Presbyterian party in 1645 and 1646. Michael Braddick, *The Nerves of State: Taxation and the Financing of the English State, 1558–1714* (Manchester, 1996), is a compelling analysis of the weight and structure of taxation in this period.

Index